59

THERE WAS ONCE A MAN CALLED ADOMAKO. HE OFTEN MADE long journeys carrying goods from one village to another and sometimes to and from the Coast.

He was travelling one day with his load and as he went he sang. His song attracted the grey parrots and they travelled along with him.

Suddenly some highwaymen jumped out at him. They seized his load and were about to kill him when he said:

'You'd better not do that. My friends are just behind and if you harm me they will catch you.'

'You're lying,' they said. 'There are no friends near by.'

'Just let me call, and you'll see.'

So the traveller shouted out at the top of his voice.

'Friends are you coming?' he cried.

'Coming, coming,' replied the parrots from the bush.

'Thieves, thieves,' he cried.

'Thieves, thieves,' cried the parrots.

'Kill them, come and kill them,' cried the traveller.

'Kill them, kill them,' replied the parrots.

The highwaymen were so scared that they ran off into the bush. The traveller burst out laughing and all around the bush was full of laughter.

The traveller was so grateful to the parrots that he made his descendants promise never to harm them. The parrot was made the emblem of their clan.

The Tortoise
and the Hornbill

THE HORNBILL IS A NOISY BIRD. YOU CAN HEAR HIM FROM MILES away in the forest. The other animals fear him for, alas, hornbills are good to eat and he attracts the hunter.

One day Tortoise lay under a big tree. It was peaceful there in the forest and from time to time he would wander off to look for a leaf to chew.

Suddenly there was a shriek from the tree above, and then another. Tortoise looked up and saw Hornbill.

'Do be quiet old chap, you're asking for trouble.'

'But I have such a beautiful voice, I must use it. Wa, wa, wa,' went the hornbill. And so he continued singing.

He was so busy showing off that he did not see a hunter who crept silently through the forest.

'Pau, pau, pau,' went the gun.

The hornbill fell to the ground.

When the hunter came to pick up the hornbill, he tripped over the tortoise, who was trying to hide in the leaves.

'Good,' he said, 'here is something else for the pot.'

He put both in his hunter's bag and turned for home.

The dying hornbill, with tears in his eyes said to the tortoise, 'I am indeed sorry, my friend, my pride and carelessness will lead to your death.'

'It's too late to be sorry,' said the tortoise. 'But at least warn others, my voice is too small.'

The bird struggled to put his head out of the bag and cried out in warning:

One man's death affects another.

Be careful that what you do does not bring sorrow to the innocent.

How the Chameleon
Won his Race

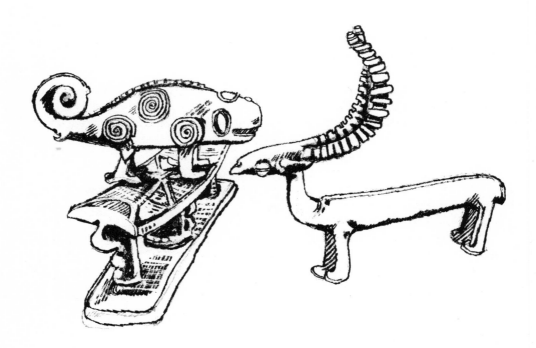

Trends in Bilingual Acquisition

Trends in Language Acquisition Research

Official publication of the International Association
for the Study of Child Language (IASCL).

IASCL website: http://atila-www.uia.ac.be/IASCL

Series Editors

Annick De Houwer
annick.dehouwer@ua.ac.be

University of Antwerp/UIA

Steven Gillis
steven.gillis@ua.ac.be

University of Antwerp/UIA

Volume 1

Trends in Bilingual Acquisition
Edited by Jasone Cenoz and Fred Genesee

EVERYONE KNOWS THAT CHAMELEON CAN ONLY WALK SLOWLY, very slowly.

One day God decided that he would find out which was the swiftest animal in the world. He called all the animals to come together for the race.

When Chameleon arrived the others all laughed. They laughed and laughed until even the hyena who was used to it got hiccoughs. But Chameleon insisted on taking part.

In the excitement of the start everyone forgot Chameleon. The animals lined up; a gun was fired and off they went. The race course was a long one and curved round in a circle. Not far from the end a low tree hung over the track and the larger animals had to lower their heads to go under it. As the bongo went under the tree Chameleon dropped on to its back. Then he crawled slowly to its tail and clung on for dear life.

The bongo was very swift and as they came to the last open stretch he drew ahead of the other animals. At the end of the course a large stool had been placed and the winning animal had to sit on it.

The bongo reached the stool and was about to sit when he heard a small voice.

'Hi, brother Bongo, do you want to sit on me?'

Bongo turned round and looked. There sat the chameleon, who had, of course, dropped off his tail.

'How on earth did you get there, brother Chameleon?' he asked in amazement. 'There was no one ahead of me.'

'I'm rather small, and you just did not see,' replied Chameleon.

Chameleon was, of course, declared victor. They all knew he could not have won the race by his swiftness, but they could prove nothing. Perhaps that is why some people think the chameleon has magic. What do you think?

King of the Birds

THE BIRDS WERE ALWAYS ARGUING AS TO WHO WAS THE strongest among them, who was the most worthy to be their leader.

Nyame the Sky God became tired of their quarrelling and called them all together.

'I will set a test,' he said, 'and whoever wins it shall be King of the Birds.'

He chose a huge tree in the forest whose great branches spread in all directions. He picked the biggest and thickest of the branches.

'Whoever can shake this branch,' he said, 'shall be king.'

One after the other the birds landed on the great branch, but even the Great Eagle was unable to move it.

At last the Allied Hornbill had his turn. He landed right on the very tip of the branch, and the branch shook.

He was so excited that he called out:

> *Mea, mea, mea, ma di hene.*
> It's me, it's me, it's me, I am king.

And so it cries to this day.

How the Mortar Got its Name

THERE WAS ONCE A CRIPPLE WHO COULD NOT WALK. WHEN HIS family went to work on the farm he had to stay in the house. To pass the time he cleaned the pots and scrubbed the stools. But the thing he loved best was the wooden mortar. How he scrubbed and cleaned it. Then he would put it on the step beside him and tell it all his troubles.

One day as he was sitting there he heard someone calling his name.

'Kwaku,' he heard, 'Kwaku.'

He looked round to see who it could be. There was no one else in the yard.

'Who is it?' he called out.

'It is I,' said the mortar.

Kwaku looked at it in surprise.

'Listen,' said the mortar, 'you have been so good to me that I am going to help you. Come and sit on me.'

'You know that is not allowed, my mother would beat me!' (In Ashanti it is taboo to sit on the mortar.)

'Nevertheless come and sit on me,' insisted the mortar.

Kwaku pulled himself up on to the mortar and sat there.

Then the mortar told him that when the family returned he was to get up and go and meet them.

'But I can't walk,' said Kwaku.

'You will,' said the mortar.

When the family returned, Kwaku's little sister came dancing in ahead of them. He stood up and walked towards the door. As he walked his legs strengthened. He was cured.

'What has happened, who cured you?' asked the family.

Kwaku pointed to the mortar.

'Owo aduro,' he replied. 'It has medicine.'

And that is how the mortar got its name: Owaduro.

71

The Gold Nugget

GUINEA FOWL AND VULTURE WERE FRIENDS. THEY DECIDED TO make drums. When they were finished they started to play. So loud and strong was the music they played that God heard them and asked them to play for him.

They drummed and they drummed and God listened to their drumming and enjoyed it very much. Since he could not decide which was the best drummer he offered them both prizes.

'I shall choose first,' said Vulture. Guinea Fowl, who was modest, agreed.

The choice was between two boxes, one clean and beautiful and one rather old and grubby. Of course Vulture took what he thought was best and Guinea Fowl went home with the old box.

Vulture collected his family around, told them of his triumph and opened the box. Alas, it contained all the filth in the world.

Guinea Fowl went home and quietly opened his box—it was full of gold and sandals and cloths and other precious things.

One day Vulture had to pay an important visit and he went to borrow some fine clothes from Guinea Fowl. He took, amongst other things, a fine gold nugget on a chain.

Guinea Fowl waited and waited for the return of his treasures but Vulture did not come. So he went round to collect them. He retrieved everything but the gold nugget. Vulture could not find it. He said his children must have swept it on to the rubbish heap.

Guinea Fowl at last was angry, very angry. He threatened to tell God what had happened unless Vulture found his gold nugget. Ever since then Vulture has been searching on the rubbish heap for the gold and Guinea Fowl cries all day:

Me pokoa, me pokoa, me pokoa.

My nugget of gold, my nugget of gold, my nugget of gold.

You Get What you Deserve

ALTHOUGH THEY LIVED TOGETHER IN THE SAME COURTYARD, Duck and Hen were always quarrelling. They disapproved of each other's habits, and like members of human political parties were always playing the game of one-up-manship. One hot day they had a particularly violent quarrel.

'You, you have a big mouth,' clucked the hen.

'As for you, when you eat you rub your beak on the ground,' quacked the duck.

'I spit on you,' clucked the hen.

The duck, quacking loudly, waddled off, but before she left she turned round and quacked so loudly that everyone could hear.

'You who wipe your mouth and I, who should gain success? I'm telling you that in future someone with a big mouth will rule over us all.' Quack, quack, quack, she waddled off and down to the stream.

I wonder?

The Leopard
and the Bush-Buck

THE BUSH-BUCK WAS ONCE THE SLAVE OF THE MANNIKINS—
small birds of the forest. He was made to work hard for them.

Now the mannikins owed the leopard money and he used to come
regularly to ask them for it. Whenever he came they only said: 'We are
not yet fully grown, see how small we are! When we are fully grown,
we will pay you.'

Time passed and the birds did not grow.

One day they scolded the bush-buck and he became very angry. He
went to the leopard and told him that the mannikins were, in fact, fully
grown. The leopard asked the birds to show him their parents.

They knew then that someone had told on them. It could only be the
bush-buck. They asked the leopard to take the bush-buck to repay the
debt.

The leopard was afraid of the bush-buck because of its horns. Also,
he did not know that it could not bite. He asked the mannikins how he
could take it.

'Go and give the bush-buck cola to chew,' they said. 'Then you will
know what to do.'

The leopard took the bush-buck a gift of cola, saying he wished to
thank it for its help. The bush-buck was greedy and took one of the
cola nuts at once to chew.

The cola was tough and it chewed and it chewed and it chewed.
Then the leopard realised that its teeth were not sharp and it could not
bite him.

The leopard sprang at the bush-buck and it was forced to flee. From
that day to this the leopard has always hunted the bush-buck.

Trends in Bilingual Acquisition

Edited by

Jasone Cenoz
University of the Basque Country

Fred Genesee
McGill University

John Benjamins Publishing Company
Amsterdam/Philadelphia

™ The paper used in this publication meets the minimum requirements of American
National Standard for Information Sciences – Permanence of Paper for Printed
Library Materials, ANSI z39.48-1984.

Library of Congress Cataloging-in-Publication Data

Trends in Bilingual Acquisition / edited by Jasone Cenoz, Fred Genesee.
     p. cm. (Trends in Language Acquisition Research, ISSN 1569–0644 ; v. 1)
    Rev. papers of the VIIIth International Congress for the Study of Child Language held
July 1999 in San Sebastián, Spain.
    "IASCL; International Association for the Study of Child Language"--Cover.
    Includes bibliographical references and index.
        1. Language acquisition--Congresses. 2. Bilingualism in children--Congresses.
I. Cenoz, Jasone. II. Genesee, Fred. III. International Association for the Study of
Child Language. IV. International Congress for the Study of Cild Language (8th : 1999
: San Sebastián, Spain) V. Series.

P118.T734   2001
401.93--dc21   2001037884
ISBN 90 272 3471 X (Eur.) / 1 58811 099 0 (US) (Hb; alk. paper)

© 2001 – John Benjamins B.V.
No part of this book may be reproduced in any form, by print, photoprint, microfilm, or any
other means, without written permission from the publisher.

John Benjamins Publishing Co. · P.O. Box 36224 · 1020 ME Amsterdam · The Netherlands
John Benjamins North America · P.O. Box 27519 · Philadelphia PA 19118-0519 · USA

Contents

Preface

We are very proud to present the first volume in the new series 'Trends in Language Acquisition Research'. As an official publication of the *International Association for the Study of Child Language* (IASCL), the TiLAR Series aims to publish two volumes per three year period in between IASCL congresses. All volumes in the IASCL-TiLAR Series will be invited (but externally reviewed) edited volumes by IASCL members that are strongly thematic in nature and that present cutting edge work which is likely to stimulate further research to the fullest extent.

Besides quality, diversity is also an important consideration in all the volumes: diversity of theoretical and methodological approaches, diversity in the languages studied, diversity in the geographical and academic backgrounds of the contributors. After all, like the IASCL itself, the IASCL-TiLAR Series is there for child language researchers from all over the world.

Although it is IASCL policy to try and link one of the two tri-annual volumes in the Series to the main topic of the preceding IASCL congress, the IASCL-TiLAR series is emphatically not intended as congress or symposia proceedings. This implies that in the volumes related to congress themes there can be contributions by IASCL members that were not presented at the congress.

We are very pleased to present the first volume of the TiLAR series, which is devoted to Bilingual Acquisition, the central theme of the 1999 IASCL Congress in San Sebastian. The volume editors, Jasone Cenoz and Fred Genesee, bring together nine contributions on various aspects of bilingual acquisition, representing three main traditions in the field. Thus rather than trying to present one unified theoretical perspective, this volume intends to bring its readership up-to-date on the most recent developments in bilingualism research. The volume concludes with a discussion chapter written by Brian MacWhinney, in which a critical appraisal of the volume as a whole is given, and the relevance of the individual chapters for present and future research are assessed.

Finally we would like to thank Brian MacWhinney, the present president of the IASCL, for his enthusiastic support in setting up the IASCL-TiLAR

Series, to Seline Benjamins and Kees Vaes of John Benjamins Publishing Company for their professional and creative input throughout the preparation of this volume as well as the series as a whole, and, of course, to the external reviewers whose constructive criticisms and judgements contributed much to the quality of this book.

'Trends in Language Acquisition Research' is made for and by IASCL members. We hope it can become a source of information and inspiration which the community of child language researchers can continually turn to in their professional endeavours.

Antwerp, March 2001

The General Editors

First words

Fred Genesee and Jasone Cenoz

The theme of this volume was inspired by the theme of the VIIIth International Congress for the Study of Child Language which was held in San Sebastián, Spain, in July 1999. The chapters in this volume are based on papers that were presented at that meeting. These chapters provide a snapshot of the current state of research on bilingual acquisition and reflect the diversity of issues, methodologies, and language combinations that can be found in contemporary work in the field. Research on the simultaneous acquisition of two languages during infancy and the early childhood years has had a remarkably long history, beginning with the pioneering work of Ronjat in 1913 and followed by Leopold's monumental classic study of his two bilingual daughters, published between 1939 and 1949. Despite the early work of Ronjat and Leopold, further research remained sparse until the 1980s. During the intervening years, beginning in the 1950s, researchers focused largely on issues pertaining to bilingualism in general. The research conducted during this era made many valuable contributions to our understanding of the social patterning of bilingualism (including language spread and loss), the social psychological and cognitive precursors to and consequences of bilingualism, and alternative conceptualizations of the diverse types of bilingualism. We are referring here to the classic works of Joshua Fishman, Wallace Lambert, John Macnamara, William Mackey, and Uriel Weinreich. The work of these scholars, and others whom we have not been able to mention because of space limitations, were relevant to bilingual acquisition, the topic of this volume, but in a relatively general and inferential way rather than directly.

Beginning in the late 1980s, there was an upsurge in theoretical and empirical attention devoted directly to bilingual acquisition. This surge in interest can be attributed to several factors. First, there is the recognition that simultaneous acquisition of two or more languages is not uncommon. While we lack definitive statistics, it has been speculated that there are as many or even more children who grow up bilingual as monolingual (Tucker 1998).

Therefore, documentation of the facts of bilingual acquisition and the development of theories to explain these facts are worthy in their own right. Second, theories of language acquisition, which currently are based largely on monolingual children, must ultimately incorporate the *facts* of bilingual acquisition if they are to be comprehensive. Much more research is needed to uncover these facts. Moreover, there is an emerging appreciation among language acquisition theorists that bilingual children provide unique test cases for important issues arising from general theories of acquisition. Slobin demonstrated the power of cross-linguistic research for our understanding of the mechanisms of acquisition and his work continues to be influential (Slobin 1997). The study of simultaneous bilinguals pushes the power of the cross-linguistic approach further since bilingual children are their own controls on a number of variables that can confound cross-linguistic studies that use different monolingual children. For example, whereas cognitive, personality, and cultural differences among individual children acquiring different languages can confound cross-linguistic studies, these individual-difference factors are essentially held constant in the case of children who are acquiring different languages simultaneously. In short, studies of simultaneous bilingual acquisition can contribute significantly to the development of a general theory of language acquisition.

While bilingual infants and children make unique subjects for language acquisition research, they are not always ideal. In addition to the inter-individual variation that any child brings to research, bilingual children bring their own unique sources of variation — bilingual children's history in each language can be frustratingly different and variable so that direct comparison of the child's acquisition in each language can be problematic, for example, in cases where developmental progress is significantly skewed towards one language relative to the other. Such variation argues for caution in generalizing the results of single case studies and for the inclusion of multiple subject designs, where feasible. Careful documentation of the child's language exposure and of the child's general level of language development at critical points in longitudinal studies is also advisable, when possible (see also De Houwer 1998a, for a discussion of methodological issues).

A final important reason for studying bilingual children is that expanding our understanding of children who acquire two languages simultaneously can expand our understanding of the human language faculty and by extension the human mind because such research permits us to examine the capacity of the mind to acquire and use more than one language (Genesee 2000). While most theories of language acquisition do not exclude the possibility of bilingual acquisition, nor do they address it explicitly or in detail — they are largely silent with respect to the acquisition of two languages simultaneously. The capacity of infants to acquire two or more linguistic systems, sometimes with radically different structural properties (e.g., English and Inuktitut in Allen 1996), has implications for our conceptualization of the neuro-cognitive architecture of the human mind that makes this possible.

Early work in the field tended to focus on the issue of language differentiation — that is the question of whether children exposed to two languages have differentiated representations of the target languages. This position is well represented in the early work of Leopold in his comments on his daughter Hildegaard's lexical development:

> The free mixing of English and German vocabulary in many of her sentences was a conspicuous feature of her speech. But the very fact that she mixed lexical items proves that there was no real bilingualism as yet. Words from the two languages did not belong to two different speech systems but to one, which was bilingual only in the sense that its morphemes came objectively from two languages.
> (In Hatch 1978: 27)

Volterra and Taeschner (1978) gave the most explicit and precise expression of this hypothesis in their claims that bilingual children go through an initial stage when they possess a single linguistic system, with gradual differentiation of the lexicon and syntax, until approximately three years of age when full differentiation was hypothesized to occur. Volterra and Taeschner's detailed formulation of the unitary language system hypothesis inspired much useful research and commentary. Meisel's contribution to this volume, which is based on his plenary address in San Sebastián, provides a comprehensive and theoretically acute analysis of the current state of the unitary language system hypothesis (see Genesee 1988 and Meisel 1989, for earlier reviews of this hypothesis). Taking advantage of current linguistic theory, Meisel explores in some detail the implications (and difficulties) of the assumptions that underlie this hypothesis. Following a thorough review of his own and other's research, he ultimately rejects it. As Meisel points out, there is broad consensus today that this position is untenable. Indeed, contemporary research on the syntactic development of bilingual children has gone beyond this position and is concerned primarily with the precise nature of the syntactic development of children acquiring two languages simultaneously (e.g., de Houwer 1990; Döpke 2000; Hulk and Müller 2000; Meisel 1990b). Meisel provides a synopsis and critique of selected studies that address this topic. The kind of careful and detailed analysis that Meisel offers is a welcome stimulation for discussion and further investigation since it is through careful analysis and precise formulation of alternatives that the scientific enterprise is advanced.

The chapters by Serratrice and Almgren and Idiazabal represent contemporary efforts to document the syntactic development of bilingual children. More specifically, Serratrice examines the acquisition of verbal morphosyntax in a child acquiring English and Italian simultaneously between 1;10 and 3;0 years of age. She focuses her analyses and comments on the lead-lag issue — that is, the hypothesis that "there is an asynchrony in the emergence of verbal inflectional morphology between poorly inflected languages, like English, and more richly inflected languages, such as Italian." Serratrice argues that previous studies on monolingual and bilingual children that have reported a lead-lag effect may be open to question because they did not use sufficiently rigorous tests of productivity. On the basis of her analyses of her young Italian-English bilingual subject, she concludes that there were more similarities than differences in his English and his Italian and, thus, that the underlying acquisitional strategy is the same in both languages. Serratrice makes a case for incremental, item by item learning of inflectional morphology and, in so doing, she contests arguments for the lead-lag effect. The Serratrice study (along with the Nicoladis study in this volume) are good examples of how empirical investigation of bilingual children can contribute to our understanding of issues pertinent to not only bilingual acquisition but also issues that have been raised by researchers studying monolingual acquisition.

Syntactic development is also the focus of the contribution by Almgren and Idiazabal. Of particular note, they examined a young bilingual child (1;07 to 4;00 years of age) who was acquiring Basque and Spanish, two typologically very distinct languages. They report differential use of imperfective and perfective verb forms in their young subjects use of Spanish and Basque, with imperfective more prevalent in Spanish and perfective in Basque. They speculate, on the basis of analyses of the input addressed to this child, that this pattern can be linked to the prevalence of imperfective forms in adult talk about pretend situations in Spanish and perfective forms for talk about real situations in Basque. The role of input which is highlighted in the Almgren and Idiazabal chapter to account for their results can be studied to great effect in bilingual children since differences in input linked to each language are often salient and, thus, amenable to careful correlational analysis.

Although the issue of linguistic differentiation has been studied exhaustively in the domain of syntax, it has been largely unexplored in bilinguals in the pre-lexical and early lexical stages of development. In particular, it remains open to question whether children exposed to two languages demonstrate differentiated linguistic representations in early phonology, either during the babbling or early one-word stages of development (see Oller, Eilers, Urbano and Cobo-Lewis 1997; Paradis 1996; Johnson and Lancaster 1998, for examples of work at these stages). The contribution by Poulin-Dubois and Goodz in this volume addresses the issue of differentiation during the babbling stage in a group of infants acquiring English and French (average age 12 months 6 days). In the only other study to study bilingual babbling, Oller and his associates (1997) examined the age of emergence and the general characteristics of babbling among Spanish–English bilingual infants. In contrast, the study by Poulin-Dubois and Goodz sought evidence for early language differentiation by looking for language-specific features in their young subjects' babbling. Their study is predicated on findings from cross-linguistic research on monolingual infants that demonstrates the emergence of language-specific segmental and suprasegmental features in the babbling of 10 month old children acquiring a variety of languages (de Boysson-Bardies 1999). Poulin-Dubois and Goodz found that the bilingual infants they examined exhibited consonantal features associated with French-monolingual babbling in both English and French contexts, and they propose that this might reflect a predominant influence of the mothers' child-directed speech — the majority of mothers in this study used French. These findings corroborate those of other studies that have similarly reported *drift* toward the features of the input language in the case of monolingual children around 10 months of age. This study represents an important first step in exploring this fascinating and critical transitional stage of language acquisition.

Another relatively unexplored aspect of early bilingual acquisition that is addressed in this volume is pre-lexical speech perception, an aspect of monolingual acquisition that has received intense attention and yielded many fascinating findings (Jusczyk 1997). The ability to discriminate between languages and the specific sound patterns that comprise the input languages is critical in the initial stages of bilingual acquisition. Research on pre-natal infants and neonates has revealed their remarkably fine-tuned abilities to perceptually discriminate language- and speech-related input; for example, neonates, and in some cases pre-natal infants, can discriminate between the mother's voice vs. an unfamiliar female voice, the native/input language vs. a non-native/foreign language, and familiar vs. unfamiliar prose text. Such early discrimination abilities provide the basis for acquiring the phonological repertoires that comprise each of the target languages in the bilingual learning environment (Genesee in press). These early perceptual experiences, arguably, are also precursors to language-specific babbling (as examined by Poulin-Dubois and Goodz) and certainly first word productions.

The pioneering research by Bosch and Sebastián-Gallés represents a first systematic foray into this domain. They report on a series of studies on the speech discrimination of 4- to 5-month-old infants who were exposed to Spanish and Catalan. Using a differential listening paradigm, they found that their young bilingual subjects, like monolingual control children who were also examined, differentiated between the maternal language(s) and a non-maternal language and they did so at the same age. Thus, the bilinguals were not delayed in their discriminant capacity as a consequence of contending with two input systems at the same time. The bilingual and monolingual infants, however, differed significantly in the duration of their listening times to the maternal language stimuli. The bilinguals' orientation latencies were shorter than those of the monolinguals to non-maternal language stimuli, suggesting that the bilingual children's perception of the input languages had already been shaped at this young age by their bilingual experience. These results provide preliminary evidence for a number of important conclusions: (1) bilingual infants possess the discriminant perceptual abilities necessary to begin the complex task of acquiring two languages from the earliest stages of language exposure; (2) these discriminant capacities are evident in bilingual infants at the same age as in monolingual infants (i.e., they are not delayed); and (3) the perceptual abilities with respect to language-relevant acoustic information are shaped by bilingual experiences very early in development. These findings provide the first exciting glimpse into this largely unexplored domain of bilingual acquisition and are likely to stimulate much follow-up investigation.

The chapter by Nicoladis on *Finding first words in the input* examines yet another early stage of bilingual acquisition, the acquisition of first words. Segmenting the speech stream into lexical units is widely recognized as one of the critical challenges of early language acquisition (Bloom 2000). The Nicoladis chapter, thus, addresses an issue that is of intense interest to researchers who focus on monolingual language acquisition. Bilingual children are particularly good subjects for examining this issue because any biases that might be associated with an individual child's predispositions to prefer or process certain kinds of linguistic input are the same for the acquisition of both languages and, thus, language-specific differences in input are enhanced. Nicoladis's findings lead her to argue that both semantic factors as well as frequency of input best explain this child's acquisitional pattern. As Nicoladis herself notes, replication of this work with more bilingual children acquiring languages with even more marked contrasts in input characteristics will serve to elucidate the role of multiple factors in early word learning in monolingual and bilingual children. We are likely to see more research that adopts this same paradigm to examine general theoretical issues in language acquisition.

The final three chapters — Quay, Lanza, and Comeau and Genesee, address socio-pragmatic and communicative aspects of bilingual development. Children in the process of acquiring two or three languages, as in Quay's case study, can reveal insights about the limits of children's communicative capacities during the early stages of acquisition since children exposed to two languages are faced with communicative challenges that monolingual children are not. For example, they must learn which language (or languages) to use with whom and when; they must learn when it is appropriate to code-mix, with whom, and how much; and they must learn when their communication with others is compromised by their language choice or some other factor, such as inappropriate selection of words or inaudible or garbled pronunciation that can plague communication with all young children. Understanding how bilingual children come to use their developing languages appropriately with others can provide us with insights about how all children come to use language in complex contexts.

Turning to each study now, Quay reports a longitudinal study of a trilingual (German–English–Japanese) child raised in Japan. This is one of a very small number of studies of multilingual acquisition (see Cenoz and Jessner 2000 for other examples). In her chapter, Quay seeks to further our understanding of trilingual acquisition by focusing on the language input addressed to this child in home and daycare settings when the child was 1;1 to 1;9 years of age. Quay describes in some detail the quantity, quality, and timing of input addressed to her young subject and notes the complex relationships between these input variables and the child's language learning and usage patterns. The most striking finding reported by Quay is this child's predisposition to favour the use of Japanese in both home and daycare settings even though his exposure to Japanese was delayed relative to his two other languages and despite the fact that Japanese was an ancillary language in the home. Quay speculates that the child made an astute language *choice* since he has opted for the language that is functional in all settings — his parents know Japanese, although they generally use English (mother) or German (father) with him in the home. Quay's chapter provides an interesting case study of how sensitive young bi/multilingual children can be to socio-cultural factors and, in particular, the power of input from same-age peers who speak the dominant societal language on young bilingual children's language choices. This is an issue that is clearly worth further investigation.

Lanza discusses the issue of language choice up closer by examining patterns of discourse between parents and their children and how these selectively promote or, alternatively, discourage code-mixing on the part of the developing bilingual child. Lanza casts her analyses clearly within the theoretical framework of language socialization and uses this framework effectively to depict how families, including children, negotiate monolingual vs. bilingual discourse styles. Building on her influential 1997 book *Language Mixing in Infant Bilingualism: A Sociolinguistic Perspective*, she argues for empirical methodologies that are appropriate to the issues at hand — in her case, methodologies that capture the fundamentally contextualized, interactional, and sequential nature of situated discourse. Lanza illustrates how the discoursal/communicative challenges of bi/multilingual acquisition can be conceptualized in ways that are fundamental to all language acquisition.

Finally, Comeau and Genesee take an even closer look at how young bilingual children negotiate language choice using a quasi-experimental investigation of child-adult dyadic conversations. In contrast to Lanza's very broadly contextualized analysis of code-mixing, Comeau and Genesee's analyses focus on the repair strategies used by bilingual and monolingual children (3 and 5 years of age) in response to breakdowns in communication that result from inappropriate language choices and other language behaviors during dyadic conversations with adults. Comeau and Genesee's study is motivated by the fact that, at times, bilingual children are faced with adult interlocutors who speak only one language and, thus, are less linguistically competent than the child. This is an unusual situation for most monolingual children who can assume that interlocutors who are older than they are are more competent. Comeau and Genesee report that the ability to repair language-based breakdowns in communication is part of the communicative competence of bilingual children, from at least 3 years of age. The sophistication of this competence is demonstrated by the children's ability to repair breakdowns in communication due to inappropriate language choice following *indirect* or *implicit* requests for repairs from their adult interlocutors despite the fact that a number of contending possibilities often exist (e.g., inaudible or garbled vocalization, poor lexical choice, or off-topic comments). In other words, bilingual children do not need explicit feedback about the source of breakdown for them to identify the relevant repair strategy. Moreover, these young bilingual children readily distinguished between language-based vs. other types of breakdowns in communication. These findings speak to a sophisticated ability to interpret complex conversational implicatures appropriately with minimal explicit input.

Finally, MacWhinney provides a synopsis of the preceding material, contextualizing them with reference to three research traditions: sociolinguistic, psycholinguistic, and developmental. MacWhinney provides an insightful and useful integration that compares, contrasts, and critiques the work in this volume. It would be redundant to provide a synopsis of his synopsis and so we will let the reader explore MacWhinney's contribution to the volume in more detail.

Like all frontline, innovative research, the research and perspectives reported in this volume will provoke much discussion and will probably raise more questions than they have answered. If this happens, then they will have succeeded since they will have stimulated other researchers to delve more deeply and broadly in order to enhance our understanding of bilingual acquisition further. It is to be hoped that the findings presented in this volume will also capture the attention of researchers for whom bilingual acquisition has not been a focus of attention so that they can enrich their and our investigations of language acquisition in the future.

CHAPTER 1

The simultaneous acquisition of two first languages[*]

Early differentiation and subsequent development of grammars

Jürgen M. Meisel

1. Introduction: The interest of studies on bilingual acquisition

The simultaneous acquisition of more than one language by a single individual has attracted the interest of an increasing number of studies, over the past 25 years. This research, initiated by Ronjat (1913), has amassed a large body of evidence indicating that this type of language acquisition qualifies as an instance of first language acquisition. The question of whether this conclusion can indeed be corroborated should be of considerable interest for those concerned with monolingual first as well as with second language acquisition. In what follows, I will therefore summarize the results of some of the research on bilingual first language acquisition, and I will highlight some current and future research issues which might be of interest for those working on other types of acquisition and, hopefully, also for those who work on bilingual development. This discussion will be focused entirely on early childhood development, i.e. on children under the age of 5;0, approximately, and it is only concerned with the simultaneous development of bilingualism (2L1); successive bilingualism, i.e. second language acquisition (L2), is, thus, only of interest to the extent that it sheds light on the simultaneous acquisition of two languages. Finally let me mention that I use the term bilingualism to include the acquisition of more than two languages simultaneously.

As an introduction to this discussion, it may be useful to begin with a few remarks on why one might want to turn to bilinguals when addressing issues in language acquisition in general, for, although bilingualism excites considerable interest, not only among scientists and the public at large, because of its political, social, and cultural relevance, one frequently cannot help but feel that it is regarded as an oddity or abnormality. This attitude is reflected in linguistic theorizing when the object of research is identified as a speaker who is not only part of a homogeneous but also of a monolingual speech community. By this remark, I do not mean to question the necessity of idealizations in defining the object and the tasks of linguistic research. But what this shows is that the ability to acquire and use more than one language is not considered as an essential but as a contingent property of the human language making capacity. Similarly, results based on bilingual data are sometimes excluded from discussions on the nature of developmental mechanisms and processes precisely because the children acquired more than one L1 simultaneously. Contrary to such views, I maintain that the human language faculty predisposes the individual to become bilingual and that adequate theories of language and of grammar need to reflect this fact.

As for language development, my claim is that research over the past decade or so has amassed solid if not conclusive evidence demonstrating that children acquiring two or more languages simultaneously, from birth or from very early on, proceed through the same developmental sequences and eventually arrive at the same kind of grammatical knowledge as their respective monolingual counterparts. In what follows, I will not attempt to demonstrate this by giving an exhaustive review of the relevant literature. Rather, I will focus on one issue, language differentiation, summarizing some findings from the last 10–15 years of research on bilingual language development and highlighting a few issues which have created controversy in the more recent debate.

A more comprehensive review of the literature would indicate that the major issues dealt with in bilingual acquisition research are of two different types. The first type investigates topics related directly to multilingualism, i.e. to the fact that more than one language is acquired and used by the same individual. In the overwhelming majority of cases, this research contrasts bilingual with monolingual L1 acquisition, and it is frequently motivated by attempts to demonstrate the success of simultaneous bilingualism. The fact that they take this perspective on bilingualism corroborates our suspicion that many researchers (as well as laymen) seem to feel that it is necessary to demonstrate that this is indeed a case of *normal* language development. Interestingly enough, work comparing simultaneous with successive bilingualism is scarce. This is surprising in view of the fact that the alleged influence of the other language, referred to as interference, transfer, mixing, etc., plays a prominent part in publications on both types of bilingual acquisition. Clearly, much more work on this issue is needed. If, for example, it can be shown that the role of the respective other language is much less important in 2L1 than in L2 acquisition — as I indeed believe is the case — this would suggest that it is not so much the presence of another language which causes differences between monolingual L1 and bilingual development; rather, different acquisitional mechanisms would then seem to come into play as a result of maturation.

The second type of research on children acquiring more than one language simultaneously focuses on the development of only one of the bilingual's languages. Some of these studies might as well have been carried out with monolinguals, and the fact that the learners are bilinguals is of no specific importance. In many cases, however, studies of this sort, although only concerned with one or the other language, provide insights which could not have been obtained by studying monolinguals, or only with much more difficulty. This applies to work investigating the role of formal properties of linguistic expressions in development. The particular value of this research focus has already been demonstrated by cross-linguistic studies such as those by Slobin and his associates; see, for example, Slobin (1985). Bilinguals offer the additional advantage of allowing for cross-linguistic comparison within the same individual, thus allowing the researcher to control a number of variables like individual maturation, processing capacity, personality factors, etc., and to tease apart structural factors from other factors in language acquisition. In other words, studies on bilingual development enable us to investigate the role of language (structure) in language acquisition.

In this chapter, I will focus my attention on the first type of research which investigates the course of development in the simultaneous acquisition of more than one language in an individual, with particular attention to language differentiation and the possibility of mutual influences between the languages during subsequent developmental phases. Although this interest is clearly marked by a monolingual perspective, I hope to be able to show that it eventually leads to insights relevant for a better understanding of language acquisition. It should furthermore allow us to call into question a position which regards monolingualism as the norm and bilingualism as some kind of deviation requiring an explanation, especially if it develops without apparent problems and with ultimate success.

2.   Language separation: Differentiation or fusion of grammatical knowledge?

2.1 The hypotheses to be examined

One of the major issues dealt with in research on bilingual language acquisition, probably the single most important one, is the question of language separation. This clearly concerns every level of linguistic knowledge, including the bilingual person's pragmatic competence. I will, however, only address the question of how and at what age children succeed in differentiating the grammatical systems they are to acquire, and I will focus entirely on morphosyntax. The issue of grammatical differentiation is obviously of prime theoretical interest since it directly concerns our understanding of the human language faculty: Are humans cognitively equipped to become multilingual, or is monolingualism the default option? In other words: Are we predisposed to differentiate two or more linguistic knowledge systems without being specially coached? These questions are of immediate practical relevance for potentially bi- or multilingual individuals and families as well as communities (indigenous, immigrant, etc.). Depending on how they are answered, different attitudes towards bilingualism will develop, and different kinds of support will become available for bilinguals, on an individual as well as on a social level.

The language separation question arises inevitably because bilingual communication normally exhibits a certain amount of mixing, most notably lexical mixing. In other words, within a conversation, a turn, and even a clause, lexical material from several languages is juxtaposed. In fact, mixing is not restricted to the lexicon; it extends to all parts of the grammar, e.g. the use of syntactic constructions from both languages of a bilingual. It is well-known by now that language mixing does not indicate deficiencies of linguistic knowledge or of the bilingual's abilities to use the languages. On the contrary, it has been shown that this type of language use is rule-governed and that it provides additional communicative means, as compared to monolingual interactions. The initial choice of language, when all participants in the interaction have more than one option, is determined by a subtle network of sociolinguistic factors. Subsequent switching between the languages is also guided by pragmatic and sociolinguistic factors, and sentence-internal switches are further constrained by grammatical ones; see the contributions in Milroy and Muysken (1995) for some recent discussions of these and related topics. All this leads to the conclusion that bilingual language use might reflect a more complex interaction of pragmatic and grammatical knowledge sources, when compared to monolingual performance.

In part, the question of whether bilingual children are able to differentiate the mental representations of their languages is motivated by a certain ignorance about how language choice and switching operate in multilingual interactions. Moreover, it is not uncommon that studies on bilingual acquisition fail to distinguish between particular types of usage on the one hand, and the underlying competence of the speakers on the other; i.e. based on the observation of mixing in language use, they jump to the conclusion that this indicates a lack of grammatical differentiation. But superficial observation cannot reveal whether language mixes follow general principles or not. On the other hand, it is not unreasonable to hypothesize that children, in order to be able to mix like adult speakers, need to acquire the pragmatic principles and the grammatical rules guiding bilingual usage. As long as they have not achieved this, during an initial phase of language development, mixing may indeed be an indication that the child has not yet differentiated the two grammatical systems (Meisel 1994b). This hypothesis appears to be corroborated by the observation that bilingual language use by some children exhibits a larger amount of mixing during an early phase which gradually decreases over time. Other findings, however, suggest that to generalize in this fashion and to claim that mixing decreases with increasing grammatical knowledge is not warranted by the empirical facts (Köppe 1997).

It is not unfair, I believe, to state that a substantial part of the debate on the language separation issue suffers from theoretical as well as methodological shortcomings. At this point, however, I will not dwell on such problems. State-of-the-art summaries of the research dealing with the problem of language differentiation are available in print, and some of them give critical assessments of the theoretical and methodological foundations of this body of work, e.g. De Houwer (1990, 1995), Köppe (1997). Let me therefore concentrate on the current discussion which can be characterized in terms of the stance people adopt with respect to each of the hypotheses (cf. De Houwer and Meisel 1996) as in (1):

(1) *Hypotheses about grammatical differentiation in bilingual development*
    1a. *Fusion Hypothesis*: The children create a new system, (randomly?) combining elements of the two or more systems.
    2. *Differentiation Hypothesis*: The children differentiate the two systems as soon as they have access to grammatical knowledge.

    2a. *Interdependent Development Hypothesis*: One of the languages serves
        as a developmental guide for the other.

    2b. *Autonomous Development Hypothesis*: The acquisition of each of the
        two languages by the bilingual individuals follows the same develop-
        mental logic which guides the acquisition of the respective languages
        by monolingual children.

As far as I can see, there is broad consensus today that the differentiation hypothesis is essentially correct when it comes to explaining grammatical development. In order to show why this is the case, in Section 2.2 I will briefly summarize some findings and arguments in support of the differentiation hypothesis, contrasting it with an early version of the fusion hypothesis, the *one-system* hypothesis. More recently, however, it has been suggested that there could be a *pre-grammatical phase* which might also be characterized by a lack of differentiation of linguistic knowledge. This will be discussed in the remainder of Section 2. In Section 3 I will then turn to the debate opposing the interdependent *vs.* autonomous development hypotheses.

2.2 One grammatical system or differentiated grammars?

Until about 10 years ago, the commonly held view was that children have to go through an initial one-system phase before they succeed in differentiating the grammatical knowledge of their languages. Although it is not always clear whether authors postulating a period of macaronic mixing are indeed referring to the children's grammatical knowledge rather than to their alleged inability to keep the languages separate in usage, only the former view is relevant for the present discussion. The most elaborate model advocating a one-system phase was proposed in the exceptionally influential paper by Volterra and Taeschner (1978) (see (2)).

(2) *The three-stage model of bilingual language development*
    I.   At the first stage, the child has only one lexical system comprising
        words from both languages.
    II. At the second stage, two distinct lexical systems develop, although the
        child still applies "the same syntactic rules to both languages"
        (Volterra and Taeschner 1978: 311)
    III. At the third stage, distinct grammatical systems develop, resulting in
        differentiation of two linguistic systems.

The authors of this paper have to be credited with making explicit a number of assumptions which had previously been entertained in a rather vague and implicit way, most notably that the alleged developmental phase characterized by a lack of differentiation is indeed referring to the children's grammatical knowledge, not merely to the use they make of this knowledge. The study has subsequently been criticized on methodological as well as on conceptual grounds, which I do not want to repeat here (Genesee 1989; Meisel 1989; De Houwer 1990). What matters in the present context is that detailed analyses of various longitudinal corpora revealed that early differentiation is not only possible but the normal case. Arguments against stage I can be found, for example, in Jekat (1985), Pye (1986), Mikés (1990), Quay (1995), Köppe (1997). As for stage II, it is by now a well established fact that children are able to differentiate grammatical systems from very early on, i.e. as soon as language-specific word order properties and inflectional morphology emerge in the children's speech (see Meisel 1989; De Houwer 1990). What these studies showed is that, in order to be able to decide on whether or not bilinguals have access to separate linguistic systems, empirical evidence is needed which fulfills at least the following requirements (cf. De Houwer and Meisel 1996) as set out in (3):

(3) *The required empirical evidence*
1. The phenomena investigated should be functionally equivalent in both target languages, but they should exhibit clear differences in their respective structural properties.
2. This requirement must also be met by the respective monolingual child languages which may be structurally identical where the adult languages differ.
3. Data claimed to constitute evidence in favor of or against a one-system phase must stem from an age period during which the children have access to grammatical knowledge; i.e. if there is such a thing as a *pre-grammatical phase*, samples from this period cannot be used in this debate.

To illustrate this point, let me quote a few examples investigating phenomena which, I maintain, do fulfill these requirements. The first one contrasts the acquisition of verb placement and finiteness in French–German bilingual children (see Meisel 1990b; 1994a). In grammatical terms, these children face, among others, the acquisitional problems outlined in (4):

(4) *Acquisitional tasks for French–German bilinguals*
1. The choice between the headedness options for all grammatical categories, e.g. head-final VP in German, head-initial in French.

2. The setting of the finiteness parameter, i.e. German as a verb-second (V2) language requires the finite verb to be raised to Comp whereas in Romance languages it moves to IP.
3. Language-specific overt markings for agreement, tense, etc.

Surface word-order patterns do not easily reveal the kind of information needed in order to be able to discover these differences. French adheres rather strictly to SVO order, but object clitics appear in preverbal position, resulting in an SoV pattern.[1] Moreover, dislocation of subjects and objects is an extremely frequent feature of the spoken language. The dislocated element appears to the left or to the right of IP, and a pronominal copy is cliticized to the verb. Since the subject rarely appears in postverbal position, placement of a constituent other than the subject in initial position results in V3 order. Aside from a number of details, French surface order thus exhibits the patterns as shown in (5), several of which deviate from the basic SVO order:

(5) *French word order patterns*
     SVO, AdvSVO, SsVO, sVOS, SoV, OSoV, SoVO

As for German, again if we ignore a number of additional possibilities, the surface orders which deviate from the underlying SOV order are mainly due to particularities of verb placement. Since the above mentioned raising of verbs to the structural second position (V2 effect) is only possible for finite verbs and is restricted to main clauses, the finite/non-finite distinction and the main vs. subordinate clause difference result in the following patterns for declarative sentences which may be expected to appear in the children's input (see (6)):

(6) *German word order patterns*
     a. matrix clauses: $SV_{+fin}O(V_{-fin})$, $OV_{+fin}S(V_{-fin})$, $AdvV_{+fin}SO(V_{-fin})$
     b. subordinate clauses: $Comp\ SO(V_{-fin})V_{+fin}$

Consequently, in order to be able to use adult-like word order, children must have access to language-specific grammatical knowledge which is not readily detectable by scanning surface sequences in the input. In French, the child has to be able to distinguish between clitics and non-clitics; in German, a distinction between finite and non-finite verbs must be made, as well as one between matrix and subordinate clauses. Moreover, one needs to distinguish between underlying OV and VO orders and between V2 and non-V2 languages.

An analysis of the language use of French–German bilingual children studied as part of the DUFDE project (*Deutsch und Französisch — Doppelter Erstspracherwerb/German and French — The acquisition of two first languages*) reveals that they indeed use different word order patterns in both languages from early on (see Meisel 1990b; 1994a). Our analyses (Meisel 1986, 1989) begin at the point of development where children start using multi-word utterances containing verbal elements, usually around age 1;10, approximately at MLU 1.75. The children only use possible target sequences as described above. But they do not use all of the surface orders present in adult speech of both languages in each of their two languages. This indicates that language-specific grammatical knowledge is already available. The data exhibit the following French–German differences (see (7)):

(7)   1.   Already during the initial phase, one finds clause-final position of verbs in German but not in French.
      2.   During this early period, one observes VOS order in French, but not in German.
      3.   Shortly afterwards, there is clear evidence for V2 constructions in German (AdvVs, OVS); in analogous French contexts, one finds target-conform AdvSV and OSV sequences (=V3) which, in turn, are not attested in the German data.

From these observations, one may conclude that language-specific headedness of syntactic categories (VP and IP) as well as the grammatical notion of finiteness and its syntactic consequences (verb raising and the different landing sites of the finite verb, IP and CP, respectively) are acquired early, with ease, and in accordance with the target grammars (see Meisel 1990a; 1994a; Köppe 1996, 1997). Since these grammars differ from each other in crucial ways, as required by the criteria defining adequate empirical evidence listed above, and since the bilingual children proceed through the same developmental sequences as the respective monolinguals, these findings constitute evidence in favor of the Differentiation Hypothesis.

A similar claim can be made based on the analysis of the acquisition of negative constructions in the speech of Basque-Spanish children; see Ezeizabarrena (1991) and Meisel (1994d). Spanish is an SVO language which allows, however, for very variable surface word order. The negator immediately precedes the finite verb, as in (8).

(8)   *no   te   me   lo   vayas a olvidar*
      NEG REFL.2SG IND.OBJ.1SG DIR.OBJ.3SG AUX   to forget
      'you should not forget this'

The syntactic structure of negatives is a controversial issue. Setting this discussion aside, I will simply assume that Neg is a functional category projecting to NegP and that its structural position is above VP. The correct surface order is achieved by the fact that the finite verb, raising to Infl, moves through Neg, and [Neg+V] subsequently raises to Infl; *no* is thus cliticized to the finite verb.

Basque verbs appear in two types of inflectional paradigms. All verbs can be used as *periphrastic* (or *analytic*) constructions that consist of a main verb and an auxiliary. In this case, the main verb carries *aspectual* information, i.e. perfective (*-0*), imperfective (*-t(z)en*), or future (*-ko*). *Tense, mood* and *person agreement*, however, are marked solely on the auxiliary. In addition to these periphrastic constructions, a small number of frequently occurring verbs exhibit *synthetic* forms. In this case, the main verb is inflected for tense, mood and person agreement. Basque is an SOV language which, although it allows for considerable variation in word order, exhibits rather strict head-final order. Sentence negation leads to a quite different situation. The negative particle *ez* together with the auxiliary precedes the verb, resulting in significant changes in word order. The neutral, unmarked order is given in (9) (a), i.e., complements of the verb (objects or adverbials) appear between the preposed auxiliary and the verb. The two following examples differ in where the focus is placed: in (b) the focus is on the verb *hartu*, in (c), it is on the subject *ikasleak*.

(9) a.   *ikasleak ez   zituen lapitzak hartu*
          student NEG AUX   pencils take
     b.   *ikasleak ez zituen hartu lapitzak*
     c.   *ez zituen ikasleak lapitzak hartu*
          'the student does not take the pencils'

The negative particle and the finite verb form a very tight unit, and it is plausible to assume that Neg is cliticized to Aux. Let us also assume that in Basque sentence structure NegP dominates VP; Neg moves to Comp via Infl where it cliticizes to Aux in the case of analytic verbs.

We know from developmental studies of a number of languages such as English, French, German and Swedish that children initially place the negator clause-externally. As soon as they have acquired finiteness, clause-internal negation appears, and the target structures are usually acquired rapidly and without apparent effort. This can be accounted for by assuming that the surface order is a result of the finite verb raising to a functional head, as mentioned above. The expected developmental pattern is also found in Spanish child language, although the hypothesis concerning clause-external placement in initial position cannot be tested empirically in Spanish. Since during early phases the subject is normally omitted, the negator precedes the verb, but it is not possible to decide whether it indeed occupies a structural position preceding the subject. Subsequently, i.e., when finite verbs are used productively, *no* follows the subject, but it consistently precedes the finite verb, thus confirming the close developmental relation between the acquisition of finiteness and Neg placement.

In Basque child language, the clausal negator *ez* appears in three out of the four logically possible positions, as is indicated in (10). Note that V_{+fin} includes auxiliaries as well as synthetic verb forms. V_{-fin} only refers to main verbs, since auxiliaries are not attested in this form (* indicates that this pattern does not exist in the data).

(10) *The position of the clausal negator in Basque child language*
    (i) V_{-fin} + NEG   (iii) *V_{+fin} + NEG
    (ii) NEG + V_{-fin} (iv) NEG + V_{+fin}

Not surprisingly, the children begin by using *non-finite* verb forms. Pattern (i), thus, appears during a period when finite verb forms are not yet attested. Patterns (ii) and (iv), on the other hand, are not developmentally ordered; in fact, three out of the four children studied here used (iv) earlier than (ii). This can be interpreted as indicating that preverbal NEG is always the result of NEG raising to Comp via Infl, as suggested above. If, however, the auxiliary is not lexically realized — a phenomenon known from children's speech in other languages — this raising operation results in a pattern like (ii). In other words, examples of a negative element positioned before the non-finite verb, as in (ii), are either (adult-like) imperatives or constructions where the auxiliary is omitted by the child. The most important observation is that one logically possible surface pattern which is, however, excluded by our grammatical analysis, is indeed not attested in the data, see (iii). This is to say that *ez* is never placed after a finite verbal element (*V_{+fin}+*ez*), i.e. the finite auxiliary cannot raise alone.

In sum, the surface orders observed in the speech of these children reflect structural properties and constraints on grammatical operations specific to each of the two languages. As with the French–German children, the directionality of syntactic categories does not seem to represent difficulties for the Basque-Spanish children, although all categories, except CP, differ in this respect in the two languages. NegP dominates VP in both languages, but, because of its right-headedness in Basque, as opposed to left-headedness in

Spanish, Neg is base-generated in post-verbal position in Basque, and, consequently, constructions with NEG following the non-finite verb appear first. Constructions with NEG following the finite element are not attested. Rather, as soon as finite forms are used, NEG + V$_{+fin}$ is raised, leading to the position of *ez* preceding the finite verbal element. In Spanish, on the other hand, NEG is always placed preverbally. Thus, the easily attained surface word order in both target languages can only be explained if one credits the children with elaborate grammatical knowledge about these languages.

Findings of this sort constitute, in my opinion, unambiguous evidence supporting the claim that bilingual children develop differentiated grammatical systems from the very beginning of morphosyntactic development. In terms of the hypotheses formulated in Section 2.1, one may conclude that the *Differentiation Hypothesis* is confirmed.

2.3 The unitary language system hypothesis during a "pre-grammatical" phase of development

This brief summary of some research on the question of early differentiation of grammatical systems should suffice to show that the *Fusion Hypothesis*, according to which the child develops a new system combining elements of the two or more target grammars, is to be rejected. There is, in fact, broad consensus on this issue since other researchers who have investigated different grammatical phenomena in various language combinations have reached similar conclusions, e.g. Genesee (1989), De Houwer (1990), Genesee, Nicoladis and Paradis (1995), Nicoladis and Genesee (1996). This is not to say, however, that the issue of language separation in bilinguals has been resolved conclusively. It seems, rather, that the problem has been shifted along the chronological axis of ontogenesis. In other words, the question arises as to whether it might not be possible to maintain some version of the unitary language system hypothesis (Genesee 1989) during *earlier* developmental phases, i.e. prior to grammatical differentiation. Another possibility is that during *later* phases, i.e. when the grammatical knowledge systems are undoubtedly separated, bilingual acquisition might be characterized by interdependent development as a result of the presence in the individual's cognitive system of more than one grammatical system. I will address the first issue in the remainder of this section and turn to the second in the following section.

In order to facilitate discussion of the possibility of an early unitary language system preceding grammatical differentiation, let me first address very briefly a problem resulting from the original *one-system hypothesis* which apparently continues to confound the current discussion. The confusion concerns the meaning of what exactly is meant by *one grammatical system*. At least three interpretations seem to be possible. A specific construction thus may

1. consist of a mixture of G_a and G_b;
2. be characterized by elements and principles which are neither part of G_a nor of G_b; or
3. reflect grammatical properties of either G_a or of G_b.

As I understand it, a unitary system defined as a case of grammatical fusion can only refer to the first option. But the way in which alleged single systems are discussed suggests that they are not necessarily understood as fused grammars consisting of elements from the two or more grammatical target systems, as defined in (1). Rather, hypotheses postulating the existence of a unitary language system have also been based on the observation that the utterances used in both language contexts, L(a) and L(b), exhibit identical structures, although the underlying principles cannot be traced to either G(a) or G(b). In this case, the nature of the non-differentiated system remains to be specified. It might contain grammatical principles erroneously attributed to the target grammars; but it might also consist of semantic or pragmatic knowledge, in which case it would not qualify as a grammatical system at all. The third option implies that the constructions in question are derived from the grammar of *one* of the languages being learned, but it is used for both languages; this is apparently what Volterra and Taeschner (1978) had in mind, at least in some of the cases mentioned in their paper, e.g. the position of adjectives. In view of the fact that the empirical evidence provided for such cases is less than convincing (see Meisel 1989 and De Houwer 1990) and given that, to my knowledge, a unitary system hypothesis defined in this way is currently not explicitly validated in the literature, I will not pursue this possibility.

This leaves us with option (2) as a possible interpretation of the claim that bilingual children rely on a single system during a phase preceding the one for which grammatical differentiation is well established, as argued in the preceding section. Remember that one of the criteria, defined at the beginning of Section 2.2, for what might constitute empirical evidence in support of a unitary system hypothesis has been that the data should stem from an age period during which children have access to grammatical knowledge; samples from a possible pre-grammatical phase have explicitly been excluded — an obvious and necessary consequence of the fact that the unitary system had

been defined as a single *grammatical* system underlying the linguistic production in both language contexts. Yet if one intends to examine the possibility of
a unitary system preceding the phase of grammatical differentiation, one must
consider the possibility that at least some of the principles underlying language
use during this period are not part of any of the target grammars. They may
either be possible grammatical principles of human languages which are,
however, not instantiated in the adult grammars of the languages to be
acquired, or they may indeed not be *grammatical* in nature. In the latter case,
the developmental phase in question can be qualified as *pre-grammatical*. The
question of whether language development includes a pre-grammatical phase
is, of course, very controversial; within the generative paradigm, it is, in fact,
not even considered seriously as a possible option. I nevertheless want to
emphasize that the plausibility of any hypothesis referring to a unitary language system preceding grammatical differentiation hinges on the problem of
defining the nature of the organizing principles of such an early single system.

A recent version of such a unitary language system hypothesis has been
developed by Deuchar and Quay (1998, 2000) and Deuchar (1999). They
argue that there is indeed one system before the differentiation of morphosyntactic systems, and they refer to it as a "rudimentary syntax, based on a
predicate-argument structure" (Deuchar and Quay 1998: 231). Their claims
are based on the analysis of the speech of a Spanish-English child; whereas
Deuchar and Quay (1998) only analyze utterances without mixing, the study
by Deuchar (1999) is based on early mixed utterances (MLU just above 1, age
range 1;6–1;10). Deuchar (1999) not only argues that early multi-word
utterances reflect predicate-argument structure, she furthermore concludes
that function words are mixed in more often than content words. She suggests
that function words are treated as non-language-specific elements by the child,
since in 85% of the mixed two word utterances she examined, the function
word does not match the context, but the content word does. In this analysis,
language context is defined according to the language used by the child's
interlocutor.

I must admit that I find certain aspects of these studies problematic. For
one thing, the high frequency of mismatches may partly be an artifact of the
data collection procedure or of the way these utterances were analyzed. Note
that these cases almost exclusively occur in Spanish contexts, i.e. the *minority
language* of a child growing up in an overwhelmingly monolingual environment. More importantly, the distinction between *function words* and *content
words* is motivated primarily by semantic considerations, the former being

defined as relational expressions or "predicates", "in the sense employed in predicate calculus" (Deuchar 1999: 25). In fact, *function words* do not correspond to some morphosyntactic entity as defined for mature grammars. They are said to belong to a closed class, but in morphosyntactic terms, they represent a rather heterogeneous class, comprising *más* 'more', *sí* 'yes', *more, gone, down, off* and *oh-dear*. Deuchar argues that these are not function words in the technical sense of the term but that they are *acategorial* elements which later drop out of the child's language as predicates, as opposed to *precategorial* words which "develop into lexical categories with the appearance of morphological marking" (Deuchar 1999: 28). With respect to their distribution in child utterances, one should note that they all seem to precede, as well as follow, their arguments.

To avoid misunderstandings, these observations are not meant to suggest that the phenomenon under discussion does not exist. Rather, it seems to be a well-established fact that children use a small set of lexical items fairly freely in both language contexts, and since more than half of the mismatches have translation equivalents in the respective other language, it is unlikely that their use could be caused merely by a lack of lexical knowledge. The question, however, is whether one can view this as evidence in support of an early unitary language system. First of all, it may well be the case that the mismatch between lexical items and language context can be explained in terms of language use in a way which does not reveal anything about underlying knowledge systems. More importantly, the term *function word* is rather misleading in this context, since it clearly does not refer to a morphosyntactic category, as opposed to *function words* in traditional grammars and *functional categories* in generative theory. If these elements do indeed express specific functions, they are more likely to be pragmatic than grammatical in nature; see Meisel (1994b) where a similar phenomenon is discussed.

As stated before, the issue hinges on the particular notion of syntax implied in this discussion. I do not mean to implore orthodoxies in grammatical theorizing, neither standard theories nor emergent ones. But it is, of course, necessary to make sure one refers to the same concepts when using the same vocabulary. As noted above, Deuchar and Quay refer to a "rudimentary syntax, based on a predicate-argument structure", and they define syntax in terms of ordered surface strings, as the "juxtaposition of two words ... in predicate-argument structures and sometimes hierarchical structure in some noun phrases containing two nouns" (Deuchar and Quay 1998: 233). The crucial problem is to define *rudimentary syntax* — is it meant to stand in contrast to *genuine syntax* or to *fully developed syntax*? If the former interpretation is intended, the underlying logic according to which children's language use is organized during this period should, in fact, be qualified as pre-syntactic or pre-grammatical, possibly relying on semantic or pragmatic principles, rather than as syntactic, as conceptualized in grammatical theories. The way in which the terms *function word* and *rudimentary syntax* are used suggests such a conclusion. However, in view of the fact that the existence of a *pre-grammatical* phase in language development is such a highly controversial topic, not favored by many authors (but see the interesting suggestion of a *protolanguage* by Bickerton 1990), it may be tempting to remain somewhat vague on the issue. This does not, of course, answer the question as to the nature of the assumed unitary language system. Interestingly enough, although they claim that their *rudimentary syntax* supports the idea of an initial single system, Deuchar and Quay (1998) nevertheless argue that the differentiation issue can only be decided upon once morphological markings are attested, i.e. around age two. In my view, the first claim is too strong since the notion of *rudimentary syntax* is not defined satisfactorily in terms of structure dependency. The second claim, on the other hand, is too weak since morphological markings need to be learned in an item-by-item fashion and do not, therefore, represent reliable evidence for the grammatical competence which underlies children's language use. In other words, children may have access to grammatical notions at a time when they have not yet learned the full repertoire of lexical items expressing these notions.

In sum, the least one can say is that the position advocated by Deuchar and Quay needs much more support, empirical as well as theoretical, in order to be considered as a strong candidate for an explanation of early bilingual language use. As for its empirical plausibility, the findings according to which the same type of predicate-argument structures is attested in both languages need to be corroborated. After all, Spanish and English share many word order properties, thus making it difficult to decide whether the two systems are separated. It will therefore be necessary to contrast languages which are structurally more distinct. Remember that evidence from Basque–Spanish and French–German bilinguals, briefly summarized in Section 2.2, indicates that the children's earliest multi-word utterances already reflect target language differences, although the specific pattern acquired by individual children may vary across individuals (see Meisel 1994c). The perhaps most detailed analysis of the emergence of multi-word utterances in bilingual L1 development has been performed by Köppe (1997: 183ff.), studying three French–German children of the DUFDE project. She presents solid evidence indicating that early multi-word constructions consistently reflect surface patterns of the respective target languages; moreover, the frequencies with which particular word order sequences are used demonstrate target-dependent preferences. This study shows, contrary to the one by Deuchar and Quay (1998), that the differentiation issue can indeed be dealt with during a phase when inflectional morphology is not yet used productively. Most importantly, Köppe's results suggest that early word order regularities reflect surface properties of the target languages rather than semantic or pragmatic principles. One might add that even if it were correct that early child utterances are organized according to pragmatic (theme-rheme, topic-comment, etc.) rather than syntactic criteria, as suggested by Bates (1976), Givón (1979) and others since, identical surface patterns found in both languages of bilinguals cannot simply be interpreted as evidence in support of one grammatical system. Finally, the notion of *rudimentary syntax* relies primarily on linear sequencing and on semantic relationships. It is not clear to what extent structure dependency is a defining property of this system. If it is not, serious doubts remain as to whether it can be construed as evidence for a one-system phase of grammatical language development.

In conclusion, then, although the idea of an early unitary system phase cannot be dismissed without further discussion, the evidence presented in its support is far from conclusive. If it can indeed be shown that the same principles determine the use of both languages of the bilingual child, the crucial question will be whether these qualify as grammatical ones as defined by an established theory of grammar. In my opinion, the currently available knowledge about this early phase of language development does not speak strongly in favor of such a conclusion. This is not to say, however, that the study of bilingual child languages during the period preceding grammatical differentiation could not be of significant interest. Rather, if it could be shown that the utterances in the two (or more) languages are organized according to principles constituting a knowledge system which is not grammatical in nature, this would give stronger support to the idea of a pre-grammatical phase of language development than the available evidence based on monolingual data. The results presented by Köppe (1997) point, in fact, into this direction. She observes that the earliest multi-word utterances lack SV and VO/OV patterns, and she argues that only with the emergence of such verb-argument sequences can one find evidence for hierarchical syntactic organization (e.g. VP), as opposed to the linear orderings found during the preceding phase. This issue clearly deserves more attention in future research, but since the outcome of this debate does not bear on the discussion of the differentiation hypothesis as formulated in 2.1 above, I will not pursue this issue further.

3. Later grammatical development: Autonomous or interdependent?

I hope to have shown in the preceding section that the *Fusion Hypothesis* is to be rejected and that there is strong support for the *Differentiation Hypothesis* as defined in 2.1, above. In other words, bilingual children are able to differentiate the two (or more) grammatical systems in their mental representations of linguistic knowledge as soon as they demonstrate performance that can be attributed to underlying grammatical knowledge. From this it follows that a possible unitary system preceding the developmental phase during which grammatical systems are differentiated is unlikely to be grammatical in nature. Whether such a pre-grammatical system is indeed a possibility and, if so, what its exact properties might be, remains unclear and largely unexplored. At this point, the issue which still needs to be addressed relates to later developments. Quite obviously, the early grammatical knowledge systems undergo subsequent important changes and may even have to be restructured in essential parts, on the way towards the mature target competences. Consequently, an obvious question to ask is whether one will find some kind of cross-linguistic influence in the course of these further developments; it is this problem which is addressed by the hypotheses on interdependent development presented in Section 2.1, above.

Surprisingly, perhaps, the picture one gets by looking at how this issue is treated in the literature reporting on bilingual first language development is not very clear, and it may therefore be useful to formulate questions for further research rather than trying to summarize findings on which there is no broad consensus. In fact, only few studies address the issue of interdependent development directly (see the following discussion). I should hasten to add that this statement is only correct if one does not consider publications on transfer or interference in L2 acquisition. In my view, they are indeed only marginally relevant for the problem under discussion, because they are mostly based on analyses of successive bilingual acquisition after early childhood, frequently of foreign language learning in the classroom — cases, in other words, which do not normally lead to grammatical knowledge equivalent to that of monolingual children. The *Autonomous Development Hypothesis*, on the other hand, assumes that, in the long term, bilinguals develop grammatical systems not different in quality from those of the respective monolinguals, and it predicts that the changes which these systems undergo in subsequent acquisitional phases are determined by the same developmental logic which guides the acquisition of the same languages by monolingual children. Whether this can be corroborated, is, of course, a matter for future research. But it should be clear that the interest of this prediction rests upon the fact that it makes strong claims about the mental representation and development of grammatical knowledge of bilingual individuals.

It is only fairly recently that the issue of autonomous *vs.* interdependent development has been addressed from this perspective, focusing on the grammatical competence of bilinguals. Paradis and Genesee (1996) formulate the relevant problems most clearly, and they investigate them by studying the emergence of functional categories related to finiteness and subject-verb agreement (Infl) and to negation in English–French bilinguals (Paradis and Genesee 1997). Importantly, interdependence, as defined by these authors, may manifest itself in three ways: as transfer, acceleration, or delay. Thus, it need not be seen as a negative factor in language acquisition. Rather, it could cause grammatical phenomena to emerge earlier in bilingual children's speech in comparison to that of monolinguals'. Assuming that certain grammatical devices are acquired earlier in some languages than in others, one could hypothesize that in bilingual development the availability of such grammatical means in one language triggers their acquisition in the other language where they would thus emerge earlier than with the respective monolinguals. Note that if acceleration of this type is indeed possible, it might lead to reorderings in otherwise invariant developmental sequences, and this would count as a qualitative change. In other words, although acceleration might be qualified as a positive influence of one language precipitated by the other, it could lead to qualitative differences between the two types of first language acquisition, contrary to our initial hypothesis; see Section 1.

Although interdependence is considered in its three manifestations, Paradis and Genesee (1996) do not find evidence supporting interdependent development, neither as transfer nor as acceleration or delay. Rather, the emergence of expressions of finiteness and agreement as well as of word order in negated utterances in English and French follows the same acquisitional pattern and develops at the same rate as in monolingual acquisition; this includes the observation that finiteness appears earlier in English than in

French. These authors therefore reject the interdependence hypothesis, where interdependence is defined

> as being the systemic influence of the grammar of one language on the grammar of the other language during acquisition. [...] By systemic, we mean influence at the level of representation or competence, sustained over a period of time. (Paradis and Genesee 1996: 3)

At the same time, they support the idea of autonomous development. Much more research of this type, contrasting patterns and rates of development in the two or more languages of multilingual individuals, is needed in order to decide conclusively on the well-foundedness of these two opposing views. As far as the developmental sequences are concerned, the research results summarized in Section 2.2 seem to support the autonomy hypothesis. If, however, it can be demonstrated that the languages contrasted in these studies develop in a parallel fashion, interdependence becomes more plausible again, provided it can also be shown that these languages develop at different rates in monolingual children. It is, therefore, necessary to reconsider the findings reported on in 2.2 in the light of these questions.

A contrary view on this issue is developed by Tracy (1995) and by Gawlitzek-Maiwald and Tracy (1996) who propose the *Bilingual Bootstrapping Hypothesis*. The idea is that

> [...] something that has been acquired in language A fulfills a booster function for language B. In a weaker version, we would expect at least a temporary pooling of resources.   (Gawlitzek-Maiwald and Tracy 1996: 903)

In other words, they assume that the two languages develop at a different pace and that the more advanced system will boost the development of the less advanced. These claims are supported by the results of a case study on one English–German child whose preferred language is German. Gawlitzek-Maiwald and Tracy (1996: 914) detected "a developmental lag" in that tense and agreement markings still lacked in English at a time when they were used productively in German. Although these authors support the ideas of early differentiation and independent development of the two grammars, they conclude, based on the analysis of mixed utterances, that the child occasionally constructs sentences consisting of a German IP and an English VP. In this way, they intend to account for the observation that in mixed utterances, "left-periphery items of main clauses are taken from German" (Gawlitzek-Maiwald and Tracy 1996: 915). In other words, during this phase, the mixed constructions always start with the German part (containing the finite verbal element), followed by the English one, but not the other way around. Conversely, English seems to take the lead in the development of infinitival constructions. I must admit that I do not find the explanation offered really convincing. Leaving aside the fact that the empirical evidence is taken from only one child, a number of theoretical problems arise. One is mentioned by Gawlitzek-Maiwald and Tracy (1996:916) themselves, namely the question of whether "one can really claim that something is missing if she appears to know very well what it is and how to fill the gap". They answer this question by referring to the implicit knowledge provided by Universal Grammar and by alluding to the well-known fact that (monolingual) children sometimes use *placeholders* before they have acquired the adequate means required by the mature target grammar. Although it may indeed be plausible to assume that the child implicitly knows that English, too, requires a functional projection above VP, the child in this case seems to know much more, for she apparently uses an English-type left-headed IP rather than the German right-headed IP. In fact, since the finite verb in German is raised to the head of CP, it is even less likely that the non-English IP allegedly combined with the English VP is imported from the child's German syntax. But I do not want to quarrel about this specific example; the more interesting question, obviously, is whether this version of the interdependence hypothesis defines interdependent grammatical development in such a way as to establish it as a conceptually attractive and empirically testable explanation of interdependent development.

Currently, the *Bilingual Bootstrapping Hypothesis* is, in my view, a plausible account of certain types of cross-linguistic influences in bilingual language use, but it needs to be spelled out more clearly and in more detail, and it requires a much broader data base and stronger supporting evidence. As a theory predicting interdependent development of grammatical competences, however, it is not particularly attractive. After all, the research findings mentioned in the preceding paragraphs and in Section 2.2 do not seem to support it. Whether this observation represents a serious problem for the idea of bilingual bootstrapping as conceptualized by Gawlitzek-Maiwald and Tracy is not obvious since, at least in its weaker version, bilingual bootstrapping need not exclude the possibility of autonomous development. On the one hand, it is not entirely clear whether the *temporary pooling of resources* postulated by Gawlitzek-Maiwald and Tracy (1996) qualifies as *systemic influence* as defined by Paradis and Genesee (1996). In other words, clarification is needed as to whether this type of interdependence is supposed to lead to grammatical fusion after all, or whether the child is said to make use of knowledge from two sources which are, nevertheless, stored separately. Since Gawlitzek-Maiwald and Tracy (1996) refer to bilingual bootstrapping as a relief strategy, the latter interpretation seems to be justifiable. In this case, bilingual boot-strapping is not in conflict with the claim of autonomy of development. It also avoids the serious problem of how to explain *re-differentiation* of partially and temporarily fused systems. Instead, it can be understood as a case of language alternation (i.e. a performance phenomenon), much like code-switching, possibly even as *covert code-mixing* if only grammatical knowledge is imported from another language whereas the lexical items are all taken from the same language. On the other hand, independently of whether one agrees with this interpretation of bilingual bootstrapping, it is clearly a phenomenon which surfaces only in specific contexts, and it is therefore of crucial importance to define those factors which favor cross-linguistic influences in general, and bilingual bootstrapping in particular. A number of suggestions have already been put forth in various studies, and more research on this issue is needed, I believe. Gawlitzek-Maiwald and Tracy (1996) consider delay in the develop-ment of one language as a crucial factor which might lead to interdependent development. This, of course, raises the question of what causes grammatical development of one language to happen at a slower pace. Structural properties of the languages, consistency of parental input, and language dominance have been suggested as causal factors in the literature discussed so far. In the remainder of this paper, I will address this issue of causal factors for cross-linguistic grammatical interaction in more detail.

Döpke (1992, 1998, 2000) agrees that grammatical differentiation happens early, and she finds that the large majority of the utterances of the English–German children in her research exhibit the morphosyntactic characteristics of the respective target languages. But she also finds utterances which appear to result from cross-linguistic influence, and, in a study in which she focuses on these "unusual structures" (Döpke 2000), she argues that the types of struc-tural differences between the languages are responsible for such influences. The phenomena studied mainly refer to the placement of finite and non-finite verbs in German (see 2.2 above). In her corpus, a number of examples are attested where the non-finite verb precedes the complement in the main clause, $*V_{fin}$ XP rather than XP V_{-fin} (11a), the finite verb follows the negator, $*$NEG V/V NEG (11b), or a non-finite verb appears to have been raised to verb-second position (11c). The latter case, however, appears to be due to the fact that these children generally have problems with the acquisition of verb morphology, as is also indicated by a fourth type of error discussed in the paper where non-finite verbs combined with a modal carry finite endings. This means that the children do not fully master the repertoire of verb forms, rather than indicating cross-linguistic influences in syntax. I will focus here on the syntactic problems.

(11)   a.   *_ich möchte tragen dich_
            I   want   carry   you
            'I want to carry you'

       b.   *_Hund nicht kommt rein_
            dog   not   come   in
            ' (the) dog doesn't come in'

       c.   *_ich sitzen   noch hier_
            I   sit+inf still   here
            'I am still sitting here'

A point which cannot be ignored in this discussion is the observation that monolingual German children have not (or only in isolated examples) been observed using patterns like those in (11). Döpke (2000: 219) attempts to explain this observed difference between monolinguals and bilinguals in terms of "cross-language cue competition on the surface of utterances". That is to say that her bilingual subjects did not organize these sentences according to structure-dependent principles such as headedness of syntactic projections and raising of finite verbs to the head of IP or CP, nor did they use abstract grammatical notions, like finiteness. Instead, she argues, they rely on surface properties of subparts of utterances in their bilingual environment. Sequences like those in (11) are thus claimed to be "neither German nor English in structure" (Döpke 2000: 220) but to be made up of chunks found in the German input, reinforced by similar sequences in English. Note that if this is correct we are not dealing with a case of cross-linguistic influence, at least not in terms of grammatical knowledge. Instead, the influence of English on German happens through the strengthening of cues found in the German input, in case (a) the V–XP ordering, because the same surface order exists in English.

This approach suffers from at least two major weaknesses. It cannot explain why other children do not behave like the ones in this study, and it is only plausible if one assumes that these children do not have access (anymore) to the human language making capacity. Döpke goes on at some length to argue that all the _unusual structures_ can be derived from the German input alone; consequently, they should also appear in the speech of monolingual

children. She asserts that this is indeed the case, although only very occasionally — a claim which is not substantiated. What is more important, however,
is the question of why other bilingual children have not been found to use
such constructions. Döpke (2000: 209) maintains that the language pair
English–German exhibits more "complexities in the overlapping structures"
than French–English or French–German. This is certainly a surprising statement. One wonders whether the English–German pair she examined is indeed
so unique, as compared to typologically-close combinations like English–
Dutch or Spanish–Catalan on the one hand, and typologically-distant ones like
Spanish-Basque, on the other. Even more surprisingly, the alleged complexities
are explained by the fact that English and German differ in headedness as well
as in the position into which the finite verb is raised. In view of the standard
assumption, shared by Döpke, that finite verbs remain in VP in English,
French and German are characterized by exactly the same similarities and
differences as English and German. The reason why Döpke does not recognize
this is that she describes finite verb raising in linear terms as "movement to
the left over negation" rather than hierarchically as movement to IP or CP.

This brings us to the second critical point, for, ironically, this analysis does
exactly what it attributes to the bilingual children, i.e. it relies on linear
orderings rather than on hierarchical structures. If, however, it is true that
"the hierarchical relationships between the subparts of the utterances were not
evident to the children *a priori*" (Döpke 2000: 224), it follows that the children
do not make use of the human language faculty. In fact, it is precisely this
reliance on surface order and on subparts of sentence structures which has
been argued to characterize adult second language acquisition, as opposed to
first language development; see Meisel (1997a; 1997b).

In conclusion, the two points of criticism are connected, i.e., these
children differ from other bilingual children mentioned in the literature in
that they use constructions typical of L2 acquisition. L2 learners, however, may
indeed not have full access to Universal Grammar (UG) understood as a
central component of the language faculty. Note that it has been suggested
before that bilingual children may occasionally behave linguistically like L2
learners. Schlyter (1993: 289 f.), for example, claims that in case of bilinguals
who do not have equal proficiency in both languages, the dominant language
develops just like that in the corresponding monolinguals, whereas the
development of the weaker language may resemble that of L2 learners. Here,
language *dominance* is defined in terms of the pace of development. Since the
children studied by Döpke (1992, 1998, 2000) use mostly English, dominance

is likely to account for their L2-like linguistic behavior, although the author herself does not find consistent developmental advantages in her children's English. Whatever the explanation may be, the rare and unusual constructions discussed here do not typically appear in the language of young bilinguals. With respect to our question about the nature of the causal factors that underlie cross-linguistic influences, the proposal put forth by Döpke is that the languages being learned share *overlapping* structures which, in turn, results in cross-linguistic strengthening of surface cues, assuming that children do not rely on structure-dependent properties of sentence structures but on surface properties of chunks of sentences. I have raised some objections to this analysis, but I certainly view this as an area where more research should be carried out in order to determine whether similar types of constructions are used by other children in various language pairs and whether an explanation in terms of cross-linguistic cue strengthening can be maintained.

I should hasten to add that at least one aspect of the work just discussed offers a promising perspective for further research. Remember that several of the studies mentioned above allude to variability of developmental pace in order to account for the alleged interdependent development of grammars. But whereas for Paradis and Genesee (1996) delay and acceleration are possible manifestations of interdependence, others view this as the cause of cross-linguistic influence. Schlyter (1993), for example, defines language dominance in terms of variability in the pace of acquisition and argues that the weaker and thus more slowly developing language is susceptible to influences from the dominant one. Similarly, Gawlitzek-Maiwald and Tracy (1996) interpret developmental lags in one language as the cause for influences from the other language. As pointed out above, however, this can at best be part of the solution to the problem of identifying causal factors for cross-linguistic grammatical interaction, for it does not explain why developmental lags occur in the first place. Language dominance, when defined in terms of quantity or quality of input, can perhaps predict the direction of possible cross-linguistic influences, but it does not reveal why certain aspects of the language system are affected whereas others are not. It is not implausible to assume that language-internal properties might favor such interactions across grammatical systems; this is why attempts at identifying the corresponding characteristics of the target languages may indeed be expected to contribute to a solution of the problem.

An interesting approach along these lines is developed by Müller (1998) and Müller and Hulk (to appear). As opposed to the authors just referred to, they are not concerned with developmental pace at all, but with transfer, the third of the possible ways in which interdependent development may manifest itself, according to Paradis and Genesee (1996). Like Döpke, Müller and Hulk identify structural areas in which the two languages overlap as the locus of possible cross-linguistic influence. But contrary to Döpke (2000) who relies on surface properties supposedly resulting in cross-language cue competition, these authors refer to bilingual children's implicit grammatical analysis of the linguistic input. The basic idea is that cross-linguistic influence is favored by structural ambiguity, the latter being defined in terms of constructions which appear to allow for more than one grammatical analysis as a result of variability in the input. In German subordinate clauses, for example, the finite verb is normally placed in final position (see 2.2); with certain lexical elements introducing the clause, however, it may have to appear in non-final position (e.g. with *denn* 'for'), or its position can vary in colloquial speech (e.g. with *weil* 'because'). If, then, a specific surface construction is found in both languages, and it is *ambiguous* in only one of them, the bilingual child "may be tempted to transfer features from the language presenting unambiguous input into the one which is ambiguous" (Müller 1998: 152). Note that according to this hypothesis transfer is predicted to operate in one direction only, from the language exhibiting the non-ambiguous construction to the one with ambiguous patterns. What is particularly interesting about this approach is, I believe, that it explores the possibility of defining causal factors of interdependent development in terms of structural properties of the language; in other words, it attempts to identify vulnerable parts of grammars rather than referring in a wholesale fashion to weaker or less developed grammars. It is important to note that according to Müller (1998) these vulnerable parts of grammars are problematic for monolingual children as well. They, too, can be led to wrong conclusions by ambiguous input constructions — but less frequently so, because there is no competing input from another language luring them into choosing the wrong option.

Müller and Hulk (to appear) elaborate on these ideas in developing a hypothesis about what they call *mapping induced influence* of one language on the other. They argue that cross-linguistic influence can occur if two conditions are met, namely, firstly, that the two languages overlap at the surface level as described above, and, secondly, an interface level is affected which connects the grammar and other cognitive systems. They further claim that it is the *C-domain* which serves as an interface of this type. Cross-linguistic influence is thus "induced by the mapping of universal onto language-specific principles, in particular pragmatic principles onto syntactic principles"

(Müller and Hulk to appear: 38). *Mapping induced influence* is understood here as a kind of *indirect* influence, as opposed to transfer which is seen as direct influence. The grammatical phenomenon studied by Müller and Hulk (to appear) is object drop in Dutch, German, French, and Italian by monolingual and bilingual children. Initially, target-deviant object drop occurs twice as frequently in the speech of monolingual speakers of the Germanic than of the Romance languages. Target-deviant object drop decreases over time with the lexical instantiation of the C system. According to Müller and Hulk, learners at early stages use a pragmatic strategy to license the empty position since the child finds evidence for object drop in Germanic as well as in Romance languages. Monolingual Romance children converge earlier with the target system than children acquiring Dutch and German because the latter are topic drop languages providing apparent evidence for discourse licensing of empty elements. As for bilinguals, they are found to drop objects frequently in French and Italian as German and Dutch monolinguals do but more frequently than monolingual French and Italian children. Müller and Hulk (to appear: 369) claim that bilinguals are indirectly influenced by the respective Germanic language. However, the difference between monolingual and bilingual children is not qualitative but only quantitative.

These hypotheses about direct and indirect cross-linguistic influence in bilingual children offer the most sophisticated accounts of interdependent developments as far as possible structural causes favoring these phenomena are concerned. But this approach is not without problems either. Note that both types of influence are defined as systemic ones as defined by Paradis and Genesee (1996), although transfer is referred to as a relief strategy (Müller 1998: 152), a term ordinarily used to designate mechanisms of language use. Here the children are said to have successfully differentiated the two grammars, but in the course of further development the grammars exhibit properties significantly different from those of monolinguals, although they are supposedly possible human grammars, i.e., they are constrained by UG. Transfer crucially implies the setting of parameters to values different from those in the respective monolingual grammars. This assumption inevitably leads into the *resetting problem* (see Meisel 1995 for a discussion in some detail), i.e., it needs to be explained how these children can eventually succeed in setting the parameters in question on the appropriate value. Müller (1998) who, herself, rejects the possibility of parameter resetting, argues that the target-deviant settings only affect *sub-parameters* which, she claims, can indeed be reset. This can hardly be qualified as a satisfactory solution. First of all, it is rather implausible that sub-parameters should be different from parameters in this respect since in both cases acquisition involves accessing knowledge provided by the human language faculty (UG) rather than knowledge attained by inductive learning. Moreover, the notion of *sub-parameter* itself is an *ad hoc* stipulation which lacks an adequate justification in terms of the theory of grammar. Let me add that the notion of *transfer* is not a felicitous terminological choice anyway, since the phenomena under discussion are claimed to appear in monolingual children as well, only less frequently; the influence of the other language thus consists of favoring one of the options offered by the target language rather than of the transfer of knowledge from the other language.

Another serious problem, as I see it, is that the notion of *structural ambiguity* is not properly defined. As mentioned earlier, Müller and Hulk are really referring to variability in the primary data. Structural ambiguity, on the other hand, is normally defined as referring to cases where one surface construction can be assigned different underlying representations. A well-known example, discussed in Section 2.2, is the syntactic analysis of SVO order where the subject and the verb may either appear in the CP as in V2 languages or in the IP, as in the Romance languages. In cases like the subordinate clause constructions discussed by Müller (1998), on the other hand, the child needs to discover that certain syntactic properties depend on the choice of a limited number of lexical items. Put differently, the learner cannot generalize to the entire set of elements belonging to the same category but needs to distinguish between subsets. This may indeed cause acquisitional problems, but children are clearly able to cope with them and are normally not induced to setting parameters to target-deviant values. In fact, in the case of clause-final verbs in German subordinates, the input is indeed unambiguous since clause-final finite verbs *plus* VO orders and V2 position of the finite verb leaves only one option, namely underlying OV ordering. All other alternatives would require movement operations not tolerated by UG. Note that similar discussions can be found in historical linguistics when it comes to explaining language change involving parameter setting. Kaiser (1998), for example, argues that ambiguity of the kind discussed here does not lead to new settings of parameters, as long as unambiguous structures are also available. This is in line with the theory of unambiguous triggers by Fodor (1998) where she argues quite convincingly that ambiguous constructions do not lead to triggering of parameter settings; instead, the child only sets the parameter to a specific value once unambiguous evidence becomes available. My conclusion thus is that these and similar problems considerably weaken the Interdependent Development Hypothesis; unless they can be solved satisfactorily, the Autonomous Development Hypothesis is to be preferred.

4.   Summary and conclusions:
Implications for a theory of language development

The simultaneous acquisition of more than one language by a single individual indeed qualifies as an instance of first language acquisition. This statement made at the beginning of this chapter has been confirmed, I believe, by the results of the research reviewed here. In view of this and similar research, there cannot really be any doubt that bilingual children arrive at the same type of grammatical knowledge as the respective monolinguals. But although the *Fusion Hypothesis* seems to be generally rejected in current work on child bilingualism and the *Differentiation Hypothesis* encounters overwhelming support, some doubts remain as to whether subsequent developments can be affected by cross-linguistic interactions of these systems. Deciding on the alternative between *interdependent* and *autonomous* development is in fact rather difficult and depends on the clarification of some points which are currently still controversial or for which insufficient evidence is available. At any rate, no one, to my knowledge, argues that developmental sequences familiar from monolingual L1 acquisition are substantially reordered in bilingual development. If, therefore, some authors support the idea of interdependent development, one needs to determine whether they are indeed referring to what has been called *systemic* influences (Paradis and Genesee 1996). This question is of crucial importance since the consequences following from the possible answers are conceptually very different and suggest also quite different practical measures, e.g. for preschool education. If, for example, one accepts the weaker version of the *Bilingual Bootstrapping Hypothesis*, this can be interpreted as evidence that cross-linguistic influences reflect the particular use a bilingual person makes of the two knowledge systems. In other words, interdependent developments of this sort need not be understood as indicating qualitatively different types of language acquisition in bilinguals as compared to monolinguals. Rather, these phenomena may well be the effect of the type of language mode of a person at a given moment. Following Grosjean (1998, 2000), the language mode is characterized by the state of activation of the bilingual's languages and language processing mechanisms. For the time being, then, I find the *Interdependent Development Hypothesis* less convincing than the *Autonomous Development Hypothesis*. There seems to be general consensus, however, that irrespective of the particular developmental route taken by bilingual children, they ultimately attain grammatical competence in each of their languages which does not differ in quality from that of the respective monolinguals.

In conclusion, the fact that multilingual development leads to multiple knowledge systems equivalent to those of monolinguals must be interpreted as strong evidence in support of the claim that the human language faculty predisposes the individual to become multilingual. Consequently, this fact should be taken into account in our thinking and theorizing about language and grammar. Let me only mention one of the numerous implications and consequences. Assuming that a theory of the human language faculty can be adequately formulated based on the idea of parameter setting, a number of consequences follow for the theory of grammar and of grammatical development which are also relevant for other types of language acquisition. One is that all values of a parameter need to remain accessible for a certain period of development, irrespective of whether a language-specific grammar is instantiated which makes use of one of the possible settings. Put differently, if children set a parameter in one language before they set the corresponding parameter in the other language, this should not count as an instance of *resetting*. This may, in fact, be a suitable definition of the *sensitive period* for language development. In other words, although it has been argued that *resetting* is not possible for second language learners, i.e., in successive acquisition of two or more languages after this age, the fact that in the simultaneous acquisition of languages a specific parameter can be set on different values in different grammars, no matter whether this happens in a synchronized fashion in both languages or delayed in one, indicates — in fact, requires — that all values remain accessible. This is to say that one should not view Universal Grammar as a system which turns into a specific grammar of a language in the course of acquisition, i.e., that UG autodestructs as a result of language-specific grammatical development, as suggested by Clahsen and Muysken (1996: 722) who claim that "Once a parametric option (consistent with the available input) has been chosen, the remaining unexercised options are no longer available." Quite to the contrary, the fact that in bilingual development each grammar develops in essentially the same way as in the respective monolingual learners explains the ease with which bilingual children, as compared to second language learners, discover structure-dependent properties of each language which are difficult if not impossible to deduce from surface phenomena. The fact that conflicting parameter settings in the two languages do not seem to represent a special acquisitional problem for bilingual learners is all the more interesting and significant in view of the large amount of variation (individual, situational, regional) which apparently does not trigger the development of separate systems in monolinguals.[2] Consequently, one might hypothesize that only certain types of variation lead to bilingualism, i.e., evidence for conflicting parameter settings causes the Language Acquisition Device to differentiate more than one system, to open a new file, using a computer metaphor, rather than to treat this information as a type of system-internal variation. If this suggestion is essentially correct, it follows, of course, that the explanation of other types of language acquisition, e.g. monolingual L1 development, will have to do without the option of a parameter being set simultaneously on more than one value. Independently of how this issue will eventually be decided upon, an adequate theory of grammar and of grammatical development must be capable of explaining multilingual development as the simultaneous acquisition of two or more first languages, i.e., an achievement of the human mind for which monolingual development is just a special case.

Notes

* This is a revised version of a plenary presentation at the VIIIth International Congress for the Study of Child Language, Donostia-San Sebastián, 15 July 1999. I want to thank Susanne E. Carroll, Fred Genesee, and Regina Köppe for reading and discussing with me an earlier version of this paper and Jasone Cenoz for helpful comments on the manuscript.

1. Small letters indicate clitic elements. The abbreviations used here and in the remainder of the paper are those standardly used in the grammatical literature: Adv=adverb; Aux=auxiliary; C, Comp=complementizer; CP=complementizer phrase; Infl=inflection; IP=inflection phrase; NEG=negator; NegP=negation phrase; V=verb; VP=verb phrase; V_{+fin}=finite verb; V_{-fin}=non-finite verb.

2. I assume without further discussion, at this point, that the various subsystems which a monolingual develops are different in nature (linguistically and psychologically) from those of *true bilinguals*; see Roeper (1999) for an opposing view of this issue.

CHAPTER 2

The emergence of verbal morphology and the lead-lag pattern issue in bilingual acquisition*

Ludovica Serratrice

1. Introduction

A number of recent studies investigating the early morphosyntactic development of bilingual children acquiring English together with another morphologically richer language have reported the existence of a developmental
asynchrony between the two languages. The common finding is that English
invariably lags behind as far as the productive use of inflected verb forms is
concerned (Gawlitzek-Maiwald and Tracy 1996; Paradis and Genesee 1996,
1997). Similarly to children who acquire English monolingually, bilingual
English-speaking children go through a protracted period of time in which the
majority of verbs appear in their bare form. At the same time as they produce
uninflected forms in English, these same children have a substantial proportion
of inflected verb forms in their other language, whether it be German, Latvian
(Sinka and Schelletter 1998), French (Paradis and Genesee 1996, 1997), or
Italian (Serratrice 1999). This lead-lag pattern in the emergence of verbal
morphology confirms the language specificity of the acquisition process and
gives further support to the *separate development hypothesis* (De Houwer 1990).

In essence bilingual children who are exposed to two languages from birth
behave as the sum of two monolinguals, at least as far as the initial stages of
morphosyntactic development are concerned.[1]

In addition to confirming the separate development hypothesis, the
observation that in bilingual children there is a discrepancy in the command
of verb morphosyntax between English and more richly inflected languages
gives credit to the idea that the acquisition of grammatical contrasts takes
place earlier in languages where morphosyntactic cues are more transparent,
reliable and consistent. In studies of monolingual acquisition researchers

working on a variety of languages other than English have proposed that from early on in acquisition, not only can children discriminate between finite and non-finite forms, but they also show productive control of subject-verb agreement (see Hyams 1986, 1992; Guasti 1993/94 for Italian; Poeppel and Wexler 1993, for German). Such crosslinguistic evidence goes against earlier claims made by researchers such as Radford (1990, 1996), Guilfoyle and Noonan (1988), Lebeaux (1988) that there is a universal initial stage in which children have no productive use of morphosyntax, and hence no abstract notion of tense and agreement. Data from the acquisition of morphosyntax in languages such as Italian, Spanish, German, and French corroborate the hypothesis of an input-driven developmental schedule which reflects the typological nature of the language the children are exposed to: the richer the morphosyntactic cues, the faster meaningful grammatical contrasts will be acquired. Conversely, the poorer the verb morphology is, the longer the acquisition process will be. In a way English-speaking children go through a stage that is missed out by children who from very early on are exposed to a multiplicity of cues whose convergence greatly facilitates the morphosyntactic acquisition process.

Paradis and Genesee (1996, 1997) present data on the acquisition of English and French in five bilingual children exposed to these two languages from birth. The syntactic phenomena analysed in Paradis and Genesee (1996) include the proportion of finite verbs, the placement of verbs with respect to negation, and the use of subject pronouns with finite and non-finite forms. With respect to finiteness and verb placement the authors observe that the English–French bilinguals in their study treat their two languages in an independent fashion, and do not apply syntactic rules from one language to the other. Similar findings are reported by Paradis and Genesee (1997) for two other English–French bilinguals. Unfortunately, however, neither study provides more than anecdotal evidence about productivity of inflected verb forms in the data they analyse. There are only a handful of allegedly representative examples of what kind of verb types the children use with various inflections, but there is no additional data on the distribution of verb inflections with different verb types, and on what verb types are found inflected for various person/number and tense combinations.

Another study that explores the issue of the separate developmental hypothesis, and indirectly of the lead-lag pattern question, is that by Sinka and Schelletter (1998). The two children in the study are acquiring English together with another more richly inflected language: German in Sonja's case, and Latvian in Maija's. For both girls inflected forms appear earlier, and are significantly more frequent and more productive in their other language than in English. On the basis of such an obvious discrepancy in the appearance and use of inflected verb forms in the corpora of Sonja and Maija, Sinka and Schelletter (1998) argue for a clear-cut case of language differentiation where the typological nature of the input drives the acquisition of morphosyntax independently of the variable represented by the other language the bilingual child is exposed to. Similarly to Paradis and Genesee (1996, 1997), Sinka and Schelletter conclude that the lead-lag pattern often observed in bilingual children exposed to two languages varying along a continuum of morpho-syntactic richness confirms the early realisation and acquisition of grammatical contrasts exactly in those languages where the convergence of complex morphophonological cues makes it more clear to the child that such contrasts exist and are meaningful.

Since crosslinguistic studies on the acquisition of verbal morphosyntax have started being conducted on a variety of languages other than English, it has become obvious that there is no reason to assume, as is done for English by some researchers (Aldridge 1989; Radford 1990, 1996), that children are unable to reproduce the person/number and tense contrasts they hear in the language addressed to them from the earliest stages of productive multiword utterances. On the contrary, there are indications that children learning a richly inflected language such as Italian can produce appropriate inflected forms from the beginning of acquisition. Children's errorless production of inflected forms has also been used by some as evidence that they master subject-verb agreement as soon as they start producing verbs.

These assumptions on the actual morphosyntactic abilities of Italian-speaking children have recently been questioned by Pizzuto and Caselli (1992, 1993, 1994). The argument at the core of Pizzuto and Caselli's work on the acquisition of Italian verbal morphology is that previous studies such as Hyams' (1986, 1992) have not subjected the data to sufficiently rigorous tests of productivity. Pizzuto and Caselli apply to the acquisition of Italian the same criteria initially proposed by Cazden (1968) and Brown (1973) for the acquisi-tion of English. For each morpheme they distinguish between *first appearance* and *point of acquisition* defined as the first of three consecutive samples where the morpheme is produced correctly in at least 90 per cent of obligatory contexts. Two additional criteria are also used in determining point of acquisi-tion: firstly, each of the samples that are crucial for scoring the acquisition point must contain at least five obligatory contexts of use. Secondly, with specific reference to verbal morphology, an inflection is considered to be used productively if it appears with at least two different verb types in each of the samples chosen for the scoring of the point of acquisition. At the same time, a verb appearing with an inflection that is used productively must also appear with at least another inflection, in order for the verb form to be used contrastively. Taken together these criteria offer a more explicit definition of acquisition than simply the criterion of 90 per cent correct forms in obligatory contexts which is all too often used as the only method to assess productive use of morphology.

Gathercole, Sebastián and Soto (1999, 2000) apply the same productivity criteria outlined above to the verbal production of two monolingual Spanish-speaking children. As for contrasts of person, number, and tense, the authors state that "it is impossible to say that one of these emerges, is learned, or is filled in before the others, there is no across-the-board acquisition of any of these" (Gathercole *et al.* 1999: 146). Another richly inflected language where there are prima facie indications that children master subject-verb agreement at an early age is Brazilian Portuguese. In this language too children start producing inflected forms from very early on and the rate of errors is extremely low, evidence that could support the hypothesis of early mastery of subject-verb agreement. Rubino and Pine (1998) have analysed data on subject-verb agreement in one child acquiring Brazilian Portuguese and have reached very different conclusions. Their findings show that although the error rate is indeed low overall, there is a significant difference between the number of incorrect singular and plural forms. This would not be expected if the child had indeed productive knowledge of how subject-verb agreement works. If on the other hand the error rates are linked to specific lexical items that have not been properly assimilated in the child's lexicon and for which he has not yet performed a suitable distributional analysis, then the results are not so surprising.

In sum, when appropriate methodological tools are used it becomes clear that even in richly inflected languages it is not appropriate to credit children with productive use of inflectional verb morphology until there is convincing evidence that they can indeed use various inflections with a variety of verb types, and that these forms are also used contrastively. Although both monolingual and bilingual children acquiring richly inflected languages produce proportionally more inflected forms than their peers acquiring English, it is not necessarily the case that this linguistic behaviour can be taken as a positive indication of adult-like command of morphosyntactic knowledge.

In this chapter data from an English–Italian bilingual child will be analysed in order to assess to what extent the child can be credited with productive knowledge of tense and subject-verb agreement, and to what extent it is
justifiable to characterise his bilingual output in terms of a lead-lag pattern. If
it is demonstrated that even in a language like Italian there is no productive
across-the-board command of finite forms, and if it is indeed the case that a
process of piecemeal learning is at work we would expect to find a certain
degree of lexical specificity whereby particular verbs only ever appear with
some inflections and not others, and some inflections are more likely to
appear with certain verbs. By this rationale children acquire inflections as part
and parcel of the verb forms they are learning, and it follows that a verb like
volere 'to want' may be more likely to appear in the first person singular
present tense (e.g. *voglio* '(I) want'), while a verb like *smettere* 'to stop', may
have a high chance of appearing in the imperative singular form *smettila* 'stop
it'. By a gradual and piecemeal process of lexical learning children accumulate
a number of verb types which tend to occur in a limited number of forms.
Initially the correspondence may even be one-to-one, one verb type always
only occurring in the same inflectional form (e.g. the verb *guardare* 'to look',
only ever occurring in the singular imperative form *guarda* 'look'). It is only
when a sufficiently large number of individually-learnt lexical items are part of
the child's vocabulary that she may begin to notice and extract paradigmatic
relations, and some productivity with at least a subset of the inflectional
paradigm begins to emerge. This idea of piecemeal learning is in line with a
number of recent studies investigating the nature of children's early verb
morphosyntax where a strong case is made for the initial lexical specificity of
children's use of verb morphology and argument structure (Tomasello 1992;
Lieven, Pine and Baldwin 1997; Pine, Lieven and Rowland 1998).

2.   Method

2.1 The subject

The data analysed in this chapter come from a case study of Carlo (C.), a
bilingual English-Italian child born in Scotland of an American father and an
Italian mother. The child has been exposed to both languages from birth on a
regular basis which qualifies this as a case of bilingual first language acquisition (De Houwer 1990). C. has two older siblings, stepbrother A., ten years his

senior and a monolingual speaker of English with some basic knowledge of Italian, and brother M., five years his senior and bilingual in Italian and English. Everybody in the family addresses C. in Italian and he uses Italian with all the members of his family and with the Italian-speaking childminders who look after him after nursery for approximately five hours a day. In this child's case then Italian is the home language, while English is the community language that he hears mostly outside the home environment. English is also spoken in the home between his parents, and between his father and his two other brothers. Approximately 45 per cent of C's waking time is spent in a monolingual Italian-speaking environment, 40 per cent in an English-speaking environment, and the remaining 15 per cent in a mixed Italian-English environment with a predominance of Italian addressed to him. This subdivision of C's time also changes significantly during visits to his maternal grandparents in Italy, during their extended visits in Scotland, and during the family's summer holidays in North America.

2.2 Data collection and transcription

Data were collected for a period of 15 months at fortnightly intervals for both languages with a number of breaks due to illness and family holidays. See Table 1 for a breakdown of the recordings selected for this study.[2]

MLU was calculated in words (MLU$_w$) rather than in morphemes in order to avoid a bias against English which is not as morphologically rich as Italian. The calculation is computed automatically, and cliticized forms (e.g. *don't*) are counted as one word.

For each language the context was kept as monolingual as possible to reflect the distinction operating in C's upbringing: Italian at home and English outside the home. In order to do so in each recording session C. typically interacted with one adult at a time, with the author in Italian, and with two monolingual English-speaking adults, K. or E. in English. Each recording lasted approximately 45 minutes and the activities during the recording sessions ranged from playing with Lego, to drawing, looking at picture books, playing with jigsaw puzzles, toy telephones, and telling stories. There was no set of structured activities as such, but the adult interlocutor tried to choose anything that was most likely to elicit the maximum amount of speech from the child at any given time.

All the data were subsequently transcribed in CHAT format as described in MacWhinney (1995). The data were transcribed orthographically except for

Table 1. Age and MLUw for the Italian and the English data

Italian			English		
File	Age	MLUw	File	Age	MLUw
1	1;10.8	1.071	1	1;10.1	1.156
2	1;10.27	1.165	2	1;10.20	1.376
3	1;11.17	1.360	3	1;11.4	1.284
4	1;11.25	1.444	4	1;11.18	1.096
5	2;0.1	1.178	5	2;0.1	1.393
6	2;0.7	1.287	6	2;0.23	1.204
7	2;0.23	1.874	7	2;2.12	1.861
8	2;1.23	1.904	8	2;2.24	1.989
9	2;2.3	1.883	9	2;4.7	2.215
10	2;2.17	2.009	10	2;4.29	1.921
11	2;3.7	2.184	11	2;7.8	2.511
12	2;4.14	2.604	12	2;9.6	2.476
13	2;5.6	2.476	13	2;10.1	2.655
14	2;5.26	2.631	14	2;10.15	2.796
15	2;9.6	2.633	15	2;10.23	2.379
16	2;10	2.465	16	2;10.30	2.649
17	2;10.18	2.735	17	3;0.3	2.381
18	2;11.12	2.873	18	3;0.16	2.934
19	3;0.3	2.690	19	3;1.25	2.588
20	3;0.17	3.306			

some child forms for which a broad phonetic transcription was provided together with the corresponding adult target. A complete morphological tagging was also added to the English data.

3.   The acquisition of subject-verb agreement in English

As is well known, English verbal morphology does not encode person distinctions in the morphological paradigm of lexical verbs, but only a number distinction. Coincidentally this number distinction is only visible in the simple present tense, while any number distinction is obliterated in the preterit where all forms are simply marked for [+past] tense. Because of the nature of inflectional morphology in the English language, clear-cut cases of subject-verb agreement on lexical verb will only be third person singular contexts where verbs take the — s suffix. Other person/number combinations are not sufficiently informative since the finite form is indistinguishable from the bare stem or the infinitive. Non-lexical verbs such as modals are equally as uninfor-

Table 2. Present tense copula *be*

Age	1SG	2SG	3SG	1PL	2PL	3PL	TOTAL
1;10.1	–	–	0/6	–	–	–	0/6
1;10.20	–	–	0/7	–	–	–	0/7
1;11.4	–	–	2/16	–	–	–	2/16
1;11.18	–	–	0/14	–	–	–	0/14
2;0.1	–	–	0/2	–	–	–	0/2
2;0.23	–	–	0/2	–	–	–	0/2
2;2.12	–	–	0/62	–	–	–	0/62
2;2.24	–	–	0/45	–	–	–	0/45
2;4.7	–	–	7/19	–	–	0/2	7/21
2;4.29	–	–	17/20	–	–	–	17/20
2;7.8	–	–	22/32	–	–	–	22/32
2;9.6	–	–	24/26	–	–	2/2	26/28
2;10.1	–	–	5/9	–	–	–	5/9
2;10.15	–	–	15/15	–	–	1/1	16/16
2;10.23	–	–	10/16	–	–	10/10	20/26
2;10.30	–	–	8/8	–	–	10/10	18/18
3;0.3	–	–	17/23	–	–	–	17/23
3;0.16	1/1	–	15/20	–	–	–	16/21
3;1.25	–	–	12/15	–	–	1/1	13/16

mative given their defective agreeing paradigm. Only auxiliaries *be* and *have* and copula *be* can provide us with additional clues to the child's mastery of subject-verb agreement.

In the next section we will investigate C's use of copula forms and aspectual auxiliary *be*, in order to assess to what extent the child shows any productive across-the-board notion that subjects and verbs must agree in number/person.

3.1 Copula *be*

Obligatory contexts for copula *be* have been calculated searching the following environments: utterances containing an expletive subject pronoun such as *it* and *there*, a deictic demonstrative pronoun such as *this/these*, *that/those*, a personal subject pronoun (*I*, *you*, *he/she*, etc.) or a subject nominal, whether a proper name or a common noun followed by an adjective, a determiner, a noun, or a negative element. This search has targeted all possible combinations in which a copula is required to occur but is omitted in the child's speech with a variety of precopular and postcopular adjectives or Determiner Phrases (DPs). DPs include proper names, personal pronouns, and determiner + common noun combinations (e.g. *that dog, a ball, my toy*, etc.).[3] In addition, all the tokens of contracted and uncontracted copula that the child actually used were also counted. The number of obligatory contexts is therefore the total number of contexts in which the child should have used a copula form (e.g. *that* (*is*) *a dog*), and the total number of contexts in which he actually used one (e.g. *that is a dog, is a big train*). The results for present tense copula *be* are summarised in Table 2.

As shown in Table 2 the only two contexts where the copula is present at all are third person singular and third person plural contexts, with the exception of one token of first person singular at 3;0.16. This is to be expected considering that all third person singular occurrences of the copula appear in one of two frames: *that's* (*a*) *x* or *it's* (*a*) *x*, and that third person plural tokens are found in the similar frame *they're* (*a*) *x*.[4] All of these frames are involved in naming objects, and they are especially frequent in the earlier stages when labelling is C's main mode of linguistic interaction. The third person singular copula makes its first appearance in the *that* (*a*) *x* labelling construction at 2;4.7, when we also find the first two plural predicative contexts where however the copula is missing.

In total there are 26 obligatory contexts for third person plural contexts, out of which the copula is correctly supplied 24 times. As for third person singular the number of obligatory contexts is considerably higher with a total of 357, only 154 of which display correct use of the copula. The overall poorer performance in third person singular contexts in absolute terms is however biased by an age effect. Third person plural obligatory contexts emerge some six months later than singular ones, by this stage C. has already been through an extended period in which the third person singular copula is missing, a situation which inflates the overall number of null copula instances. By the time obligatory contexts in the plural emerge there is reason to believe that C has begun to realise the obligatoriness of the copula, at least in restricted naming contexts. If we compare C's performance on third person singular contexts with his performance on third person plural contexts from 2;4.7 onwards then we find that 154 out of 203 third person singular contexts display use of the copula, a proportion of 74.87 per cent of copula tokens in obligatory context. This figure is still lower than 92.3 per cent (24/26) of occurrences in obligatory contexts that we find for plural copula forms but it is nevertheless a more comparable figure, particularly if we take into account the fact that the number of singular contexts is almost ten times that of plural contexts (203 vs. 26).

As for the contexts in which the copula is used, there is a clear lexically-specific effect. Within the larger copular construction of the type *DP* + *copula*

+ *Adj/DP*, C. only uses a small subset where the precopular slot can only be filled by *that*, *it* or *they*, while the postcopular position is open to a variety of different adjectives or DPs. Because the copula is so severely limited as to the range of subjects with which it appears (*that*, *it* and *they*), there is reason to believe that the child's knowledge at this stage is not knowledge of a larger copular construction of the type *DP + copula + Adj/DP*, but of a much more lexically-specific construction *that/it/they + copula + Adj/DP*. As the child learns that elements other than *that*, *it* and *they* can occupy the precopular slot position, an ever larger inventory of lexically-specific constructions should accumulate in his linguistic repertoire until the kind of subject is no longer subject to lexical restrictions.

As we noted previously, the child engages in a substantial amount of naming, especially in the earlier stages, an activity involving third person referents which, particularly initially, are for the most part singular. Until 2;9.6 86 per cent of all of C's DPs are found in predicative position following a copula; it is only from 2;9.6 onwards that DPs start to appear in argument position as the subjects and objects of verbs. Naming constructions are also frequent in the adult language C. is exposed to: an average of 16 per cent (847/5161) of all adult utterances are naming constructions (e.g. *she's pretty*; *that's a cat*; *these are beavers*; *they are naughty children*, etc.). In the initial phases C. uses a predicative construction where a dummy placeholder (*this* or *that*) is juxtaposed to an adjective or a noun, optionally preceded by a determiner. Slowly this predicative construction turns into a copular construction when the contractible form of the copula starts appearing in singular contexts and then in plural ones. There is reason to believe that for C. the copula is nothing more than the filling out of a slot inside a construction. Firstly, the two main elements of the copular construction are identified: the precopular DP and the postcopular DP which in an initial phase are only divided by an intonational break to indicate that the pronoun *that* and the noun following it are not part of the same constituent, but two distinct entities.

(1)   (1;10.20)
      *CAR: dat # bunny.
(2)   (1;11.4)
      *CAR: dat # ball.

At a later stage, presumably once C. has been exposed to a sufficiently large number of examples of contractible copula, and once he is able to produce the

/ts/ cluster, he is in a position to start reproducing with greater accuracy what he hears in the input.

(3)   (2;4.7)
      *CAR: that's my shoe.

There are no subject-agreement errors throughout the whole corpus, but this in itself is not a sufficient reason to credit him with any productive knowledge. Rather one could simply characterise this as a sign of extreme conservatism whereby the child limits himself to reproduce what he hears in the adult input. As Tomasello and Brooks (1999: 168) have suggested, "the consistent ordering patterns used by children are very likely direct reproductions of the ordering patterns they have heard in adult speech, not productive syntactic symbols".

In sum, the fact that C's use of the copula is so strictly dependent on a lexically-specified construction indicates that his knowledge is best character- ised in usage-based terms, rather than in terms of an abstract notion of subject-verb agreement.

Similar conclusions are reached by Radford (1990) in an in-depth analysis of a large corpus of utterances from monolingual English children. Just like for monolingual English-speaking children, for this bilingual child the significance of the emergence of copula forms can only be assessed within the context of the constructions they appear in.

3.2 Aspectual auxiliary be

Although copula *be* and aspectual auxiliary *be* are homonyms, there is some evidence that C. treats the two differently. Firstly, unlike for the copula, where the only two person/number combinations for which there are obligatory contexts are third person singular and third person plural, for the aspectual auxiliary all person/number combinations with the exception of second person plural have a number of obligatory contexts ranging from 3 for first person singular, to 80 for third person singular. The obligatory contexts for aspectual auxiliary *be* forms were identified by the appearance of an overt subject (e.g. *doggie going away* identifies an obligatory context for a third person singular form of the auxiliary, while *I playing with my toys* identifies an obligatory context for a first person singular form of the auxiliary and so on). Once again third person singular is the person/number combinations for which there is the largest number of obligatory contexts and the largest proportion of correct instances. Table 3 below reports the data on aspectual auxiliary *be*.

Table 3. Present tense aspectual auxiliary *be*

Age	1SG	2SG	3SG	1PL	2PL	3PL	TOTAL
1;10.1	–	–	–	–	–	–	–
1;10.20	–	–	–	–	–	–	–
1;11.4	–	–	–	–	–	–	–
1;11.18	–	–	–	–	–	–	–
2;0.1	–	–	–	–	–	–	–
2;0.23	–	–	–	–	–	–	–
2;2.12	–	–	–	–	–	–	–
2;2.24	–	–	0/2	–	–	–	0/2
2;4.7	–	–	–	–	–	–	–
2;4.29	–	–	–	–	–	–	–
2;7.8	–	–	3/3	–	–	–	3/3
2;9.6	–	–	19/22	–	–	–	19/22
2;10.1	0/1	–	–	–	–	–	0/1
2;10.15	0/1	–	18/21	–	–	2/2	20/24
2;10.23	0/1	–	17/17	–	–	2/2	19/20
2;10.30	–	1/1	3/3	1/4	–	–	5/8
3;0.3	–	–	5/6	–	–	2/3	7/9
3;0.16	–	0/2	4/4	1/1	–	–	5/7
3;1.25	–	–	2/2	–	–	2/2	4/4

The preponderance of third person contexts is most likely due to the nature of the activities C. is engaged in during the recording sessions. Both C. and his adult interlocutors often comment on the actions being performed by characters in a book, or by toys they play with. A total of 15 different verb types in the progressive form are found with aspectual *be*, thus indicating some degree of flexibility in the extent to which C. uses the auxiliary (*crossing, going, coming, bringing, falling, crying, swimming, getting, putting, making, playing, eating, raining*). It must be noted however that out of 82 inflected forms of the auxiliary *be*, 12 are combined with the verb *doing* in the formulaic question *what's x doing?*. In fact *doing* is the only verb that appears in this question construction, where the only variable element is the subject. Another 40 inflected forms of *be* are found with *going*, hence two verb types alone account for over 60 per cent of all progressive forms accompanied by the aspectual auxiliary.

In the case of the aspectual auxiliary, like in the case of the copula, there is little empirical evidence that C. is able to extend the use of the inflected verb form to a significantly large number of contexts. The child obviously knows something about the progressive construction *x + aspectual be + V-ing*, but his knowledge is still very much tied to a small number of person/number combinations as far as the aspectual auxiliary is concerned (mainly third person singular contexts). Moreover, although the total number of verb types that can occur with the progressive — *ing* marker includes 15 different verbs, two verbs alone (*going* and *doing*) account for almost two thirds of all of C's progressive constructions. These facts taken together suggest that, even by the end of the period of observation (3;1.25), C's knowledge about the aspectual auxiliary system and the agreement between subject and finite verb is still a small subset of the target adult knowledge. Such knowledge is usage-based in the sense that it is shaped by the contexts in which the child finds it necessary to use these verb forms, namely third person contexts, and specifically third person singular contexts, where two thirds of the time the progressive verb is either *doing* or *going*. An additional limitation in the range and number of verb types that C. uses is also due to the fact that the child was recorded in play situations which involved a restricted and fairly repetitive set of activities such as looking at picture books, assembling jigsaw puzzles, playing picture domino, drawing, etc. The opportunity to document his language use in other daily activities such as getting ready to go to nursery, eating, or bathing did not arise as the child is exclusively addressed in Italian at home. It must therefore be acknowledged that a partial explanation for the child's somewhat restricted verb vocabulary is also due to a sampling artifact.

3.3 The marking of subject-verb agreement on English lexical verbs

The observations reported in the previous sections reveal a picture of C.'s grammar where there is a progressive increase in the number of inflected forms over time, although the number of person/number combinations is extremely limited, and the use of forms is embedded in lexically-specific constructions. The fact that there are no commission errors in the data must not necessarily be interpreted as meaning that the child actually knows anything about the inflectional paradigm and the agreement requirements of the various forms. Given the overall indications of the limitation of his system we are inclined to treat the absence of errors as an indication of conservatism.

As Gropen, Pinker, Hollander, Goldberg and Wilson (1989) suggest, speakers tend to be conservative in the way they use lexical items. On the basis of experimental findings they show that adult speakers are inclined to use lexical items in the same constructions they have heard them being used by others before. A recent experiment by Akhtar (1999) on the use of novel verbs in canonical SVO order and non-canonical SOV and VSO order with mono-lingual English-speaking children also shows that children prefer to use a new verb with the same ordering pattern as they have heard it used by the adult experimenter. There are quite clear indications that children's strategy seems to be to repeat what they hear with minimal variations and only when they have reason to do so, i.e. when they encounter a new lexical item that does not fit in previously heard and stored constructions. If this is the case, then one must be careful when inferring target-like competence from children's error-free performance.

After this cautionary note on the assumptions that can be reasonably made on the basis of error-free production, it remains to be seen if C. has any productive agreement system on lexical verbs. Following Kayne (1989) and Ingham (1998) we consider the — s suffix on English lexical verbs and on the periphrastic *does* form as a marker of agreement rather than of tense. Because of the homonymity between the bare stem and the non-third person present tense forms in English, the only context in which agreement is morpho-phonologically visible is precisely third person singular. For this reason only third person singular contexts will be analysed here to assess to what extent C.

Table 4. Proportion of English inflected and bare verb forms in third person singular present tense contexts

Age	Inflected forms	Bare forms	Proportion in obligatory contexts
1;10.1	–	–	–
1;10.20	–	–	–
1;11.4	–	–	–
1;11.18	–	–	–
2;0.1	–	–	–
2;0.23	–	–	–
2;2.12	–	3	0/3
2;2.24	–	–	–
2;4.7	–	–	–
2;4.29	–	–	–
2;7.8	–	–	–
2;9.6	2	2	2/4
2;10.1	–	–	–
2;10.15	–	–	–
2;10.23	–	–	–
2;10.30	–	2	0/2
3;0.3	5	10	5/15
3;0.16	–	15	0/15
3;1.25	3	1	3/4

has any productive subject-verb agreement notion with lexical verbs. The results for present tense third person contexts are summarised in Table 4.

The conservative estimate of third person singular contexts reveals that C.'s overall performance is rather poor, out of 44 obligatory contexts only eight verbs are correctly inflected. What is more, only two verb types (*come* and *go*) ever appear inflected. As far as periphrastic *do* is concerned, there is only one instance of *doesn't* in a negative sentence throughout the whole corpus:

(4) (2;10.30)
  *CAR: no doesn't go there.

As for questions, there are only twelve where auxiliary *do* is required: four yes/no questions, two *what* object questions, five *where* adjunct questions, and one *why* question. All but one of the questions are auxiliaryless:

(5) (2;10.15)
  *CAR: where I put it?

(6) (3;0.16)
  *CAR: where this donkey go?

(7) (3;0.16)
  *CAR: why do not fit?

Although the very small number of wh-questions including a lexical verb makes it difficult to draw any definitive conclusions regarding the status of auxiliary *do*, the evidence that is there suggests that C. has not yet realised the requirement of an inverted and inflected auxiliary in root questions involving a simple present lexical verb.

In sum, the evidence reviewed here shows that this bilingual child has virtually no command of agreeing verb forms in English by the age of 3;1.25. A very small proportion of lexical verb types are inflected for agreement (*come* and *go*), for a total of only 8 tokens altogether, and auxiliary *do* forms are virtually non-existent.

4. Subject-verb agreement in Italian

4.1 A note on Italian verb morphology

Italian is a person-marking language where each person/number combination is uniquely identified by an inflectional ending. Verbs are classified into three conjugations: the -*are* conjugation which is also the largest verb class and tends to include newly coined verbs (e.g. *faxare* 'to fax'), the -*ere* conjugation (e.g. *battere* 'to hit'), and the -*ire* conjugation (e.g. *dormire* 'to sleep'). Most irregular verbs belong to the -*ere* conjugation, a much smaller number to the -*ire* conjugation, and there are only four, but highly frequent irregular verbs in the -*are* conjugation (*andare* 'to go', *dare* 'to give', *fare* 'to do/to make', and *stare* 'to stay'). Italian verbs never appear as unmarked bare stems like English verbs. The full inflectional system includes 21 simple and compound, finite and non-finite tenses, 16 of which are commonly used. Compound or periphrastic forms require the use of auxiliary *essere* 'be', or *avere* 'have', and are followed by a past participle. With *essere* the past participle must agree in gender and number with the subject. If *avere* is used the past participle is in its unmarked form (masculine, singular), but it must agree with the object of a transitive verb if the object is in its clitic form. Progressive forms employ the auxiliary *stare* and an invariable gerundival participle. The Italian copula is homonymous with the auxiliary *essere*.

4.2 The emergence of copula forms in Italian

A search for all Italian copula forms was performed and supplemented by a search for obligatory contexts. Potential obligatory contexts include all those predicative constructions containing a null or overt subject (be it a pronoun, a proper noun, or a common noun), and a nominal or adjectival predicate in the general construction *DP + copula +Adj/DP*. The results for present tense copula are summarised in Table 5.

Similarly to what was observed for the English copula, the only two contexts for which there is a significant number of obligatory contexts, and a corresponding proportion of tokens, are third person singular and third person plural. Once again the strong bias towards third person usage is to be found in the kind of activities C. was engaged in which resulted in such a large number of third person tokens.

Unlike in English, where the production of copula forms never reaches significant proportions, C.'s use of copulas in Italian is substantial as early as 2;1.23. In the Italian copular constructions as in the English ones, the precopular DP slot is typically filled by a demonstrative pronoun such as *quello* 'that', or *questo* 'this', or by a null subject. As far as the distribution of copula forms is concerned, while in English their presence is restricted to copular

Table 5. Present tense copula *essere* in obligatory contexts

Age	1SG	2SG	3SG	1PL	2PL	3PL	TOTAL
1;10.8	–	–	–	–	–	–	–
1;10.27	–	–	3/3	–	–	–	3/3
1;11.17	–	–	5/7	–	–	–	5/7
1;11.25	–	–	6/11	–	–	–	6/11
2;0.1	–	–	0/1	–	–	–	0/1
2;0.7	–	–	16/24	–	–	–	16/24
2;0.23	–	–	66/96	–	–	0/2	66/98
2;1.23	–	–	12/13	–	–	–	12/13
2;2.3	–	–	14/16	–	–	–	14/16
2;2.17	–	–	35/37	–	–	–	35/37
2;3.7	–	–	17/17	–	–	1/3	18/20
2;4.14	–	–	16/18	–	–	–	16/18
2;5.6	–	–	28/28	–	–	1/1	29/29
2;5.26	–	–	64/64	–	–	5/6	69/70
2;9.6	2/2	–	41/42	–	–	1/1	44/45
2;10	–	–	14/14	–	–	5/5	19/19
2;10.18	–	–	39/39	–	–	10/10	49/49
2;11.12	–	–	14/14	–	–	5/5	19/19
3;0.3	–	–	12/12	1/1	–	10/10	23/23
3;0.17	–	–	23/23	–	–	8/8	31/31

constructions, in Italian there are also a number of existential constructions including the copula:

(8) (2;2.3)
    *CAR: c'è la volpe.
    %eng: there is the fox.

In English it was noted that C. never committed any commission errors, but only omission errors; in other words, whenever a copula form is used it always correctly agrees with the subject in person and number. In Italian, on the other hand, there is a small error rate of 1.7 per cent, which at first one might be tempted to discard as a performance effect. If however one looks at the distribution of these agreement errors, an interesting pattern emerges. Firstly, all commission errors are with plural subjects. In 7 cases a third person plural subject requiring a third person plural copula is found with a third person singular copula.

The fact that tokens of the plural copula are rarer should not necessarily imply any difference in the error rate. If subject-verb agreement is a mechanism which is productive across the board, there should be a comparable error rate between singular and plural forms. Furthermore, when one looks at the contexts in which 5 out of the 7 errors are committed the picture is even clearer. They are of the form *c'è* + *plural DP*, 'there is + plural DP':

(9)   (2;0.23)
      *CAR: c'è i gufi.
      %eng: there's the owls.

(10) (2;2.17)
      *CAR: c'è le pecore.
      %eng: there's the sheep.

It seems obvious that C. has learnt a *c'è* + *DP* construction where *c'è* is analysed as an invariable element in construction-initial position typically followed by a singular DP, but optionally also by a plural DP. C. relies on a partly flexible construction where the first element is invariable and is not specified for either singular or plural number, and the second is variable and includes both singular and plural DPs. In this sense the string *c'è* behaves as an existential placeholder which is not specified for person or number, as suggested by Groat (1995) for English existential *there*, and as such can be followed by any DP regardless of whether it is singular or plural.

Although C. displays limited knowledge of the agreement paradigm of copula *essere*, mainly restricted to third person contexts, there is some evidence that from 2;5.6 onwards he can use imperfect tense forms contrastively. Out of a total number of 34 imperfect tense copula tokens, 30 are third person singular, 2 are first person singular, and 2 are third person plural. Almost half of the third person singular forms are found with existential *ci* 'there', and are strictly correlated with the emergence of narratives in the past:

(11) (3;0.17)
      *CAR: c'era una volta un cavallo che [/] che andava qua dentro.
      %eng: there was once a horse that went inside here.

(12) (3;0.17)
      *CAR: poi una volta c'era un ippopotamo.
      %eng: then once there was a hippo.

Although the number of imperfect tense copula forms is only 7 per cent of all copula tokens, nevertheless they are used appropriately to refer to past events, and they are used contrastively with present tense forms. The relative high proportion of *c'era* 'there was', forms could prima facie seem problematic. They are typically used in stereotyped beginnings of story telling, corresponding to English *Once upon a time there was a...*, and as such one might reasonably suspect that C. has memorised them as longer chunks which he uses when he wants to start telling a story. Examples such as (7) however testify to the fact that C. must indeed be sensitive to the tense specification of a form such as *era* 'was'. The verb *andava* '(he) went', in the relative clause is also in the imperfect tense and it matches the copula in the main clause in both agreement and tense specification.

In sum, the data presented here show that C. can use both present tense forms of the copula *essere*, and imperfect past tense forms, albeit the past tense forms emerge later and are much less frequent. Neither for present tense, nor for imperfect tense forms there is across-the-board mastery of the paradigm. It is only third person singular contexts, and to a lesser extent third person plural contexts that are represented in a significant way. Moreover there is a certain degree of lexical specificity in C's copular constructions, especially noteworthy the absence of subjects realised by DPs containing a determiner and a common noun, proper names or pronouns. The limited number of subject DPs containing a determiner and a common noun or a proper noun is also reflected in the speech of C's adult interlocutors. Only 4 per cent (37/884) of copular constructions in the adult speech include either a proper name or a DP with a determiner and a common noun. In all likelihood the shared context of the face-to-face adult-child interaction biases the speakers towards the use of deictic devices such as pronouns in preference to proper or common nouns.

Overall the indications are that C. is working on the copula in a construction-specific way which is also informed by a considerable degree of lexical specificity.

4.3 The emergence of inflectional morphology in Italian

In line with previous studies on the acquisition of morphology in Romance languages, the relative proportion of correct and incorrect tokens of inflected verb forms for the present indicative in Table 6 reveals low error rates.

The mean error rate for C's present indicative forms is 3.6 per cent, ranging from 0 per cent for first person plural forms, to 10 per cent for third person plural forms. These figures are similar to those reported by other studies on the acquisition of morphology in Romance languages such as

Pizzuto and Caselli (1992, 1994) and Rubino and Pine (1998). C. is very accurate from the very earliest recordings: out of a total of seven sessions with 0 per cent error rate, five are found before 2;2.3. It is nevertheless important to emphasise once again that low error rates without any indication of actual productivity cannot be taken as good evidence of real mastery.[5] It could very well be the case that C's accuracy is simply the result of careful rote learning and conservative use. It is therefore necessary to investigate to what extent error-free production is also a sign of productivity across the board.

Until 2;2.17 there is virtually one verb form per verb type per session. Starting from 2;2.17 there is an observable tendency for more verb forms than verb types, and this trend becomes particularly clear from 2;5.6 onwards. When there are more forms than types it is not clear whether it is the case that one verb type appears with a large number of forms, or whether there are several verb types which minimally appear with one inflection. This is a subtle

Table 6. Proportion of incorrect verb tokens in the Italian present indicative and error rate

Age	1SG	2SG	3SG	1PL	2PL	3PL
1;10.8	–	–	–	–	–	–
1;10.27	–	–	0/1	–	–	–
1;11.17	1/5	–	0/7	–	–	–
1;11.25	3/0	–	0/3	–	–	–
2;0.1	–	–	–	–	–	–
2;0.7	0/1	–	0/4	–	–	–
2;0.23	0/2	–	0/4	0/1	–	–
2;1.23	–	–	0/2	–	–	–
2;2.3	1/4	0/1	0/4	0/3	–	–
2;2.17	0/1	0/1	1/10	0/1	–	1/1
2;3.7	0/1	–	2/7	–	–	1/1
2;4.14	2/13	–	0/22	–	–	–
2;5.6	0/28	0/1	0/33	–	–	1/4
2;5.26	0/12	1/10	0/33	0/5	–	0/1
2;9.6	1/31	0/5	0/24	0/8	–	–
2;10	1/16	0/3	0/1	0/3	–	–
2;10.18	0/11	0/4	1/9	–	–	0/5
2;11.12	0/12	0/9	0/22	–	–	0/2
3;0.3	0/15	0/7	0/23	0/7	–	0/15
3;0.17	3/10	–	–	0/1	–	1/11
Total N/ tokens	12/161	1/41	4/209	0/29	–	4/40
Error rate	7.5	2.4	1.9	0	–	10

but interesting difference in that it would reveal two different acquisitional strategies. In the case in which the larger number of verb forms were due to one, or two, verb types appearing with multiple forms it would look as if the child were filling in a paradigm on a verb-by-verb basis. By contrast, if one found that a large number of verbs appear with only one or two different forms, it would suggest that the child is using the inflections in a more across-the-board, paradigmatic fashion. In the former case it is as if the child were filling in the slots of the paradigm for a particular verb ; in the latter it is as if the child were filling in the verbal paradigm itself, with less regard to the build-up of a repertoire of inflected forms for specific verbs.

A closer inspection of the distribution of multiple inflections across verb types reveals that 17 verb types out of a total of 82, occur with four or more forms across the 20 Italian files (*andare* 'to go', *avere* 'to have', *cadere* 'to fall', *chiudere* 'to close', *dare* 'to give', *dire* 'to say', *dovere* 'must', *fare* 'to do/to make', *giocare* 'to play', *girare* 'to turn', *guardare* 'to look/to watch', *mangiare* 'to eat', *mettere* 'to put', *potere* 'can', *prendere* 'to take', *trovare* 'to find', *volere* 'to want').[6] This distribution of verb forms gives some credit to the hypothesis of verb-specific learning. It does appear as if C. is working around a small number of verbs for which he learns a large number of inflected forms, while the vast majority of verbs in his vocabulary only ever appear with one or at most two inflections. Interestingly, there are indications that most of the small group of verbs for which C. is using four or more forms overlap with Ninio's (1999) group of *pathbreaking* verbs. Pathbreaking verbs are highly transitive, frequent, generic verbs which appear early in acquisition because of their semantic lightness and because they typically encode meanings that are pragmatically important to children (Clark 1978). According to Ninio's (1999) classification, C. uses six *obtaining* verbs (*dare* 'to give', *fare* 'to do/to make', *trovare* 'to find', *mettere* 'to put', *prendere* 'to take', *volere* 'to want'), one *consumption* verb (*mangiare* 'to eat'), and one *perception* verb (*guardare* 'to look'). Like the 14 Hebrew-speaking children and the English-speaking child in Ninio's study, C's early verb vocabulary also revolves around a small number of so-called pathbreaking verbs. Although the nature of the interactions in which C. engages with his adult partners contributes to restrict the type of verbs that the child is likely to use, nevertheless it is surely not simply a sampling artifact that C. is starting to use a large number of inflected forms with this specific set of verbs rather than others. A combination of factors biases the child's focus on these verbs: pragmatic factors, the verbs' semantic lightness and their generality, and ultimately their high transitivity.

Despite the fact that C. is approaching the acquisition of morphosyntactic contrasts on a verb-specific basis, it is also necessary to establish whether any paradigmatic learning is also taking place at the same time, as a result of the broadening of the child's lexical knowledge. Although at 2;2.17, 2;3.7, and 2;4.14 the third person singular present indicative inflection is used productively, it is not until 2;5.6 that the first contrasts emerge. A number of contrasts make their appearance simultaneously: there is a mood contrast between infinitive and indicative; a person contrast between third person singular and third person plural in the present indicative; an aspect contrast between present indicative and the present progressive, another person contrast in the present progressive between third person singular and third person plural, and finally a tense/aspect contrast between third person singular present indicative and third person singular present perfect. Table 7 schematizes the appearance of person, number, tense, aspect and mood contrasts over time. Appearance of a grammatical contrast, is a measure of productivity of verbal inflections. Productive use of for example a person inflection is identified at a given time point as the presence in a transcript of at least two inflected verbs with a given inflection (e.g. *parla* '(he/she) speaks', and *mangia* '(he/she) eats'), and the presence of at least another inflected form for at least one of the verbs which already appear with the inflection under investigation (e.g. *mangio* '(I) eat') (Pizzuto and Caselli 1994).

What is striking about the data in Table 7 is that, although tense/aspect contrasts start to become productive at the same time as person contrasts in the present between third person singular and third person plural, they are limited to third person singular until 2;10.18, when a contrast between first person plural present, and first person plural present perfect appears for the first time. Following the method outlined above we were in a position to establish whether an inflection was used productively (at least 2 verb types with the same inflection, and the same verb root with at least two distinct inflected forms). By this rationale, if at least two person inflections can be said to be used productively, we can say that there is also contrastive use emerging, e.g. the second person inflection present indicative contrasts with the third person inflection present indicative.

The largest number of contrasts that are added over time are person contrasts, mainly in the present tense, but also in the present perfect, and to a lesser extent in the present progressive. It must be noted that there is however an important qualitative difference between the acquisition of person inflections in the present tense paradigm, and the acquisition person contrasts in

Table 7. The emergence of grammatical contrasts in Italian

Age	Person	Number	Tense	Aspect	Mood
2;5.6		3SG/3PL.PRES*	PRES/PRES	PRES/PRES.	INF/IND
		3SG/3PL.PRES.	PERF	PROG/PRES	
		PROG		PERF	
2;5.26	1SG/2SG/3SG PRES	1SG/1PL	PRES/PRES	PRES/PRES.	
			PERF	PROG/PRES	
				PERF	
2;9.6	1SG/2SG/3SG PRES	1SG/1PL PRES	PRES/PRES	PRES/PRES.	INF/IND/**IMP**
	1SG/3SG PRES.PROG		PERF	PROG/Pres,	
				PERF	
2;10	1SG/2SG PRES	1SG/1PL PRES	PRES/PRES	PRES/PRES	INF/IND
			PERF	PERF	
2;10.18	1SG/3SG PRES	3SG/3PL PRES	PRES/PRES	PRES/PRES/	INF/IND
			PERF	PRES PERF	
2;11.12	1SG/2SG/3SG PRES	**3SG/3PLPRES**	PRES/PRES	PRES/PRES	INF/IND
	1SG/3SG PRES PERF	**PERF**	PERF	PERF	
3;0.3	1SG/2SG/3SG PRES	1SG/1PL.PRES	PRES/ PRES	PRES/PRES	INF/IND
	1PL/3PL.PRES	3SG/3PL.PRES	PERF	PERF	
	1SG/2SG/3SG PRES	**1SG/1PL.PERF**			
	PERF				
3;0.17	1SG/2SG.PRES	3SG/3PL.PRES	PRES/PRES	**PRES.PERF**	INF/IND
	1SG/3SG.PRES PERF		PERF/**IMPERF**	**IMPERF**	

Bold indicates the appearance of new contrasts

periphrastic forms. All that is required there is to learn the inflectional paradigm of an auxiliary verb, either *essere*, *avere* or *stare*, rather than a completely new inflected form.

Although one might be tempted to credit C. with the mastery of person contrast, and hence awareness of agreement, there is no evidence that it is relevant across the board, apart from present tense and present perfect tense. In the present progressive, person contrasts are limited to first person singular, third person singular and third person plural, and in the imperfect the only productive person inflection is third person singular. Moreover, only 37 per cent of the 53 verb types that occur in the present indicative, are found with two or more inflections throughout the period of observation, 63 per cent only ever appear with only one person inflection.

As for tense and aspect contrasts, they start to emerge together with the first person/number (third person singular vs. third person plural) contrasts in the simple present and in the present progressive. For the present progressive, first person singular, third person singular and third person plural are productively contrasted with simple present and present perfect. While for the present perfect first person singular, second person singular, third person singular, first person plural and third person plural all contrast with the corresponding persons in the simple present by file 2;11.12.

5.   Discussion

Crosslinguistic studies of monolingual and bilingual language acquisition have often reported an asynchrony in the emergence of verbal inflectional morphology between poorly inflected languages like English, and more richly inflected languages such as Italian and Spanish where bare stems are not allowed, and each person/number combination is uniquely identified by an inflectional affix. Children acquiring English both in a monolingual and in a bilingual setting are known to go through a protracted period of time in which they produce uninflected bare stems in root contexts, rather then target-like inflected forms (Wexler 1994, 1998). This behaviour has variously been attributed to the setting of the stem parameter (Hyams 1986, 1992), to the optionality of abstract tense and agreement in the children's grammar (Schütze and Wexler 1996), to a grammar that only includes lexical categories (Radford 1990), to the underspecification of number (Hoekstra and Hyams 1998), or more generally to children's inability to extend verb-specific patterns to a verb-general category (Tomasello 1992; Lieven *et al.* 1997; Pine *et al.* 1998).

At the same time, some researchers have advanced the hypothesis that children learning a person-marking language like Italian do learn the verbal inflectional system earlier than their English-speaking peers (Hyams 1986, 1992; Guasti 1993/94). These speculations are largely based on the fact that Italian-speaking children produce a variety of inflected forms from the earliest stages of acquisition and by and large they use them appropriately. Hence the conclusion that they have productive command of inflections as a system reflecting a higher level of organization in their grammar.

Similar claims have been put forward by researchers working with bilingual children. A lead-lag pattern has also been observed in children acquiring English together with another more inflected language from birth. The

developmental discrepancy observed in the acquisition of inflectional morphology in such children has been at the core of the argument for the separate
development hypothesis (De Houwer 1990). If children's profiles are so
different when it comes to the production of finite inflected forms, then surely
they must be treating the two languages as two independent systems whose
properties are learnt in a language-specific way.

Although this is most likely the case, it does not necessarily imply that
children who produce language-specific inflected forms, can also be said to
master those forms at a paradigmatic level, especially not if their output does not
meet the requirements imposed by strict methodological criteria. This point has
been convincingly argued for by Pizzuto and Caselli (1992, 1994) for the acquisition of Italian morphology, by Gathercole *et al.* (1999, 2000) for the acquisition
of Spanish morphology, and by Rubino and Pine (1998) for the acquisition of
subject-verb agreement in Brazilian Portuguese in monolingual children.

This case study of English–Italian bilingual acquisition confirms the
conclusions reached by these studies in monolingual settings, and questions the
idea of a developmental lead-lag pattern in the early stages of bilingual first
language acquisition. We found more similarities than differences in the
acquisition of C's verbal system in English and Italian, the underlying acquisitional strategy is essentially the same in both languages: slow and gradual
verb-specific learning. In English morphological marking on lexical verbs is
virtually restricted to aspectual -*ing*, while third person singular -*s* in the
habitual present tense reaches insignificant proportions in obligatory contexts.
Some contrastive use of third person singular and third person plural copula
forms was observed, albeit limited to one specific predicative construction
whose precopular slot is limited to only three types of subjects: *that*, *it* and *they*,
while the postcopular slot is filled by a variety of DPs.

In Italian the situation looks somewhat different, however close inspection
of the data reveals a number of similarities with C's acquisitional strategy in
English. Although in Italian there is a greater absolute number and a greater
proportion of correctly inflected forms than in English, the vast majority of
verb types appear with only one or two inflections, and only a small number of
verbs, some of which are highly irregular, appear with four or more inflections.

The English and Italian data discussed in this chapter point to a complex
picture of bilingual language acquisition. On the one hand, language-specific
properties of the morphology and the syntax of the language being acquired
inevitably shape the emergence of grammatical contrasts. There is a predictable
discrepancy in the age and in the extent to which verbal inflectional morphol-

ogy makes its appearance in the child's linguistic output in the two languages. On the other hand, there is a more subtle acquisitional strategy which seems to be language-independent. The degree of conservatism and language specificity observed in C's data has been reported in a number of recent studies focussing on a data-driven approach to language acquisition (Tomasello 1992; Olguin and Tomasello 1993; Lieven *et al.* 1997; Akhtar and Tomasello 1997; Tomasello and Brooks 1999; Rubino and Pine 1998; Goldberg 1998; Akhtar 1999).

The common argument at the core of these studies using both experimental methods and observation of naturalistic interaction is that children's language production is much less creative than one would expect if they actually operated with an abstract syntactic category of verb. Neither in naturalistic nor in experimental settings are children able to move away from verb-specific and construction-specific usage before the age of 3 (Tomasello 2000). It is not until they have accumulated a sufficient number of exemplars that they can begin to organize them into what will eventually become more abstract classes.

Goldberg (1998) makes exactly this suggestions regarding the organization of the verb lexicon. As children learn more and more construction-embedded verbs, it is anti-economical to keep learning them item by item. Children then begin to notice similarities: semantically similar verbs have a strong tendency to appear in the same argument structure constructions, it seems therefore reasonable to speculate that they will proceed to clustering these verbs into subclasses.

The idea that reorganization of the grammar is driven by lexical growth is also central to the *critical mass* argument put forward by Marchman and Bates (1994) and Bates and Goodman (1997, 1999), according to which lexical and grammatical growth are inextricably connected. The claim is that the achievement of a lexical *critical mass* provides the child with a dataset which is large enough and representative enough to extract general (morphological) patterns.

If this is along the right lines, a usage-based model of acquisition that pays close attention to what constructions the child uses over time and with what verb types will provide us with sensitive tools to uncover the mechanisms that are at work in the initial stages of language development.

6.   Conclusion

This case study of bilingual first language acquisition in two typologically different languages such as English and Italian has questioned the actual

existence of a lead-lag pattern in the acquisition of verbal inflectional morphology. A careful analysis of the data has shown how even in Italian, where
the number and the proportion of correctly inflected forms is by far larger
than in English, there is a considerable degree of lexical specificity at the
construction level.

The absence of errors cannot be taken as an ultimate proof of either adult-
like competence or of imitative behaviour we are however inclined to opt for
the second option. The behaviour of a child who, for example, makes no case-
marking errors in the use of subject pronouns is certainly target-like but it
does not necessarily follow that it reflects adult-like competence in the
nominative case-marking of subjects (Pine *et al.* 1998). In addition to error-
free production the child must also show that he can use a variety of personal
pronouns correctly, not just one or two, and he must also show that nominative pronouns are used constrastively with accusative and oblique case pronouns. A child who uses *I* correctly must also use *me* and *my* appropriately, if
she does not the possibility exists that she has only learnt about a specific
lexical item in a specific preverbal position. This is why it is necessary to have
criteria of productivity as the ones proposed by Pizzuto and Caselli (1994).
Point of acquisition must be surely determined not only by error-free production, but most importantly by evidence suggesting that the child has gone
beyond purely lexically specific knowledge and is able to apply what he knows
about familiar items to new ones. To this purpose experimental work is
necessary and complementary to the collection and analysis of naturalistic
data. The use of novel words in testing conditions is similar to using a tracer
which can help the researcher disentangle the level of abstraction the child has
reached from the specifics of knowledge tied to individual lexical item.

The extreme degree of lexical specificity in C's data is therefore a better
indicator of the extent to which he can actually go beyond what he hears in the
adult input. Although an analysis of the input addressed to the child is beyond
the scope of the present chapter, there are a number of naturalistic and
experimental studies that have successfully correlated children's earliest
linguistic production with adult input and have reached the conclusion that
much of children's early multiword utterances are nothing more than careful
replication of what they hear in the adult input (Rubino and Pine 1998;
Gathercole *et al.* 1999; Akhtar 1999).

Further research is needed crosslinguistically both in monolingual and in
bilingual children on the issue of lexical and construction specificity across
languages to investigate to what extent children acquiring languages typologi-

cally different from English can be shown to follow fundamentally similar strategies despite their superficially different profiles.

Notes

* I would like to acknowledge the enthusiastic participation of Carlo, his family, Karen Kay and Eric Laurier in this project. Many thanks to Gina Conti-Ramsden and the editors of this volume for helpful suggestions on an earlier draft of this chapter, and to Antonella Sorace, Ronnie Cann, Caroline Heycock, and Annick DeHouwer for comments on previous research this chapter is based on.

1. Recent work has suggested the possibility that there may be some sort of language transfer between a bilingual child's two languages, despite the existence of two separate grammatical systems (Döpke 1997a; 1997b; 1998; Müller 1998; Hulk and van der Linden 1997, 1998). The hypothesis that young bilingual children acquire two separate systems does not automatically imply that these two systems are necessarily impermeable to one another, some degree of contact can potentially be envisaged. However, although the possibility of language transfer may indeed exist at later stages of language development, it will not be of immediate concern in this investigation of a child's earliest multiword utterances.

2. A number of recordings not included here were also carried out at the two nursery schools C. attended in order to obtain information on what kind of English input the child was exposed to from the nursery staff.

3. The procedure adopted for identifying all possible copula contexts is the following: firstly a list of possible subjects is compiled including proper nouns, common nouns, personal pronouns (*I, you, she*), indefinite pronouns (*someone, noone*), demonstrative pronouns (*this, that*), existential pronoun (*there*), possessive pronouns (*mine, hers*), locative adverbs (*here, there*). The corpus is then automatically searched for all possible copula contexts identified by strings containing one of the potential subjects immediately followed by one of the following: adjective (e.g. *he naughty*), common or proper noun (e.g. *that baby, that Eric*), determiner (e.g. *there the girl, that my teddy*), personal pronoun (e.g. *that you*), possessive (*teddy mine*), locative adverb (e.g. *dolly there*), preposition (baby *over there*), negation (*doggie not nice*).

4. There are also 13 occurrences of *what's that?* (Files 10–18), and 4 occurrences of *where is it?* (Files 14–17) which must be treated as instances of rote-learned frozen forms. There are no examples in the data in which a subject other than *that* is found in the object wh-question, or other than *it* in the adjunct *where* question.

5. Antelmi (1997: 143) reports errorless verb production in the early stages of acquisition (1;6–1;8) for Camilla, a child acquiring Italian monolingually, followed by a very high agreement error rate between 1;9 and 1;11 (43–51 per cent of incorrectly agreeing forms).

6. Note that verbs such as *fare* 'to do/to make', *andare* 'to go', *dare* 'to give', *stare* 'to stay', *potere* 'can', are highly irregular and must be learnt on a form by form basis by the child, with little reference to a consistent inflectional paradigm.

Chapter 3

Early language differentiation
in bilingual infants[*]

Laura Bosch and Núria Sebastián-Gallés

1. Introduction

Large groups of infants around the world are exposed from birth to more than
one language and for them, linguistic diversity is the norm rather than the
exception (McLaughlin 1978). Besides the well-known extension of bilingualism in some countries of Europe, Asia and Africa, as well as in Québec and
other areas in Canada, English-Spanish bilinguals account for at least 10 per
cent of the US population, a country in which monolingualism has always
been considered the norm (Menn, O'Connor, Obler and Holland 1995).
Bilingual exposure is, therefore, not so uncommon as the general literature on
children's language acquisition seems to suggest. Nevertheless research on that
population can still be considered as comparatively underdeveloped. Within
this area of investigation a number of crucial questions remain unanswered,
one of them being the differentiation issue (i.e. how early and to what extent
the bilingual's two languages are distinguished). The answer to this central
issue is not simple and information both from carefully designed perception
and production studies is required before one gets a detailed picture of the
differentiation processes in bilingual acquisition. A fast revision of the early
literature on the production domain shows a predominant position favoring
a late language differentiation in bilinguals or what has been identified as the
one-system hypothesis (see, for instance, Leopold 1954; Redlinger and Park
1980; Volterra and Taeschner 1978). According to these authors, children's
capacity to fully differentiate the two languages of exposure would not
generally be attained until the third year of life, once functional categories
have emerged. In general, the main argument for this lack of discrimination is
the extent of language mixing in children's utterances and although differentiation is thought to begin by the end of the second year, its completion would

be reached past the end of the third year (see Lanza 1997, for a detailed review of these and other related studies). As the literature on bilingual development has been substantially increased and more studies on children's early linguistic stages have been developed, positions favoring a somewhat earlier differentiation have emerged (as in De Houwer 1990; Genesee 1989; Genesee, Nicoladis and Paradis 1995; Meisel 1989; Pearson, Fernández and Oller 1995). Reanalyses of early data in the literature (as in Paradis 1996, who offers evidence of an early phonological differentiation in Leopold's daughter data) argue in the same direction. From this more recent perspective, disagreement with what has been identified as the unitary system hypothesis can be found and empirical evidence of an earlier differentiation is offered. Children's production of distinct words from each of their languages very early in development, i.e. in the one-word stage, is taken as one of the arguments for differentiation. In the absence of data from speech perception studies with bilingual infants, it was suggested (Genesee 1989) that languages might be distinguished at the point in development when infants begin to utter single words. This statement was grounded on the evidence derived from language discrimination studies with monolingual infants, whose capacities had started to be analyzed (Bahrick and Pickens 1988; Mehler, Jusczyk, Lambertz, Halsted, Bertoncini and Amiel-Tison 1988). However, the time course and the nature of the speech perception processes in pre-lexical bilingual infants remained unexplored.

Increasing current knowledge on bilingual language acquisition and its impact on the initial stages of linguistic development is required even from a social and educational perspective. More information about the implication of raising children bilingually and, more specifically, about the possibility that a certain delay in the milestones of speech development could arise from early bilingual exposure, is lacking. A recent study regarding early vocal behavior in prelinguistic infants (Oller, Eilers, Urbano and Cobo-Lewis 1997), indicates that vocal precursors to speech develop independently of certain specific conditions of rearing, among them bilingual experience. Consequently, a bilingualism deficit hypothesis is not supported by this work, but the possibility exists that slight delays, important differences or even some advantages in the perceptual domain are present in this initial period. Comparisons between infants from monolingual and bilingual environments at different age periods during the first year of life should be undertaken in order to assess the existence of these differences/delays in the developmental milestones in speech perception. Specific characteristics of the initial speech and language perception processes in bilingual exposure can only be revealed through carefully designed experimental studies because they may be temporary and eventually disappear by the age when a child begins to utter the first words. It is thus clear that much remains to be done before these early processes are fully characterized.

One last point that should be mentioned in this introduction refers to the fact that even in simultaneous exposure a language dominance may eventually arise. In particular, some data from French-English highly proficient adult bilinguals who were asked to perform fragment detection and speech segmentation tasks, gave evidence of a language dominance, that is, subjects did not respond as monolinguals in both languages but rather they showed a monolingual pattern only in one of the languages, something that was interpreted in terms of the availability of general vs. restricted segmentation procedures (Cutler, Mehler, Norris and Seguí 1992). If this language dominance and its implications on speech processing mechanisms is shown to be representative of bilingual language acquisition in general, then the study of infants' initial capacities becomes crucial if one wants to trace back this phenomenon and analyze its generality.

The work to be presented in this chapter focuses on the speech perception capacities of bilingual-to-be infants in their pre-linguistic period, especially those relative to the language differentiation issue and native-language recognition processes during the first semester of life. In order to gain a better understanding of the specific characteristics of the perceptual development of this population, data from infants growing up in monolingual environments will also be presented to enable comparison. This chapter, thus, deals with what has been identified as simultaneous bilingualism (Romaine 1995), that is, simultaneous exposure to two languages from birth. Bilingual infants in our studies are being simultaneously exposed to Spanish and Catalan, a pair of Romance languages that have important similarities concerning prosodic structure but with differences both at the segmental and syllable structure levels. All the infants that have been tested in the University of Barcelona belong to families that live in the metropolitan area of Barcelona. The community is officially bilingual, although areas where monolingualism prevails can easily be found (both Spanish and Catalan). From the different types of childhood bilingualism that have been described (Romaine 1999), our bilingual groups may be better classified as type 6, that is, parents are generally bilingual as well as sectors of the community, although the match with this type is not perfect, as the strategy one-parent-one-language (which corresponds to type 1) is very frequently and spontaneously applied: the parents speak their own native language to the child from birth. Therefore, code-switching is certainly restricted, and mainly depends on a change of speaker. At the same time, language mixing is not a widespread phenomenon among the families in our studies.

The chapter is organized as follows. The first section below reviews monolingual data on infants' early language discrimination capacities in experiments using different language contrasts. The next section deals with the differentiation issue in Spanish–Catalan bilingual infants and data from two different experiments will be discussed. In the following section native-language recognition processes, based on orientation latency measures, are analyzed and data from two different age levels (4 and 6 months) are compared. The final section of the chapter offers a summary of the main findings and draws the lines for future research. Although restricted to a single pair of languages, the experiments reported in this chapter represent a first step in the characterization of the initial speech perception processes in bilingual language acquisition.

2.   Language discrimination in pre-lexical infants: an overview of monolingual data

Before presenting bilingual data, reference should be made to the few studies that have dealt with the initial capacities to discriminate languages in infants growing up in monolingual environments. The literature on this topic is rather limited (just a few language comparisons have been studied and no more than three age levels have been involved), but taken as a whole the studies offer a coherent picture of these early language perception abilities, their changes during the first months of life and some hints about the mechanisms involved. This information is needed if one wants to compare the nature and the time course of these abilities in infants from bilingual environments.

2.1 Contrasting languages with different rhythmic properties

Language discrimination studies in infants were first analyzed in the pioneering work by Mehler and colleagues (Mehler *et al.* 1988). In their 1988 article two different age groups (French newborns and American 2-month-olds) participated and two pairs of languages (French–Russian and English–Italian) were employed. The selection of languages is a central aspect of this and subsequent work because different predictions can be established depending on the rhythmic properties of the target languages. In this case, the comparisons were made between languages that are considered to belong to different rhythmic categories.[1] To briefly summarize their results and taking into account the reanalysis of the data that was undertaken some time after the original experiments were published (Mehler and Christophe 1995), the main conclusions indicated that if at birth infants were able to discriminate rhythmically different languages (as in the pairs above mentioned), even when the language of the environment was not involved (as in the pair English–Italian for French newborns) by two months discrimination was only achieved when the familiar language was present in the testing situation (English–Italian for the American 2-month-olds, but no discrimination was found between French and Russian, both non-familiar languages). Almost at the same time, the results from another infant study with American 5-month-olds tested on the Spanish–English contrast confirmed this capacity to differentiate languages that are considered distant in prosodic–rhythmic terms (Bahrick and Pickens 1988).

The change in behavior between newborns and 2-month-olds is worth considering. This behavioral difference has been interpreted as an indication that by two months of age infants have already built an initial representation of the maternal language which is closely related to the prosodic properties of that language. Consequently, 2-month-old infants are probably classifying the utterances they hear in the testing situation as belonging to either their maternal language or to an undefined foreign one, while newborns, in the same testing situation, would simply classify any sentence-token into a language-type, regardless of whether one of the languages is familiar or not (Mehler and Christophe 1994). The use of low-pass filtered speech material in the above mentioned experiments, usually with a cut-off frequency of 400 Hz which eliminates most of the segmental information while leaving intonation and rhythm intact, reinforces the idea that infants rely on prosodic cues to achieve discrimination and use them as a basis for the building of this initial language representation.

A number of other studies on the same topic have been developed since these first results were published. English–Spanish discrimination was assessed in newborns (Moon, Cooper and Fifer 1993) and not only discrimination between the materials was found, but also a preference for the sentences in the maternal language. In another investigation, English–French discrimination (again a stress-timed vs. a syllable-timed language contrast) was assessed in 2-month-old American and French infants, using normally recorded utterances, low-pass filtered material and also in a scrambled word condition where the prosodic organization of the utterances was destroyed (Dehaene-Lambertz 1995). Evidence of differentiation was obtained and what is more, the results with the prosodically unstructured material confirmed the predominant role of prosody in continuous speech processing in young infants, because in this condition no discrimination could be obtained.

To deal with these perceptual aspects and to serve as a theoretical framework for infant language discrimination studies, the TIGRE proposal (Time and Intensity Grid REpresentation) was developed (Mehler, Dupoux, Nazzi and Dehaene-Lambertz 1996). The proposal takes as a starting point the observed capacity of infants to perceive rhythmic units and to extract and represent the prosodic structures of languages. This capacity is considered part of the biological endowment and its role may be crucial for infants growing up in multilingual environments. A simple mechanism is hypothesized, which seems to rely on robust acoustic cues present in the speech signal that can be easily extracted to build a primary level representation. This primary representation is said to be grounded on the sequence of vowel nuclei in the speech stream and it is deemed to retain not only sequential information but also the duration and intensity indexes for every vocalic element in the sequence (Mehler *et al.* 1996). Intervocalic duration is also thought to be reflected in the representation so that the periodic characteristics of the language can be captured.[2]

The TIGRE proposal gives rise to a series of predictions about infants' capacity to discriminate between languages. Because this capacity is said to rely on periodic information in the speech signal, discrimination should be difficult for pairs of languages that are classified in the same rhythmic class. On the contrary, differentiation for languages that belong to separate categories should be comparatively easy and straightforward. This is precisely what had been observed in the above mentioned infant studies.

2.2 Contrasting languages with similar rhythmic properties

The analysis of discrimination capacities for languages of the same rhythmic class has been undertaken more recently and the results do not question the predictions derived from the TIGRE proposal. In one study, French newborns could not discriminate between two stress-timed languages such as English and Dutch (Nazzi, Bertoncini and Mehler 1998). Moreover, when a combination of sentences from pairs of languages was employed (either English–Dutch vs. Italian–Spanish, or English–Italian vs. Dutch–Spanish) infants were able to dishabituate only when the material was grouped according to the rhythmic class, that is, from English–Dutch to Italian–Spanish (Nazzi *et al.* 1998). Results were interpreted as favoring the prominent role played by global prosodic information in the discrimination between languages.

A second study that is worth mentioning here tackles these discrimination abilities in 2-month-old infants. Babies from English homes were presented with different language contrasts that involved familiarity and phonological class variables (Christophe and Morton 1998). They were able to distinguish English from Japanese but they did not detect a change from French to Japanese, both non-familiar languages belonging to two separate rhythmic classes, neither of which matched the native one. Surprisingly, Dutch (non-familiar) was discriminated from Japanese and, as expected, it was not distinguished from English. The authors' interpretation of these results was that infants at two months have already built an initial representation of the native language and that this is enough to make them treat non-familiar material as irrelevant to their language learning. This could be the reason for why French was not discriminated from Japanese, although French and Japanse are two languages that certainly differ in their rhythmic properties. At the same time, because of prosodic similarity, infants treated Dutch as a native language, and consequently discrimination from Japanese could be observed. The information to retain here is that distinctions between languages from the same rhythmic category do not seem to be available at this early age, probably because the properties of this initial language representation are simple and coarse-grained and do not allow for more fine-grained distinctions beyond prosody–rhythm.

A third study that deals with the capacity to differentiate within-class languages has employed a pair of syllable-timed languages, i.e. Spanish and Catalan, selecting older infants than the ones in the study above mentioned (Bosch and Sebastián-Gallés 1997a). 4.5-month-old infants from monolingual environments, either Spanish or Catalan, were tested on utterances from these two languages produced by a bilingual female speaker. Results indicated that differentiation was possible, either using normally recorded speech (Bosch and Sebastián-Gallés 1997a), low-pass filtered speech with a cut-off frequency of 400 Hz (Bosch and Sebastián-Gallés 1997a, 1997b) and also using multispeakers and male voices (Bosch, Cortés and Sebastián-Gallés 2001). On the other hand, unpublished data recently obtained at the LSCP in Paris indicate that French newborns cannot distinguish Spanish from Catalan material, thus indicating that prosodic differences between these two languages are not so notorious and probably require exposure to one of the languages in order to be detected.

These results suggest that discrimination between languages that belong to the same rhythmic class seems to be attained during the first semester of life, although it requires a certain refinement of the perceptual capacities that may not be present during the first two to three months of life (as in Christophe and Morton 1998). Results from a recent study with American five-month old infants also point in the same direction (Nazzi, Jusczyk and Johnson 2000). Different within-class contrasts were tested and evidence of differentiation was obtained for British English vs. Dutch and for British vs. American English, while the Dutch–German contrast could not be distinguished. The data support the notion that by five months of age a sharpening in infants' processing of prosodic information has taken place and consequently, some within-category language discriminations can be reached. However, exposure (or acquisition) seems to play a crucial role because non-familiar languages still cannot be differentiated, as in the case of the Dutch–German contrast.

A last point to be mentioned here refers to the type of acoustic information that infants rely on in order to be able to differentiate between languages. The notion of a perceptual refinement from the second to the fourth month of life has been put forward, but whether the cues for discrimination are still found in the rhythmic–prosodic characteristics of the language or whether other distinctive cues are available, relative to the distributional properties at the segmental or syllable structure levels, remains an open question.

To summarize, the investigations just reviewed are congruent with the notion of a gradual refinement in infants' capacities to identify their native language and to differentiate it from other languages, even rhythmically similar ones, during the first months of life. Within-class distinctions are not considered to be available until the infant has reached 4 to 5 months of age. All the investigations also point out that the main cues for early discrimination seem to derive from prosody, although more precise analyses are needed if one wants to specify the type of acoustic information that is relevant for discrimination in every language comparison. Specific manipulations of the speech signal prove to be helpful in establishing what elements are being attended to by the young infant (Ramus and Mehler 1999; Ramus, Nespor and Mehler 1999).

3.   The analysis of early perceptual differentiation under conditions of bilingual exposure

Understanding the mechanisms for discrimination is certainly important if one turns to the situation of infants from bilingual environments. In fact, the crucial point is how and when an infant discovers the existence of two different sound patterns in the ambient language. If utterances drawn from two different languages are wrongly considered to arise from the same underlying structure, then language learning would be compromised because of the improbability that specific structures match the requirements of utterances from both languages. Obviously, this may have negative consequences for the language acquisition process. The possibility exists that infants might be delayed in the perceptual milestones achieved during the first year of life, as described in the studies with monolingual infants (see Werker and Tees 1999, for a summary of current knowledge on infants' initial speech perception capacities, their reorganization during the first year of life and the beginning of word learning processes). Some parents seem to be aware of this possibility when they express their mixed feelings about early simultaneous bilingualism, despite the lack of evidence showing that it causes a delayed language acquisition onset.

From a theoretical perspective, and taking into account data on monolingual infants summarized in the previous section, two opposite outcomes can be derived from the simultaneous exposure to two languages. These mainly depend on their proximity in prosodic terms. In its simplest version the argument is the following one: Prosodic similarity between the languages of exposure should result in a late differentiation, while just the opposite prediction would hold for languages from different rhythmic categories. This position is in agreement with predictions derived from the TIGRE proposal (Mehler *et al.* 1996). The argument is, thus, that prosodic similarity can make both languages indistinguishable and that unless infants refine their perceptual analysis of the input — something that may eventually be reached through extended exposure — no separate representation is possibly being built. However, an alternative prediction is also tenable, that is, simultaneous exposure to two languages could lead to an enhanced language discrimination capacity. In bilingual environments infants may have increasing opportunities to detect inconsistencies in their somewhat complex input, in which certain incongruent cues or heterogeneous sound patterns might often be present. The detection of these cues could result in a refinement of the infant's discrimination capacities, making this language differentiation precóciously available.

Until recently, no answers could be found regarding this issue as no research had been specifically designed to deal with these early language and speech perception processes in infants from bilingual environments. Although in Bahrick and Pickens' study (1988) a group of bilingual infants from

English–Spanish bilingual homes was included in the sample, their data were not comparatively analyzed, as this was not the primary concern of their investigation. Moreover, those infants were 5-month-olds and the language contrast implied two rhythmically different languages, which, as has been said before, is far from being the most challenging situation for discrimination.

Research at the University of Barcelona has begun to address the issue of perceptual differentiation for rhythmically similar languages at four months of age in bilingual-to-be infants. A series of experiments has been designed accordingly and the main results will be presented and discussed in the following sections.

Previous research based on language familiarity
As a first approach to the differentiation issue, a group of 4.5-month-old infants from Spanish–Catalan bilingual environments (half of them had a Spanish-speaking mother and the other half a Catalan-speaking mother) was tested on Spanish and Catalan utterances for discrimination (Bosch and Sebastián-Gallés 1997a). The methodology that was employed was the same that had been proved successful in testing discrimination for this pair of languages in infants from monolingual families. The procedure was based on previous work in the research field of infants' visual attention (Johnson, Posner and Rothbart 1991). It had been adapted to assess preference for auditory stimuli based on familiarity, taking as a measure the latency of the first ocular saccade towards a lateral sound source (Dehaene-Lambertz and Houston 1998). Reaction time measures have been rarely used in infant auditory perception studies (for an exception, see Morgan 1994) although they are clearly indicative of the amount of information required to generate a response. In Dehaene-Lambertz and Houston's study (1998) faster orientation latencies towards the maternal language were observed and they occurred in utterances that were as short as 1.2 s on average. This means that the cues in the speech signal that enable the infant to identify the language as familiar can be reliably extracted with ease and speed, and they are probably redundant and distributed along the utterances.

In this exploratory experiment, the first one done to compare monolingual and bilingual infants' behavior, no significant differences were found in the bilinguals' orientation latencies to either Spanish or Catalan material, while the Spanish and Catalan monolingual groups had given evidence of differentiation by orienting faster towards material in the native language (Bosch and Sebastián-Gallés 1997a). The flat pattern found in the bilingual group could not be explained by the averaging of the orientation latencies of the maternal-Spanish and maternal-Catalan subgroups of bilingual infants. In both cases, the differences between Spanish and Catalan material were less than 80 ms, while for monolinguals they almost reached 200 ms. Results from the bilingual group, with similar orientation latencies for both languages, could be interpreted as an indication that no differentiation had been established, favoring the position that simultaneous exposure makes the infant unable to tell the languages apart. But recall here that this measure is based on familiarity and assesses preference, at least in the case of infants from monolingual environments, so the results can also be interpreted as indicating the absence of a language dominance in these infants: as they were equally familiar with Spanish and Catalan, similar orientation latencies were observed. Because discrimination could not be properly addressed by this methodology that had proved useful in the monolingual situation, a different procedure was to be selected.

4. Testing a within category differentiation: Spanish–Catalan discrimination

A second methodology had to be devised in order to properly address the discrimination issue in our bilingual population (see Bosch and Sebastián-Gallés 2001). The experimental paradigm was developed after Jusczyk and Aslin's familiarization-preference procedure (Jusczyk and Aslin 1995). It combines features of the extensively used Head-turn Preference Procedure (Kemler-Nelson, Jusczyk, Mandel, Myers, Turk and Gerken 1995) plus features characteristic of the word monitoring and auditory priming paradigms used in research with adults. Initially designed to test infants' word segmentation strategies (as in Jusczyk and Aslin 1995), it has been successively readapted to be used in different word and rule learning infant studies (Marcus, Vijayan, Bandi Rao and Vishton 1999; Saffran, Aslin and Newport 1996). The familiarization-preference procedure uses an extended familiarization phase and a test phase in which listening times to different passages/materials are monitored. If discrimination is reached, differential responses based on the duration of infants' visual fixation on an image on a screen are expected to novel materials compared to the familiarized ones.

A series of experiments was run with monolingual and bilingual infants to assess the methodology and to enable the comparison between both populations. In the following sections just data from the bilingual study are summarized (see Bosch and Sebastián-Gallés 2001, for a full description of the experimental series).

4.1 Method

4.1.1 *Subjects*
A group of 28 infants from Spanish–Catalan bilingual families participated in this experiment. They were divided into two subgroups according to the language predominantly used by the mother in everyday mother-child interaction (Spanish-dominant bilingual and Catalan-dominant bilingual subgroups). The bilingual status of the families was carefully assessed through a questionnaire and only cases in which the distribution of daily exposure to both languages ranged from 50–50 per cent to 65–35 per cent were included in the sample. Mean age was 135 days and 139 days for the Spanish-dominant and the Catalan dominant groups, respectively.

4.1.2 *Procedure*
Materials in this experiment were eight different three-sentence passages, four in Catalan and four in Spanish. Sentences in the passages had been produced by a bilingual female speaker. Two different passages in the same language were used in the familiarization phase until the infant accumulated two minutes of sustained attention. Each infant was familiarized with the maternal language (i.e. the Spanish-dominant group was familiarized with Spanish and the Catalan-dominant group with Catalan). One trial consisted in the presentation of a passage twice, with a total duration slightly below 30", so that infants needed at least three trials on each passage to reach criterion. Passages were presented from a hidden loudspeaker (either on the left or right side) whenever the infant fixated an image on the corresponding left or right screen. Listening time was monitored based on infants' visual fixation on that image (trial duration was under infant control: if she looked away for more than 2 seconds the trial was over, if not, presentation went on until its completion).

In the test phase the infant was presented with four novel passages of similar duration, two in the same language as the one used in the familiarization phase and two in the other language. These four novel passages were repeated twice until the completion of eight test trials. Recall that the rationale behind the procedure is that if infants have reached/extracted a common representation from the sentences in the familiarization phase that matches their representation of their native language, they may show a novelty detection effect for sentences in the non-familiar (or in the other) language.

4.2 Results

Data from the two bilingual subgroups showed longer listening times for the non-familiarized language in the test phase thus indicating that discrimination was reached in both cases: infants familiarized to Spanish could detect a change to Catalan when it was presented in the test phase and also infants familiarized to Catalan were able to detect a change to Spanish in the corresponding test trials (see Figure 1). The ANOVA indicated a highly significant interaction between the language of the passages and the maternal language ($p < 0.0001$). Planned t-tests revealed significant differences in mean listening times to familiarized vs. non-familiarized language for both subgroups and only five out of the twenty-eight infants tested did not show a higher listening time for the passages in the novel language, which suggests that the effect is fairly robust (Bosch and Sebastián-Gallés 2001).

Additionally, when data from these bilingual subgroups was statistically compared to previous results obtained in two groups of monolingual infants (Spanish and Catalan), using the same procedure and materials, the only significant effect that was found was again the interaction between language in the test phase and maternal language, that is, the language of the familiarization phase (see Figure 1). No differences could be found in the behavior of

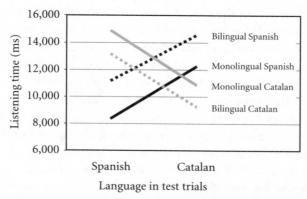

Figure 1. Mean listening time to test passages for the different groups of monolingual and bilingual infants tested in the Catalan–Spanish discrimination experiment with the familiarization-preference procedure (adapted from Bosch and Sebastián-Gallés 2001)

these four groups with different linguistic background (Bosch and Sebastián-Gallés 2001).

4.3 Discussion

The results in this experiment can be interpreted as indicating an early perceptual differentiation of the two languages of exposure in bilingual environments. Infants slightly below five months of age show evidence of detecting a language change for the Spanish–Catalan contrast. Moreover, the comparison with data from monolingual infants gives no indication of a significant delay in these early perceptual processes. It should be stressed here that the two familiar languages for these bilingual infants were considered most challenging for their perception and discrimination capacities, and the straightforward prediction was that distinction would probably take place later in development, perhaps with the building of the first lexicon. Our results favor the opposite position, i.e. an early discrimination, and they provide no support for a bilingual delay in language discrimination capacities.

How can we account for these results? Which cues in the speech signal make this distinction precociously available? From a prosodic perspective Spanish and Catalan would be grouped together: both are syllable-timed languages and similarities exist in their prosodic structure. If any, differences might be found below the phonological phrase level in the prosodic hierarchy. The presence of vowel reduction only in Catalan may be responsible for rhythmic differences at the clitic group or phonological word levels. Besides possible rhythmic differences, Spanish and Catalan also differ in their vowel repertoires (i.e. five vowels in Spanish [a, e, i, o, u] vs. seven in Catalan plus a schwa [a, ɛ, e, i, ɔ, o, u and ə], and moreover, vowel reduction has important consequences on the vocalic distribution in connected speech (in unstressed syllables only three vowels — [i, u, and ə] — are used). Central vowels in Catalan (/a/ and /ə/) account for more than 60 per cent of the vocalic nuclei in fluent speech, while in Spanish a more balanced distribution of the five vowel sounds is found. Therefore, cues that enable differentiation might be found in the metrical but also in the distributional properties of these languages. Even though we know that infants do not represent speech as a sequence of vowels and consonants, it is possible to hypothesize that attention to the distributional properties of vowels could be helpful in making the distinction between these two languages available. Further experiments are certainly needed to shed light on the mechanisms underlying these discrimination capacities and the type of cues that are used in the different language comparisons.

5. Native-language recognition processes: monolingual *vs.* bilingual comparison at four months

The differentiation issue is just one aspect in the study of speech perception processes in bilingual language acquisition. Unfortunately, the whole picture is far from complete but there is more information to be included here as it is relevant to the processing mechanisms underlying these native-language recognition and discrimination capacities.

In the first series of experiments developed in our laboratory, when we used the orientation latency measure (i.e. measuring the time the infants need to visually orient towards a lateralized sound source from where utterances were presented), an outstanding difference appeared when the behavior of our two types of population (monolingual vs. bilingual) was compared (Bosch and Sebastián-Gallés 1997a). In one of the testing conditions materials were selected to establish a contrast between the familiar language (Catalan or Spanish) and a rhythmically distant non-familiar one (English). Monolingual and bilingual infants were tested with the same materials, although for the bilingual subgroups the familiar language was just one of the two languages heard at home (they were grouped according to their *maternal* language — the language predominantly spoken by their mother). Because the selected non-familiar language was English, which is prosodically different from either Spanish and Catalan, differentiation should pose no problem, and therefore we predicted faster orientation latencies towards the utterances in the familiar language in all cases. What we found was that *only* the monolingual infants behaved in the predicted way, while bilinguals offered longer latencies for the utterances in the maternal language (Bosch and Sebastián-Gallés 1997a). Statistical analyses revealed that significant differences corresponded to the orientation latencies towards the familiar material, while the time needed to orient towards the English utterances was similar in both groups (see Figure 2).

The same pattern of responses was obtained when bilinguals were tested using Italian as a non-familiar language (Bosch and Sebastián-Gallés 1997a). This later result seems to suggest that the rhythmic properties of the languages in the test are not determinant in the observation of the response pattern (it was found both when a rhythmically distant and a rhythmically close language were employed).

The possibility exists that this peculiar pattern was an artifact of the methodology and that it does not reflect a systematic tendency in the way utterances are processed, but simply shows up in a task that implies frequent changes in language presentation. To clarify this issue, the bilingual data were reanalyzed in search of any evidence that could explain these slower latencies. A possible hypothesis would be that longer latencies might reflect activation/inhibition processes of the separate language files that the bilingual infant has already built at four months of age. In this case, longer latencies would always appear after a language switch but not in consecutive trials using the same language. However, results from this reanalysis were inconclusive, so this tentative hypothesis had to be discarded. It was then decided to test older infants to see whether this response pattern was still present.

6.   The orientation latency measure at six months

To further analyze the slower orientation latencies towards the maternal language found in bilingual infants when presented with utterances from two different languages (one familiar and the other non-familiar), an experiment was run at six months following exactly the same procedure that had been applied at four months (Bosch and Sebastián-Gallés 1997a), that is, testing maternal language (either Catalan or Spanish) vs. English, with the orientation latency measure.

6.1 Method

6.1.1 *Subjects*
Two groups of healthy, full-term, 6-month-old infants participated in this study. In the monolingual group, ten infants that belonged to monolingual families (half were Spanish and half were Catalan) were tested. The bilingual group also included ten infants, half with a Spanish-speaking mother and the other half with a Catalan-speaking mother. Mean age was 197 days (range 183–207) for the monolingual group and 190 days (range 181–205) for the bilingual group. As in all of our infant studies, the linguistic status of the families was assessed through a questionnaire that reflected the daily amount of exposure to Spanish and Catalan so that global exposure could be esti-

mated. All bilingual infants in the sample ranged from 50–50 per cent to 35–65 per cent distribution of daily time of exposure to both languages. On the other hand, monolingual infants belonged to families in which only one language was spoken at home and exposure to the non-familiar language had to be considered sporadic, with an incidence below 20 per cent of the total time.

6.1.2 *Procedure*

Infants were tested with a modified version of the visual orientation procedure (Dehaene-Lambertz and Houston 1998) with exactly the same materials that had been employed in the 4-month-old infants' study (Bosch and Sebastián-Gallés 1997a). The testing included the presentation of a maximum of 28 utterances, half in the maternal language and half in English, divided in two blocks. The infant was seated on a special seat facing a central monitor flanked by two identical photographs of a woman that hid the lateral loudspeakers from where the utterances were presented. On every trial, after the infant had visually fixated the image that appeared in the central monitor, the presentation of the auditory stimulus began (on one side) and the time the infant needed to visually orient towards the lateral sound source could be monitored. The presentation was computer-controlled, and every 16 seconds a new trial began until the completion of the first block (14 utterances). The second block, with the remaining 14 utterances, started after a short pause and went on until its completion or until the infant's attention was not directed towards the visual and auditory stimuli for more than five consecutive trials. The side (left or right) and the type of language (maternal or English) was randomized for every subject with the following restrictions: no utterance was ever repeated, no more than three successive presentations could be played on the same side and no more than two utterances from the same language could appear in a row. The whole session was video-recorded and the orientation latencies were coded off-line to obtain the measures for every valid trial.

6.2 Results

Mean orientation latencies to utterances in the maternal language and in English were computed for every infant in the study. From a maximum of 28 test trials the average number of valid trials for the Monolingual group was 17.8 (SD=4.4) and for the Bilingual group it was 15.9 (SD=2.5). Monolingual infants correctly oriented in 73.8 per cent of the trials, and bilingual infants did so in 62.1 per cent of the trials. No significant differences between the two groups were found.

For the monolingual group, mean orientation latencies to utterances in the maternal language were 1184 ms (SD=395.9) and to English 1452 ms (SD=385.1); for the bilingual group, mean orientation latencies to maternal language were 1904.4 (SD=682.4) and to English 1631.6 (SD=563.7) (see Figure 2). Data from the two groups were submitted to an ANOVA. No clearly significant effects were found for group (monolingual vs. bilingual) [F (1,18)= 3.936, $p<0.063$] or for type of language (maternal vs. English) (F<1) but a highly significant interaction effect between the factors analyzed was observed [F (1,18)=30.902, $p<0.0001$]. In both cases a paired t-test indicated a significant difference between latencies to maternal vs. non-familiar material (monolingual group: t (9)=3.32, $p<0.009$); bilingual group: t (9)=−5.19, $p<0.001$).

As expected, monolingual infants showed a faster reaction for utterances in the maternal language and a slower latency to orient towards material in a non-familiar language. For bilinguals we replicated the finding previously observed at four months: orientation latencies to utterances in the maternal language were slower than latencies towards material in the non-familiar language. Independent t-test analyses indicated that a significant difference was only present in the maternal language comparison (t (18)=2.885, $p<0.01$)

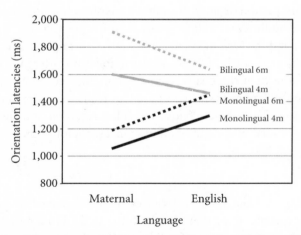

Figure 2. Maternal language recognition in monolingual and bilingual infants at four and six months of age: mean orientation latencies to English sentences and sentences in the maternal language (either Spanish or Catalan)

but not when latencies to English utterances were compared ($t < 1$). Thus, monolingual and bilingual infants' responses were similar for utterances in the non-familiar language but when the maternal language was presented they clearly differed in the speed of their orientation responses.

An additional analysis was done taking into account data from our previous study with 4-month-old infants (Bosch and Sebastián-Gallés 1997a). The analysis included two factors (age and type of environment) with two levels each (4 and 6 months; monolingual and bilingual environment). The ANOVA showed a significant effect of environment ($F_{(1,36)} = 8.34$, $p < 0.007$) and a highly significant interaction between language in the test and type of environment ($F_{(1,36)} = 52.54$, $p < 0.0001$). These results indicate that bilingual and monolingual infants differ significantly in their responses to the language materials. Slower orientation latencies are found in the bilingual group but they are restricted to the presentation of utterances in the maternal language as no significant differences are found when responses to English utterances are compared. No differences appeared related to the age factor, which can be taken as an indication that the pattern of responses we have obtained is rather stable.

6.3 Discussion

Taken as a whole, results from monolingual and bilingual infants can be interpreted as a clear indication of a difference in native-language recognition processes when both populations are compared. This difference seems to be relatively independent of the prosodic distance between the languages that are contrasted and it does not seem to be sporadic as the same pattern has been obtained at two different age levels. The data suggest that the underlying mechanisms that are activated in this language recognition task may differ and that these longer latencies for the maternal language seem to be specific to the bilingual situation. However, a proper explanation for this particular phenomenon remains to be found, as well as its generalization to different types of bilingual exposure: Is the proximity of the languages that the infants hear regularly the determining factor in these longer latencies to the maternal language or are they a characteristic feature of bilingual infants regardless of the properties of the languages they are exposed to? One tentative explanation refers to the possibility that the nature of these native language recognition processes implies a certain cost for infants that have been exposed to two languages right from birth. This cost, which would translate into the slower orientation latencies for the utterances in the maternal language when only one of the two familiar languages is presented, might be the consequence of two types of processing activities involved, namely, recognition of a familiar pattern plus its identification. This tentative explanation implies that differentiation has already taken place, something that has been corroborated by the Spanish–Catalan discrimination experiments (Bosch and Sebastián-Gallés 2001). In the case of monolinguals these two operations reduce to one because these infants would be building a single native-language representation. Whether bilinguals are actually forming separate representations for the two languages of exposure and whether the constitutive elements of these primary representations are equivalent in both monolingual and bilingual infants are issues that are far from being solved at the present time. All that can be said for the moment is that different underlying processes seem to be activated in the specific testing situation that has been employed, although their precise nature still remains unrevealed.

7. Conclusion

The aim of this chapter was to offer a synthesis of a series of experiments that have specifically addressed the issue of early language differentiation in bilingual language acquisition by analyzing the speech and language perception abilities in the first months of life. The studies that have been described give evidence of an early perceptual differentiation between the languages of exposure in the most challenging situation, when both familiar languages are rhythmically close.

Although we were certainly aware of the impressive speech and language discrimination capacities in infants from monolingual environments, *a priori*, simultaneous exposure to two similar languages from birth should be considered as a possible problem for the infant that is beginning to develop language. Now that empirical evidence for perceptual discrimination has been obtained, the precise mechanisms that enable differentiation remain to be fully specified.

How does the infant find out that there are two languages in his/her environment and not just one? And, once perceptual differentiation has been reached, how is it related to the language acquisition processes for the two languages in the bilingual infant? These are general questions that have motivated the research line whose results have been described in the previous sections.

The crucial finding is that evidence favoring an early differentiation has been obtained and, what is more, no specific delay has been identified concerning these initial language discrimination capacities. As the bilingual situation that has been analyzed implies two rhythmically close languages (i.e. Spanish and Catalan) for which discrimination is considered to be most challenging for infants' capacities, the results we have obtained could possibly be generalized to other bilingual situations. However, further research is needed in different bilingual contexts to confirm this hypothesis.

Can we offer an answer concerning the mechanisms that make possible this early differentiation for two prosodically close languages? If languages belonged to different rhythmic categories (for instance, Spanish vs. English) an explanation could be found in terms of clear surface cues that make the distinction available, as data from newborns have shown. But a rhythmic classification of languages would group Spanish and Catalan together, so as a first approximation, coarse-grained rhythmic similarities should prevail over differences (see Bosch and Sebastián-Gallés 1997a, for a discussion of the locus of differences between Spanish and Catalan in the prosodic hierarchy framework). However, extended exposure may gradually enable a more refined analysis of the input language, leading to the detection of differential cues between these two syllable-timed languages. If this argument is applied to the bilingual situation, instead of a perspective that enhances confusion between languages, one could say that because of increased variability in the input and the presence of explicit inconsistencies in the signal from the very beginning (discrepancies which in the monolingual situation would require longer exposure to the native language in order to be detected), an early division of the input into two separate files may be favored. The one person, one language strategy employed systematically by many families could help in facilitating and maintaining the distinction, but it should not be considered the primary mechanism. The origin of the distinction should be found in the metrical and/or distributional properties of the signal itself and in the readjustment of infants' initial language file specification due to complex (i.e. bilingual) input. Ongoing research in our laboratory using other within-category language contrasts (i.e. contrasting Italian both with Catalan and Spanish) has been designed to further explore young bilingual infants' language discrimination capacities.

A second aspect that has been indirectly analyzed refers to the language dominance issue. As it has been pointed out, psycholinguistic research with highly competent adult bilingual speakers has offered the idea that, even in an extremely balanced situation, a language dominance has been established and its origin may be found in the perceptual organization that takes place during the prelinguistic period (Cutler *et al.* 1992). Research in our laboratory does not offer evidence for the early establishment of a language dominance in these bilingual-to-be infants. Recall that when they were tested on the Spanish–Catalan contrast, no preference was found and similar orientation latencies to utterances in both languages were obtained (Bosch and Sebastián-Gallés 1997a). Recent unpublished data from two groups of 4.5-month-old bilingual infants tested on the Spanish–Italian contrast reveal no differences in the response pattern observed regardless of the *maternal* language (Bosch and Sebastián-Gallés in preparation). As far as data obtained in our laboratory with different groups of infants from bilingual environments goes, no evidence of the establishment of a language dominance has been obtained.

Finally, we would like to draw attention once more to the differential behavior between monolinguals and bilinguals when orientation latency measures or reaction time measures are obtained. Indeed, this is an area in which further research is clearly needed because it concerns the underlying mechanisms that are active in speech and language processing tasks. Perhaps a parallellism can be found in other areas of bilingual infants' language development in terms of language selection and the behavioral costs of language switching, but this is work that will have to be done in the lexical acquisition domain, with infants older than the ones that have participated in our research project.

Notes

* This work has been supported by a research grant (DGICYT PB97–0977) from the Ministerio de Educación y Ciencia (Spain), and the *Grup de Recerca Consolidat* (5120-UB 05) from Generalitat de Catalunya (Spain). We thank X. Mayoral for technical support and C. Cortés, G. Pérez and M. Rodríguez for assistance in testing infants. We also thank the parents and infants that participated in this study and the following people and institutions: Dr. Lailla and Dr. Jiménez from the *Hospital de Sant Joan de Déu*; Dr. V. Molina from the *Institut Universitari Dexeus*; Dr. Llauradó from *C. A. P Les Corts*; the staff nurses and midwives from *C. A. P. Manso*, the *Hospital de Sant Joan de Déu* and the *Hospital Clínic i Provincial de Barcelona*; M. Colilles and M. Cequiel from the *Centre Vincles*; N. Jiménez from the *Institut d'Educació*.

1. The classification of languages into rhythmic classes has been proposed by linguists (among them Abercrombie 1967; Ladefoged 1975) and three main categories have been established: Stress-timed languages such as Germanic, Slavonic and Arabic languages; syllable-timed languages, such as Romance languages; and mora-timed languages which

include Japanese and Tamil. Although initially rhythm was considered the consequence of the isochrony of syllables or related to inter-stress intervals, recent work has shown that a crucial variable in determining rhythmic differences can be found in the vowel/consonant temporal ratio (Ramus and Mehler 1999; Ramus *et al.* 1999). The recent identification of reliable acoustic characteristics that serve to classify languages according to their rhythmic patterns brings empirical support to the broad categories previously defined by linguists and used by psycholinguists to interpret the behavior of both infants and adults in a wide range of speech perception tasks.

2. Ultimately, the rhythmic properties of the language of exposure will determine the type of speech processing mechanisms that will be active when listening to the language. Evidence of such language-specific processing mechanisms is found in cross-linguistic adult speech perception studies from which the term language specific listening has been proposed and whose origin is traced back to the initial experience with the language in early infancy (Cutler, Mehler, Norris and Seguí 1983; Cutler and Otake 1994; Mehler, Frauenfelder and Seguí 1981; Otake and Cutler 1996; Pallier, Sebastián-Gallés, Dupoux, Christophe and Mehler 1998; Sebastián-Gallés, Dupoux, Seguí and Mehler 1992).

CHAPTER 4

Language differentiation in bilingual infants
Evidence from babbling[*]

Diane Poulin-Dubois and Naomi Goodz

1. Introduction

Throughout the twentieth century, the issue of whether early exposure to two languages negatively affects the process of language acquisition has been a preoccupation not only for researchers and theorists but also for educators and for parents wishing to raise their children with two languages. The most basic concerns are whether bilingual children will show the same ages of onset for the major language milestones and whether their rate of language development will be comparable to that of monolingual children (Leopold 1939, 1949; Romaine 1999). To date, few studies have been aimed at investigating these questions but the available data suggest similar ages of onset for canonical babbling and other vocal performance measures, and for emergence of first word, and multi-word combinations (Oller, Eilers, Urbano and Cobo-Lewis 1997; Goodz 1994).

Although questions about rate and onset of language development have been major concerns for parents and educators, researchers have been more interested in investigating whether bilinguals are able to differentiate their two languages in a systematic way. At least two opposing points of view have been proposed. On the basis of their study of two children, Volterra and Taeschner (1978) proposed a three-stage process of linguistic differentiation, also known as the single system hypothesis. According to this view, the bilingual child begins with one lexical system which includes items from both languages (Leopold 1978; Taeschner 1983). In the second stage, the child distinguishes two different lexicons but applies the same syntactic rules to both languages. In the third stage, the young bilingual has two separate linguistic codes, differentiated in both lexicon and syntax. Volterra and Taeschner present two main lines of evidence from their longitudinal study of two children in support for the unitary system hypothesis; failure to find translation equivalents in early lexical productions, and use of elements from the two languages in some multi-word utterances.

The claim that young bilingual children reject cross-language synonyms in their early lexicons has been challenged by recent longitudinal studies using diary records, video recordings and standardized parental questionnaires (Mikes 1990; Vihman 1985). For instance, in a recent study on the early lexical development of 27 English–Spanish bilingual children, translation equivalents were reported in all children tested and represented an average proportion of 30 per cent of all words coded in the two languages (Pearson, Fernández and Oller 1995). Similarly, in a case study of an infant acquiring Spanish and English from birth, Quay (1995) reported equivalent terms in her subject's two languages even in the first few months of lexical acquisition. Interestingly, a reanalysis of Volterra and Taeschner's data (Quay 1995) provides even more evidence of the early use of translation equivalents.

The extent to which bilingual children mix elements of their two languages, as well as the interpretation of such mixing has been the focus of much research and debate. Language mixing in the early stages of bilingual acquisition has been reported in almost all studies (see McLaughlin 1978 and De Houwer 1995, for reviews) and several forms, including phonological, lexical, and morphosyntactic mixing, have been observed. However, some studies have found either no evidence of mixing at all or only a very small proportion of mixed utterances (De Houwer 1990; Goodz 1994; Meisel 1990b; Lanza 1992).

The existence of language mixing has been of crucial interest in the debate about early language differentiation and interpretations differ significantly. Until the end of the 1980s, the use of two languages within a single utterance was considered to be a reflection of children's failure to differentiate their two languages and even a sign of language confusion. More recently, other explanations have been offered. Foremost among these is the extent to which parents may model mixed utterances in speech directed to their children (Goodz 1989), parental success in negotiating a bilingual environment with their children (Lanza 1992), and disparities in the children's level of competence in each of their two languages (Genesee, Nicoladis and Paradis 1995; Goodz 1994).

In the latter connection, Genesee *et al.* (1995) have noted that bilingual children are more likely to show mixing when using their non-dominant language. Similarly, Goodz (1994) has reported that even children who speak only one of the two home languages exhibit language mixing when interacting with the parent speaking the child's non-dominant language. In cases where such mixing occurs, it appears to be due to the children's attempt to meet the parent on a common linguistic ground by introducing items from that parent's native language. These children typically do not mix when interacting with the parent speaking their dominant language.

The evidence that bilingual children show signs of differentiation of their two languages at the very early stages of language production raises the possibility that such distinction might emerge even before children begin to produce their first words (De Houwer 1998a). The basis for this possibility comes from studies of infants exposed to only one language. It is well established that infants have developed sophisticated abilities in speech perception by the end of the first year and that their vocal production gradually incorporates phonological and prosodic elements in their linguistic environment during that period (Jusczyk 1997). From a very early age, infants appear to have some ability to recognize some general characteristics of utterances in their native language, such as prosodic features relating to the intonational and rhythmic properties of speech. This is illustrated by the fact that even newborns can distinguish utterances in their native language from those in a foreign language (Mehler, Jusczyk, Lambertz, Halsted, Bertoncini and Amiel-Tison 1988). The fact that the same pattern of results is observed when low-pass filtered speech is presented to infants suggests that this distinction is based on the recognition of prosodic, and not phonetic, features.

A few months after birth, infants have developed a sensitivity to the phonetic and phonotactic characteristics of their native language. Between 6 and 9 months, infants distinguish words in their native language from words in another language on the basis of the presence and ordering of specific phonetic segments (Jusczyk, Hohne, Jusczyk and Redanz 1993). In sum, the literature on speech perception in infancy clearly shows that infants possess the skills necessary to distinguish between their native language and a foreign language. In fact, studies by Werker and her colleagues (Werker and Tees 1984) reinforce this conclusion by demonstrating that towards the end of their first years, as they increasingly target the language of their environment, infants show a decreasing sensitivity to contrasts which are not phonemically relevant in that language. Thus, we can hypothesize that by the end of the first year, infants raised in a bilingual environment can distinguish between their two native languages and therefore have the potential to begin to treat the two languages in systematically different ways.

There is some evidence that infant babbling varies as a function of the linguistic environment. Some cross-linguistic studies of vowel production, consonantal repertoire, and intonational contours in babbling have revealed significant differences across linguistic groups, similar to the differences found across the target languages (de Boysson-Bardies and Vihman 1991; de Boysson-Bardies, Vihman, Roug-Hellichius, Durand, Landberg and Arao 1992; Whalen, Levitt and Wang 1991). For example, using acoustic, instrumental and phonetic transcriptions, it has been found that infants raised in a French linguistic environment exhibit a greater frequency of rising intonation in their babbling than do infants in English environments (Whalen *et al.* 1991). Similarly, comparisons of the babbling of infants exposed to English, French, Swedish, and Japanese with the speech of adult speakers of these languages have revealed similarities in frequencies of certain place and manner categories of consonants and vowels (de Boysson-Bardies *et al.* 1992). These findings, although charac-terized by large individual differences within each linguistic group, have been interpreted as support for the *babbling drift* hypothesis which asserts that there is a progressive resemblance of infant babbling to the phonetic and prosodic characteristics of the language to which they are exposed (Brown 1958; cf. Oller and Eilers 1982; Eilers, Oller and Benito-Garcia 1984).

To our knowledge, only one study has investigated the babbling produc-tions of infants reared in bilingual environments (Oller *et al.* 1997). However, only the age of onset and quantitative measures of vocal performance were examined in that study of Spanish–English infants. Thus, the objective of the present study was to examine the babbling productions of 12-month-old infants raised in a bilingual environment. More specifically, we examined the distribution of consonants in the babbling productions of French-English bilingual infants.

2.   Method

2.1 Participants

The sample included in the present study was composed of thirteen infants, seven boys and six girls, all raised in bilingual French and English families living in Montreal, Canada. There were two identical male twins included in the sample. The average age of the children was 12.60 months, ranging from 9.82 to 13.95. All families were Caucasian and from middle-class socioeco-nomic status. Eight of the 13 children were first-born. There were ten French-speaking and two English-speaking mothers included in the sample.

The names of potential participants were drawn from birth lists provided by a governmental agency. In recruiting participants for the study, it was necessary to assess the linguistic environment of each potential participant with some precision. During a telephone interview, an assessment of exposure to each language was conducted, taking into account the languages spoken by each caregiver as well as the amount of time spent by the child with that person. Using a questionnaire developed specifically for this purpose, one parent (usually the mother) was asked to assess the total amount of the child's waking time spent with each caregiver by the child in a typical week, both alone and with other caregivers. The collected information was then used to calculate the child's overall percentage of exposure to French and English. A criterion of at least 20 per cent exposure to the non-dominant language, that is, the language they were least exposed to, was used. This relatively liberal cut-off point has been used in the selection of participants in another study on bilingual children (Pearson *et al.* 1995). Ratio of dominant-to-nondominant language exposure varied across subjects from 76: 24 per cent to 56: 43 per cent. The mean percentage exposure time was 54.0 per cent for French and 54.3 per cent for English.

In half of the families, the child was spoken to in a one person-one language fashion. In the other families, French was spoken to the child by both parents (N=1), or both parents used the two languages equally (N=3), or one parent spoke both languages and the other spoke only one language (N=1). With regard to the broader linguistic environment of these children, the data from the questionnaire revealed that, except in two cases, both parents were fluent in French and English. However, English was the language spoken at home in the majority of families.

2.2 Materials

The babbling sample was recorded with a Marantz audiotape recorder with a Sony multidirectional ECM 909-A microphone. Spectrographic analyses were completed with a CSL 4300 Kay Elemetrics sonagraph, a CSL 6300 palatometer, a Zenith Data Systems PC and an AIWA double stereo WX 220 Cassette Deck.

2.3 Procedure: data collection

Recording of babbling sample took place at home, in the absence of the investigators. All participants were recorded in both a French and an English context. The parents were given written instructions about the recordings. For example, they were instructed to choose a time for recording when the infant was likely to be alert and known to babble (e.g., meal and bath time). They were also instructed to hold the microphone at about 20 cm from the baby and to prevent the presence of external noise during the recordings. Two 20-minute recording sessions were completed: one with one of the parents and a second one with the other parent. During each session, parents were instructed to be alone with the child and to speak exclusively the language they typically used with the child throughout the entire session. They were also instructed to stop talking as soon as the baby started to vocalize. The twins' babbling was recorded while both infants were together; therefore, their babbling sample was treated as data from one participant in the data analyses.

2.4 Phonetic transcription

Utterances containing CV, VC, and CVC syllables were selected for analysis. No other productions typical of the vocal play period (i.e., squeals, growls, etc.), emotive sounds (i.e. crying, laughing, etc.) or vegetative sounds (i.e., coughs, sneezes) were used. Utterances were defined as an individual syllable or string of syllables separated from other utterances by an interval of at least 500 ms. There were 1,341 babbling utterances coded, 696 of which were produced in the French-speaking context and 641 in the English-speaking context. Each utterance was transcribed by a trained phonetician fluent in French and English, using the International Phonetic Alphabet. In addition, all utterances were digitized and sonagrams inspected by the coder in order to provide reliability of the transcriptions. In order to compare the vocal production of our bilingual infants to that of the French- and English-speaking monolingual infants described by de Boysson-Bardies and Vihman (1991), consonantal productions were classified according to manner and place of articulation. Only true consonants were considered, that is, glides and glottals were excluded. For manner categories, consonants were classified according to four categories: stops, fricatives, nasals, and liquids. For place of articulation, consonants were classified into three categories: labials (including labiodental), dentals (including alveolar and palatal) and velars (including uvulars).

3.   Results

In the first analysis, we tested the hypothesis that linguistic context will modify the distribution of place and manner of articulation of consonants in bilingual infants' production. A shift in the distribution of categories of consonants across linguistic contexts would provide some evidence for an early attunement of children to the phonetic differences between the two linguistic systems. Intergroup comparisons were also carried out to determine the similarities and differences between the babbling of monolingual and bilingual infants. For the intergroup analyses, we used for comparison the published data of the consonantal productions of five monolingual French and five American babies with the same mean age as our bilingual infants (de Boysson-Bardies and Vihman 1991; de Boysson-Bardies *et al.* 1992). In the longitudinal study by de Boysson-Bardies and her colleagues this monolingual sample corresponded to the recording session in which infants produced an average of four words. Tokens of each consonant were tabulated for each bilingual subject for each of the two recording sessions (French and English) and the percentage of each type of consonants was calculated and averaged across bilingual infants for each session.

Consonants produced by adult speakers of French, English, Japanese and Swedish have been compared in the literature (de Boysson-Bardies *et al.* 1992). Although there are few differences in the consonants produced by adult French and English speakers, English speakers have been found to have a higher percentage of stops in their speech than French speakers. On the other hand, French speakers have been reported as producing more labials than English speakers. With regard to infant babbling, similar comparisons across these four linguistic groups have yielded differences in the percentage of stops, with more stops found in English than in French babbling and more labials in French babbling than in English babbling (de Boysson-Bardies and Vihman 1991).

Table 1 shows the mean percentage and standard deviation of place and manner consonants in each of the two linguistic contexts. For each of the

Table 1. Mean frequency and percentage (and standard deviations) of consonants in babbling of bilinguals in French and English context

| | Context | | | |
| | French | | English | |
Consonants	Frequency	Percentage	Frequency	Percentage
Labials	33.6	38.0 (16.9)	32.7	36.2 (12.5)
Dentals	53.9	46.6 (21.3)	44.4	51.3 (19.8)
Velars	16.4	15.3 (12.9)	13.4	12.5 (11.5)
Stops	62.8	56.0 (16.3)	54.3	58.2 (13.4)
Fricatives	15.0	14.6 (9.8)	12.9	14.4 (7.7)
Nasals	16.3	19.3 (11.3)	15.8	18.5 (15.5)
Liquids	9.8	10.1 (11.9)	7.5	8.9 (3.8)

seven types of consonants a paired t-test was calculated to identify a possible difference between the percentages across the two contexts. Results indicated no difference between the two contexts for any of the seven comparisons, all ts < 1, n.s. In other words, the percentages of consonantal productions were similar, whether the infant was interacting with a French- or an English-speaking parent.

As the large standard deviations suggest, there was a wide range of percentages of consonants across children. This intersubject variability can be illustrated with data from individual children, with a focus on the proportions of stops and labials across the two contexts as these two categories have been found to differ in frequency across French and English adult speakers. Only three infants showed a percentage of stops higher in English than in French. Of these three infants, two were more exposed to English than to French (67 per cent and 68 per cent) and one was more exposed to French (59 per cent). In the case of the labials category, only one subject showed the expected pattern of a higher proportion of labials in the French context and this child's dominant linguistic environment was French. In summary, the babbling of the bilingual infants was almost undistinguishable in the two contexts with regard to consonantal production.

The second important question to consider is whether the infants' babbling showed a pattern of consonant distribution more similar to the French or to the English distribution. Indeed, the lack of difference across contexts observed so far does not inform about the phonetic structure of the babbling produced. We therefore compared the distribution of consonants in each of the two contexts to the monolingual group exposed to the same language.

Table 2. Mean percentage (and standard deviations) of consonants in babbling of French monolinguals and French–English bilinguals in French context

Consonants	Groups	
	Bilinguals	Monolinguals
Labials	38.0 (16.9)	53.4 (32.9)*
Dentals	46.6 (21.3)	40.9 (30.3)
Velars	15.3 (12.9)	5.7 (7.1)*
Stops	56.0 (16.3)	62.7 (18.5)
Fricatives	14.6 (9.8)	13.5 (13.4)
Nasals	19.3 (11.3)	16.5 (9.6)
Liquids	10.1 (11.9)	7.3 (14.7)

*$p < .05$

Table 2 shows the percentage of consonants of each type for the bilingual infants in the French context and the corresponding monolingual French data at the same age, as reported by de Boysson-Bardies and Vihman (1991). A series of one-sample t tests were performed on each pair of means and revealed only 2 significant differences (out of 7) between the bilingual and monolingual infants. The monolingual infants produced more labials than the bilinguals, t (11)=−2.89, $p < .01$, and the bilingual infants produced more velars than the monolingual infants, t (11)=2.34, $p < .05$. All the other percentages did not differ across the groups, all ts < 1.3.

Similar analyses were conducted in order to compare the distribution of consonants for the bilingual infants in the English context with such distribution in the monolingual English infants studied by de Boysson-Bardies and her colleagues. In contrast to the French data, there were more differences in the babbling of the two groups. As shown in Table 3, the two groups differed in five out of seven percentages of consonantal categories. There were more labials, velars, and stops produced by the monolingual infants: labials, t (11)=2.98, $p < .01$; velars, t (11)=2.74, $p < .05$; and stops, t (11)=2.62, $p < .05$. Furthermore, the bilingual infants produced more dentals and more fricatives than the monolingual infants, t (11)=3.55, $p < .0001$, and t (11)=3.45, $p < .01$, respectively. The two groups did not differ with regard to the proportions of nasals and liquids.

In conclusion, the consonants observed in the babbling of the French-English bilingual infants resembled more the babbling of monolingual French infants of the same age than that of monolingual English infants. In particular, bilingual infants were found to produce fewer stops than English-learning

Table 3. Mean percentage (and standard deviations) of consonants in babbling of English monolinguals and French–English bilinguals in English context

Consonants	Groups	
	Bilinguals	Monolinguals
Labials	48.0 (23.7)**	36.2 (12.5)
Dentals	29.1 (25.5)**	51.3 (19.8)
Velars	22.5 (19.0)*	12.5 (11.5)
Stops	69.3 (16.0)*	58.2 (13.4)
Fricatives	6.0 (1.9)**	14.4 (7.7)
Nasals	16.3 (16.3)	18.5 (15.5)
Liquids	8.3 (7.4)	8.9 (3.8)

*$p < .05$; **$p < .01$

monolingual infants, a category of consonants that has been reported to differ across French and English adult and infant populations with more stops in English than in French language samples. There was no clear pattern observed between amount of exposure to a given language and differences in babbling across linguistic contexts.

4. Conclusion

The study of bilingualism has often focused on the potentially negative effects of early bilingual experience, such as delay or deviance, in comparison to the monolingual experience (see Romaine 1999; De Houwer 1995 for recent reviews). One important issue concerns whether the language of young bilingual infants consists of an initial unitary language system or whether language differentiation is present from the beginning (Genesee 1989; Pearson *et al.* 1995; Pye 1986; Vihman 1985, 1986). The present study addressed the issue of early language differentiation, but at a period of speech development that has never been studied in the context of the early differentiation debate, that is, the babbling stage.

The major question motivating this study was whether infants exposed to two languages (French and English) from birth would babble differently depending on whether they were interacting with a French-speaking or an English-speaking parent. It was hypothesized that such babbling differences would provide strong support for the possibility that infants are sensitive to systematic differences in parental input even at the prelinguistic stage.

Since the only study to date dealing with the babbling of bilingual infants was concerned only with whether exposure to two languages from birth, in this case, Spanish and English, would influence the onset and developmental course of babbling, no direct evidence is as yet available. However, cross-linguistic studies reporting babbling differences both at the segmental and suprasegmental levels in infants exposed to several different languages lends support to this possibility.

Although the present work hardly resolves controversies, it provides some evidence relevant to the debate on early language differentiation, albeit such evidence is limited at the present time. Concerning the issue of the timing of the differentiation of linguistic systems in bilingualism, the present findings suggest that bilingual infants babble in a dominant *language*. We found that most infants produced consonants more frequently found in the babbling of monolingual French-learning infants than in the babbling of monolingual English-learning infants. In other words, our young bilinguals did not babble differently as a function of the linguistic context, which would provide the stronger evidence for early language differentiation. On the other hand, our very young bilinguals did not produce a blend of French and English babbling across the two contexts, or the equivalent of language mixing at later stages of language development. Instead, the babbling of these babies was similar across the two contexts, in that it contained the distribution of consonants more typical of French than of English. This dominance of French was not systematically related to the total amount of French language that the infants were exposed to as amount of exposure varied quite widely across children.

How can such an unexpected dominance be accounted for? The fact that the mother was French-speaking in the majority of cases might suggest that the infants *selected* the mother's language in their babbling because some aspects of maternal speech (e.g., prosody) were more salient than those of the speech produced by the other caregivers. Although infant-directed speech is used widely with infants, there is some evidence suggesting variability across caregivers, particularly across mother and father, in the quality of infant-directed speech. For instance, Fernald, Taeschner, Dunn, Papousek, de Boysson-Bardies and Fukui (1989) have reported, in a large cross-linguistic study of the prosodic features of speech to preverbal infants, that mothers used a wider mean frequency range in speech to infants in comparison to fathers. Given the evidence that the wide pitch excursions common in infant-directed speech are important in eliciting and maintaining infant attention, it is possible that the mother's language was more attractive than the father's language in the environment of these babies, even more than the relative amount of exposure to the mother's and father's language. This interpretation of our findings remains, of course, speculative since no analysis of the parental speech was carried out. Another tentative explanation for the observed dominance of French in the babbling of our bilingual infants might be related to the different suprasegmental properties of French and English. French is more based on the syllable as the rhythmic unit than English is. In other words, bilingual infants in the babbling stage might adopt one of their two languages on the basis of the more regular suprasegmental properties of the two languages. Finally, it is possible that the larger number of differences observed between the monolingual and bilingual English samples might be an artifact created by the unique features of the English language spoken in Montréal. Comparative studies of American and Québec English have revealed that they are different in many respects, including the presence of French phonological features in Québec English (McArthur 1998). A follow-up study that would include a monolingual sample of English-learning infants from Québec would be necessary in order to determine if this variable played a significant role in the present pattern of results.

Of course, the fact that we collected only one sample of babbling and that we restricted our analyses to consonants limits the scope of the present study and suggests caution in the interpretation of the present results. The one-time sampling design does not exclude the possibility that the babbling of our 12-month-old infants corresponds to a first stage of bilingual babbling development and that at later stages, the consonantal distribution will differ from what we observed. In other words, a longitudinal study of bilingual babbling might reveal that infants begin to adapt their babbling to the linguistic context later on or that the consonantal distribution differs from the distribution of both French or English monolingual babbling. In sum, the present findings need to be replicated with other linguistic properties, particularly with analyses such as the vowel formants, and the intonational contour of babbling.

In conclusion, this first analysis of the babbling of bilingual-to-be infants provides some tentative support for the hypothesis that these infants develop differentiated language systems during the babbling period. The dominance of French in the babbling of 12-month-old infants raised in French-English bilingual environments provides such support as infants seemed to have selected one of the two languages, presumably on the basis of prosodic features. However, the absence of the use of babbling in contextually sensitive ways, as shown in the similar consonantal distribution of the babbling across linguistic contexts, suggests caution in the interpretation of our findings. Future studies, including investigations of bilingual populations exposed to phonologically more dissimilar languages, will be required in order to disambiguate the present findings.

Notes

* This research was supported by a grant from the Natural Sciences and Engineering Research Council of Canada to the first author. We thank Lisa Lebel for her help in collecting the data, and Bengovesta Maneva for completing the phonetic transcriptions.

CHAPTER 5

Past tense verb forms, discourse context and input features in bilingual and monolingual acquisition of Basque and Spanish[*]

Margareta Almgren and Itziar Idiazabal

1. Introduction

A steadily increasing amount of studies on language acquisition offers data from a great number of different languages, including analyses of bilingual acquisition. On this occasion, our aim is to contribute to this extensive corpus by looking into the acquisition of past tense verb forms in Basque and Spanish, exploring data from longitudinal studies on Basque–Spanish bilingual and Basque-speaking monolingual children.

Our data will make possible a comparison of the simultaneous acquisition of two structurally very different languages by one subject and will also contrast this process with that of monolingual acquisition. By doing so, the possible cross-linguistic differences in language acquisition need not seek explanations on the basis of inter-subject differences in general cognitive development, but can be found in language specific or input specific features (De Houwer 1997).

Shirai and Andersen (1995) discuss two factors that may determine the development of verbal tense and aspect marking: the role of inherent semantics and that of features in caretakers' speech. In this study, we will not only deal with the well-known *aspect-before-tense* hypothesis and features in input, but also take into account a broader perspective on discourse type. For this purpose, we will analyse the emergence of past tense morphology in the productions of a Basque–Spanish bilingual boy and a Basque-speaking monolingual girl within specific discourse contexts, such as temporal references to past activities in interaction with adults, or imaginary play situations. We will reflect some of the characteristics of the terms *tense, aspect* and *Aktionsart* which are most commonly emphasised in the *for-and-against* debate referring to the *aspect-before-tense* hypothesis. We will also have a look at the definitions of different types of discourse and their implications for the distribution of verb forms. Finally, we will refer to studies which have stressed the importance of certain features in the adult input for the distribution of verb forms in children's productions. This will give us the opportunity to analyse similarities and differences due to language specific features as well as discourse context and adult input.

2.   Tense, aspect and Aktionsart

It is generally admitted that verb tenses encode temporal functions, most commonly classified in past, present and future categories. In addition, verbal morphology generally also contains aspectual and modal references.

The main point stated by different authors (Lyons 1968; Comrie 1985) is that *tense* is a grammatical category which expresses location in time, taking the present moment — or any other point — as the deictic centre. *Aspect*, on the contrary, does not serve deictic purposes, but refers to internal situational characteristics such as duration, completion, iteration and so forth. The third category, *mood*, refers to the probability, obligation or necessity of what is stated, according to the point of view of the speaker (Comrie 1976; Aksu-Koç 1988).

The *aspect* category, however, is often used to cover different phenomena. Morphological or grammatical aspect has to do with the way languages mark aspectual values in verbal inflection, whereas *Aktionsart* or lexical aspect, refers to the inherent semantic properties of the verb (Smith 1983; Schlyter 1990). Aktionsart, or the correlation between inherent semantics and verb forms, has been particularly emphasized in studies on the acquisition of verbal morphology. It has thus been stressed by those who support the *aspect-before-tense* theory that perfective past tense forms emerge with verbs which express a sudden change of state, while present tense forms are related to state verbs and activity verbs adopt progressive forms, which is particularly evident in the acquisition of English (Bloom, Lifter and Hafitz 1980).

The classes of semantic categories established by Vendler-Mourelatos have been generally accepted, with a few additions (Andersen 1989). Furthermore, it should be taken into account that the semantic features in question do not only refer to properties of the verbs, but also to the characteristics of the situations, processes or actions described. The categorization of verb classes and types of processes has been reviewed by Bronckart (1996), who finds that the following features should be considered relevant:

– *state verbs* refer to stable, non-changing situations.
– *activity verbs* refer to dynamic, durative and non-resultative processes.
– *accomplishment verbs* refer to durative but resultative processes.
– *achievement verbs* refer to non-durative and resultative processes.

The non-resultativity is also known as *atelic* and the resultative category frequently appears as *telic* or *change-of-state*.

It has also been pointed out that the categories established may be perceived differently by individual speakers, and as testing results by Bonnotte, Kaifer, Fayol and Idiazabal (1991) show, they may be less stable and more elastic than first imagined. Differences in child and adult use may thus to a certain extent be explained by differences in the perception of semantic categories (Aksu-Koç 1988: 183).

3. Tense and aspect in studies on language acquisition

When specifically the acquisition of tense and aspect has been dealt with, in monolingual as well as in bilingual contexts, two general trends can be distinguished:

a. Authors who analyse the acquisition of languages with richly developed and differentiated tense-aspect systems, for example Slavic languages, tend to find a simultaneous acquisition of both tense and aspect. Weist, Wysocka, Witkowska-Stadnik, Buczowska and Koniecza (1984) and Smoczynska (1985, 1996) report a simultaneous appearance of perfective and imperfective past tense forms in Polish.

b. Authors who analyse the acquisition of morphologically poor languages like English, or languages with morphemes which do not encode tense and aspect separately, seem to interpret the appearance of aspect as previous to that of tense. In an experimental study on French children's use of temporal morphology, Bronckart and Sinclair (1973) found that verbal inflection initially served to indicate the aspectual characteristics of the situations referred to, rather than deictic tense relations. Bronckart (1976, 1982) also found a strong correlation between the kind of processes described and the verb forms used in French child language. In these studies, the degree of accomplishment and the difficulty of achievement of the activities seemed to be the most relevant features.

One of the most frequently mentioned longitudinal studies when it comes to the *aspect-before-tense* hypothesis was carried out by Antinucci and Miller (1976), with reference to Italian and English. It was supported by De Lemos (1981) for Portuguese, Jacobsen (1986) for Peruvian Spanish and Aksu-Koç (1988), with reference to aspect and mood in Turkish, where multifunctional morphemes adopt aspectual and modal functions before temporal use.

When going deeper into these questions, however, some authors point out that the apparent contradictions may not be more than two sides of the same coin. Shirai and Andersen (1995) found that early development of tense-aspect morphology in English was strongly influenced by the inherent semantics of the verbs in a relative sense: the majority of verbs with past or perfective inflections in the children's productions were telic.

Acording to Bickerton's (1981) interpretation of Bronckart and Sinclair's (1973) and Antinucci and Miller's (1976) findings, children first encode the punctuality of an action when using past tense morphology. This is because they are bioprogrammed for the state-process and punctual-nonpunctual distinctions.

Shirai and Andersen, however, question whether the bioprogram is really the answer to the issue, and draw the attention to the distribution of verbal morphology in the adult input children are exposed to. The quantitative analyses they carried out proved that the mothers' speech really contained past tense forms with achievement verbs in more than 60 per cent, and progressive inflections with activity verbs in about 60 per cent of the cases. This distributional bias was also reflected in the children's speech, making input specific features seem a more convincing factor than the bioprogram for children's use of morphology.

According to Shirai and Andersen (1995), the development of past tense morphology supports the *aspect-before-tense* hypothesis. An additional explanation to the restricted use of verbal morphology is offered: the prototype of the past tense category used by children (and adults) initially contains the three features, +resultative +punctual +telic. Since perfective aspect is difficult to distinguish from the category *prototypical* past, what is interpreted by some authors (Bronckart and Sinclair 1973; Antinucci and Miller 1976 for instance) as the marking of aspectual values, may have been given the value of past tense by others (Weist *et al.* 1984; Smoczynska 1985, 1996; López-Ornat 1994), thus creating a contradiction which is more apparent than real.

In bilingual acquisition studies, several references to aspect and tense can also be found. Meisel (1994c), analysing the emergence of grammar in three

German-French bilinguals aged 1:05 to 3:00, finds a strong correlation between inherent semantics and verb forms during the early stages. Previous to 2:06 (average age), the usual correlation *change-of-state verbs/past participle* and *stative verbs/present tense* forms is attested. In the following phase, a transition towards more adult-like systems, the most relevant feature of verb form markings for the children seems to be ±perfectivity of action. Tense marking in its proper sense is considered a late acquisition, emerging with the perfect tense forms in German at around 2:07–2:08. In French, however, these participle forms are first used more like adjectives, making it difficult to determine the exact moment when tense marking appears.

One more study which may shed some light on these apparent contradictions needs mentioning. Schlyter (1990) found inter-linguistic points in common but also differences when two tense and aspect systems, French and German, were acquired simultaneously by three bilingual children. Although in this case French was a weaker language in two of the children, aged 1:10 to 3:04, some general tendencies are clear. On the one hand, the relation between semantic categories and verb forms seems to hold, at least up to the age of approximately 2:10. The distribution of the forms, however, displays some inter-linguistic differences. The relation *change-of-state verbs* or perfective aspect and past participle is above all attested for the French *passé composé*, whereas in German the most evident relation is between present tense forms and verbs that do not imply a change: *geht nicht* '(it) doesn't work/(it) isn't possible'; *fehlt* '(it) is missing'.

Schlyter (1990) draws attention to the fact that the same kind of *clusters* between verb forms, semantic categories and time references are language specific features, and as such also interwoven in adult input. In this sense, the forms used by the children could partly depend on specific features of the input language.

On the other hand, Schlyter (1990) points out that even if the child starts out with an *Aktionsart* system before acquiring adult time concept and tense relations, there need not be a *black-and-white* difference between the *aspect-before-tense* interpretation and the restricted tense system or Event Time System, as viewed by Weist *et al.* (1984), in which the event can slightly precede or follow Speech Time, but where Reference Time is frozen at speech time. It seems to Schlyter that the real difference between child and adult systems lies in references to events outside the narrow frame of Speech Time, the so-called remote past or remote future, which are absent in child language before (approximately) age 3.

4. Typology of discourse and distribution of verb forms

The idea that verbal morphology does not emerge independently of its discursive context is certainly not new, but less attention may have been paid to this aspect than to others in studies on acquisition.

Nevertheless, several attempts have been made to formalise a theory of discourse types and their influence on the choice of verb forms. In 1982, Bronckart identified three types of discourse, each of which is characterised by its specific verb forms: discourse in situation, theoretical discourse and narration. The discourse in situation, or dialogue, is closely related to the communicative situation and generates present tense, *passé composé* (present perfect) and future simple verb forms, in addition to temporal adverbs such as *today, tomorrow* or *yesterday*. Narration, on the other hand, is seen as the most extreme example of temporal and spatial separation from the communicative situation.

When analysing the use of verb forms in narrative texts produced by French school children, Fayol (1985) and Dolz (1987) confirmed the opposition *imparfait/passé simple* established by Benveniste (1966) which characterises written narrative in French. This analysis was extended to Italian, Catalan, German and Basque in subsequent studies (Dolz, Plazaola, Rosat, Schneuwly and Trevisi 1988; Dolz 1990), establishing inter-linguistic differences in the use of verb forms in different types of text.

Further studies on the subsystems of verb tenses in different types of texts in different languages have lead to the formulation of a theory of discourse types organised according to a subsystem of verb tenses which contributes to its cohesion (Bronckart 1996). Four types of discourse can be grouped together in two *blocks: raconter* or tell (a story) and *exposer* or expose.

The interactive discourse or dialogue, part of the *exposer* block, with its subsystem of present/present perfect verb tenses, can be expected in child language, as well as the interactive or contextualised relating. In fact, anybody familiar with children's initial language stages knows that the most common types of texts produced consist of comments on objects and on actions performed by the child or the adult interlocutor. When the first examples of *story-telling* emerge, these are generally comments on picture books in dialogues with the adult interlocutor. Even when the first references to past events (near or remote) appear, these are normally guided by adult questioning. In a study of English cohesion in the speech of children aged 2 to 5, Bennet-Kastor (1986) found that *state* and *action* verbs tend to appear in narratives, although autonomous narration is not common at a very early age.

There is, however, a specific context to be taken into account: that of pretence activities or imaginary play situations. Some authors have focused on the importance of imaginary play situations. Gili Gaya (1972: 162), for example, explicitly mentioned the emergence of the imperfective past in Spanish for this purpose.

(1)   Este   era un ladrón   y nosotros éramos los
      this one be-IMP-PAST a thief and we be-IMP-PAST the
      guardias
      policemen
      'This one was a thief and we were the policemen'

Antinucci and Miller (1976) observed the appearance of the imperfective past in Italian children's speech in fictional story-telling contexts and Aksu-Koç (1988) also found that one of the first uses of the Turkish multifunctional morpheme -miç was applied to story-telling. With reference to the acquisition of Dutch verbal morphology, De Houwer and Gillis (1998) point out the difficulty of determining exactly when children acquire tense distinctions. The present perfect of lexical verbs is used by children and adults to express past time references, whereas simple past forms of lexical verbs occur very rarely before the age of four, "and if they do occur, they tend to be used with a 'pretend' irrealis meaning" (1998: 34).

As a matter of fact, data referring to the use of verb forms in child language have frequently been drawn from narratives based on the well-known *Frog story* (Mayer 1969; Berman and Slobin 1994). Among others, Sebastián (1989) and Aksu-Koç (1988), who used the *Frog story* for their studies, emphasise that the analysis giving account of verb forms produced in this specific context, may not be directly comparable to those produced elsewhere.

Applied to bilingual children, some data concerning clause linking devices or semantic roles in Turkish-French, Turkish-English or Turkish-Dutch bilinguals aged 5 to 10 have been based on the rendering of the *Frog Story* (see Aarsen, Akinci and Yagmur 2001; Akinci 2001). The early stages of the tense-aspect emergence, however, are difficult to explore using this story. As Sebastián (1989) points out, children younger than 3:06, bilingual or monolingual, do not normally produce narratives: they limit their productions to the description of the pictures.

5.   Input features

Specific features of adult input as a factor which contributes to the child's selection of verb forms was already taken into consideration when we referred to the work carried out by Schlyter (1990) and Shirai and Andersen (1995). Data which very convincingly argue in favour of this hypothesis are presented by De Houwer (1997) in an investigation on the use of past tense forms in Dutch and (American) English by a bilingual child. In both languages, simple and complex verb forms can be used in references to past time events, and a parallel development might be expected. However, this did not prove to occur: while in English the simple past forms predominated, in Dutch the complex present perfect forms were the most frequent. Since in this case, cross-linguistic influence or cognitive developmental level could be disregarded as determining factors, the most plausible explanation was based on input frequency. It was then shown that the distribution of the simple and complex forms in English and Dutch input was strongly correlated to the child's production. In Dutch, 72 per cent of present perfect lexical verbs in the input corresponded to 43 out of 63 past tense forms produced by the child, whereas the same proportion of simple past forms in the English input corresponded to 44 out of 62 tokens in the child's utterances. The author finds the input frequency explanation much more satisfactory than the aspectual category hypothesis.

The importance of distributional frequencies in the adult input as a factor which at least to some extent determines the early use of past tense verb forms has also been proposed by Krasinski (1995).

6.   Spanish and Basque past tense morphology

In the following brief review of Spanish and Basque, two languages with rich but quite different verbal morphology, only features relevant to young children's productions will be taken into account.

Spanish, being a Romance language, has developed morphologically simple or synthetic forms for present, past and future tenses. In particular for simple past tenses there is a duplicity of forms: on the one hand there is the perfective form *pretérito indefinido*, and on the other the imperfective form, the so-called *pretérito imperfecto*. As can be seen from the examples below, there are no separate aspect and tense morphemes in these simple past tense forms, as shown for the third person singular (2–3):

(2) (Él) com-ió
      eat-PAST-PERF
  'He ate'

(3) (Él) com-ía
      eat-PAST-IMPERF
  'He ate'

Both these simple past forms can make progressive contrasts, using perfective and imperfective auxiliaries:

(4) (Él) estuvo   comiendo
      AUX-PAST-PERF PRES.PARTICIPLE
  'He was eating'

(5) (Él) estaba   comiendo
      AUX-PAST-IMPERF PRES.PARTICIPLE
  'He was eating'

The progressive forms, however, are less frequent in Spanish than in English and some of their functions are covered by the imperfective past tense. The perfective progressive form will not be found in children's productions at the age of 3 or 4, according to findings by Sebastián (1989).

Differently from Spanish, Basque clearly separates aspect and tense morphemes. Aspect is marked by the following suffixes (with phonological variations), added to the lexical verb stems: *tu* perfective and *tzen* imperfective, as in (6) and (7).

(6) har**tu**   du
      take-PERF AUX-TRANS-PRES
  '(He) has taken it'

(7) har**tzen**   du
      take-IMPERF AUX-TRANS-PRES
  '(He) takes it'

Tense is marked by auxiliaries for present and past, and marked differently for transitive and intransitive verbs. Basque, being an ergative language, has developed morphologically different systems for absolute and ergative case marking, an issue which in this case is relevant only because it brings with it two different tense auxiliaries, much in the same way as in French and German the *être/sein* and *avoir/haben* auxiliaries ((8)–(11)):

(8) Hartzen   **du**
     take-IMPERF AUX-TRANS-PRES
     '(He) takes it'

(9) Sartzen   **da**
     come-IMPERF AUX-INTRANS-PRES
     '(He) comes in'

(10) Hartzen   **zuen**
      take-IMPERF AUX-TRANS-PAST
      '(He) took it'

(11) Sartzen   **zen**
      come-IMPERF AUX-INTRANS-PAST
      '(He) came in'

Progressive aspect can also be formed in Basque using periphrastic constructions containing the particle *ari* ((12)–(13)):

(12) Sartzen   **ari da**
      come-IMPERF PROG AUX-INTRANS-PRES
      '(He) is coming in'

(13) Sartzen   **ari zen**
      Come-IMPERF PROG AUX-INTRANS-PAST
      '(He) was coming in'

Thus, present and past tenses are clearly distinguished through their auxiliaries, and marked separately from the aspectual suffixes.

Basque, however, also maintains a small set of the so-called synthetic or
simple inflected forms in present and past tenses of a few verbs. In acquisition
contexts very few of them will appear, except for the copula *izan* (14) and *egon*
(15) 'to be':

(14) da   zen
      BEING-PERMANENT-PRES BEING-PERMANENT-PAST
      '(he) is'   '(he) was'

(15) dago   zegoen
      TEMPORARY-BEING-PRES TEMPORARY-BEING-PAST
      '(he) is'   '(he) was'

The synthetic verb forms have been assigned the aspectual value *punctuality* by grammarians (EGLU 1997), but studies on the distribution of Basque past tense forms in different types of discourse have shown the difficulty of determining the exact values of the three past tenses in Basque, i.e. the perfective, the imperfective and the synthetic forms (Plazaola 1993).

7. Present perfect tense or perfective aspect?

The status of the present perfect tense seems to create the same problems in Basque and in Spanish as in other languages, as far as its use as perfective/resultative aspect or for temporal references to the past is concerned. Furthermore, in the variety of Spanish spoken in the Basque Country, the present perfect covers uses which correspond to the past *indefinido* in other areas of Spain.

The present perfect in Spanish is often used for temporal references to a *near* past, even in combination with temporal adverbs or expressions:

(16) Ha   traído   el periódico hace una hora
AUX (he) bring-PART the newspaper ago an   hour
'He brought the newspaper an hour ago'

In Basque, the perfective present forms fulfil similar functions. As to morphology, though, it should be remembered that transitive and intransitive verbs use different auxiliaries, and also that the order of appearance of the elements is the opposite to Spanish, an interesting fact when it comes to bilingual acquisition:

(17) Egunkaria   ekarri   **du**   orain dela ordu bat
newspaper-the bring-PERF AUX-TRANS ago   hour one
'He brought the newspaper an hour ago'

(18) Irakaslea   ikasgelan   sartu   **da**
teacher-the classroom.the.in come-PERF AUX-INTRANS
'The teacher has come/came into the classroom'

No doubt, the differences in the distribution of tense and aspect features in Basque and Spanish make the analysis of their emergence very interesting in bilingual acquisition context. But as stated in the introduction, our aim in this study is also to address two further questions: the implication of discourse context for the distribution of verb forms and the reflection of certain features of adult input in the children's production.

8. Corpus

The data for this study have been drawn from two different sources. The bilingual boy M. was videotaped as part of the HEGEJH-BUSDE (*Basque–Spanish Bilingual Children's Language Acquisition*) project carried out by the Universities of Hamburg and the Basque Country for the longitudinal study of bilingual first language acquisition (Mahlau 1994). In all, 42 transcripts of productions in Basque and 45 in Spanish have been used for the present investigation, covering the ages 1:07–4:00 in both languages.

A Basque-speaking monolingual girl, B., was videotaped by a second investigator (Zubiri 1997), who used the same guidelines for sequences and transcriptions (38 in all) as the HEGEJH-BUSDE project: fortnightly sessions of 30 to 40 minutes, where at least one of the parents took part in natural everyday activities and play situations at home. These data cover the ages 1:06–3:00.

The Basque–Spanish speaking child is a privileged little boy in bilingual acquisition contexts. He was born in a middle-class family where the *one person, one language* principle was followed by his Spanish-speaking father and his Basque-speaking mother, and also by other adults of his environment when interacting with him alone or with him and his 2-year-older sister. We believe he can be considered a good example of well-balanced early bilingualism. It should be added that when all four members of the family are involved in linguistic interaction, the conversations are carried out in Spanish, the only language spoken by the father.

The monolingual little girl, an only child, was always spoken to in Basque by her parents and other adults and it is quite certain that before the age of 3 she had practically no contact with Spanish. This fact makes her a very interesting subject for comparison with M., since so far there are very few studies on Basque-speaking monolingual children.

Normally, one recording per month was transcribed by native speakers, either by the investigator who carried out the recording and revised by a second investigator, or vice versa. In some cases, the parents also contributed by communicating their specific knowledge of their children's language use, thus increasing reliability.

For the present study, all the children's utterances containing present perfect and past tense forms were selected and analysed, always in their context of production. They were also coded according to semantic features. As to adult input, past tense forms and present perfect forms in references to past events appear already in the first session in Spanish, and from the fourth recording in Basque. However, the most relevant factor seems to be the presence or absence of specific past tense forms used in the context of imaginary play situations. An exhaustive quantitative classification of these forms has not yet been carried out, but some data will be given in points 10 and 11.

9. The first morphological contrasts in Basque and Spanish productions

The order of appearance of the first contrasted forms in Spanish produced by our subject corresponds to the pattern found in other studies, where the contrast present tense–present perfect was first attested (Hernández Pina 1984; López Ornat 1994; Aguirre 1995).

The first perfective forms emerge both in Basque and Spanish and in both children with clear aspectual correlation to Aktionsart: they are all bound to resultative verbs. At the initial stage, some of the examples are bare participles and almost all of them refer to objects or toys which fall down, break or roll under the sofa. In other words, they are invariably comments on the immediate communicative situation:

(19) (M 1:11–Spanish)
      se   ha   caído
      REFL AUX fall-PART
      '(It) has fallen (down)'

(20) (M 1:11–Basque)
      Hau   apu(r)tu   da
      this.one break-PERF AUX-INTRANS
      'This one has broken'

(21) (B: 1:10–Basque)
      Hau   (e)rori
      this.one fall-PERF
      'This one has fallen'

(22) (M: 2:00–Spanish)
      se   ha   meti(d)o
      REFL AUX go.under-PART
      'It has gone (in) under'

(23)   (M: 2:00–Basque)
Beittu zabaldu   dut
look   open-PERF AUX-TRANS
'Look I have opened it'

(24)   (B: 2:00–Basque)
Hola(n) ken(d)u   dut
like.this take.away-PERF AUX-TRANS
'I have taken it away like this'

Aguirre (1995) finds a short period of aspectual use of the verbal morphology in her Spanish monolingual subjects, but in the interpretation of the data offered by López Ornat (1994), temporal and aspectual use is considered to appear simultaneously, since perfective and imperfective suffixes are not restricted to specific semantic categories. It should be added that neither of these authors refer to any specific discourse context.

In our case, however, the temporal value of the above mentioned present perfective forms emerges relatively late in both languages, and it is difficult to determine the precise moment. This is also the case in Dutch, as explained by De Houwer and Gillis (1998) and French, according to Schlyter (1990) and Meisel (1994c). When these forms are combined with adverbs or other time expressions, they can be considered as having temporal value in the sense that they refer to events outside the frame of the communicative situation. By the end of the period analysed in this study, around 10 per cent of the present perfect forms (tokens) produced in Spanish have a clear temporal value. In Basque, this percentage is higher: 20 per cent in M. and 25 per cent in B.

(25)   (M 2:09–Spanish)
En la   escuela me ha   tirado   una
at the school me AUX throw-PART one
'At school (some)one has thrown me (down)'

(26)   (B 2:10–Basque)
Atzo   ibili   ga(ra)   ta
yesterday use-PERF AUX-INTRANS because
'Because we (have) used it yesterday'

(27)   (M 3:05–Spanish)
Ya   se   me ha   olvidado
already REFL me AUX forget-PART
'I have already forgotten (it)'

(28)   (M 3:09–Basque)
Ikusi   dugu   lehen
see-PERF AUX-TRANS before
'We have seen it before'

In addition to the pattern of semantic values being similar to that of other languages, it is interesting to observe that M. does not seem to have any difficulty in maintaining the opposite order of the elements (aux. + participle in Spanish/participle + aux. in Basque), nor in using transitive and intransitive auxiliaries in Basque.

10. Past tense morphology in Spanish in the bilingual child's productions

In the studies on the acquisition of Spanish verbal morphology already mentioned (Hernández Pina 1984; Jacobsen 1986; López Ornat 1994; Aguirre 1995), the order of appearance of the perfective and imperfective simple past tense forms has been established as *pretérito indefinido* 'perfective past' > *pretérito imperfecto* 'imperfective past'.

It was therefore a surprise to discover that when M. produced his first past tense forms in Spanish at the age of 2:07, these were without exception imperfective forms. In looking for an explanation we considered some kind of transfer from Basque would seem plausible, bearing in mind the recent exploration of common linguistic structures and their possible transfer in bilingual language acquisition, carried out by Müller (1998). But as we shall see, both children start out by producing perfective past tense forms in Basque. So, the explanation must be found elsewhere.

As a matter of fact, in their *peer commentaries* on Müller's (1998) article, both De Houwer (1998b) and Lanza (1998a) point out input factors as a more plausible influence than transfer. In our case, the imperfective past forms appeared in a specific discourse context: that of imaginary play. The use of past imperfective forms for pretence activities has also been a constant feature of adult input in Spanish: M's father used these in every session from the start of our data collection, as we can see already in M 1:07: *¿Ahí pasaban las noches, no? Los coches . . .* 'There they used to spend the nights, didn't they? The cars . . .', *Ahora yo era el señor que venía por el coche* 'Now I was the man who came to get the car'.

Most sessions in Spanish also contain some references to real past events in adult input, where both perfective and imperfective past tense forms are attested. In two sessions, however, only imperfective forms for pretence activities appear. M. does not pay too much attention to these expressions, until the age of 2:07, when he starts reproducing them.

(29) (M: 2:07)
> V: ¿Y qué era, un.. iban   todos detrás de uno,
> and what was.it, a.. go-PAST-IMPERF-they all   after of another
> en caravana?
> in a.convoy?'
> 'And what was it, a . . . did they all go one after another in a convoy?'
> M: Si xx iban.
> yes, xx they.go-PAST-IMPERF
> 'Yes, xx they went (they did)'

From this moment on, the overwhelming majority of the past tense forms produced by the child in Spanish correspond to pretence activities in imaginary play situations.

(30) (M 2:08)
> Tenía   el cristal   roto
> have-PAST-IMPERF the windscreen broken
> '(It) had the windscreen broken' [a toy car he is "repairing"]

(31) (M 2:10)
> Esto era   un monte
> this be-PAST-IMPERF a mountain
> 'This was a mountain'

(32) (M 3:02)
> Pero el pollito quería   subir
> but the chicken want-PAST-IMPERF climb.up
> 'But the chicken wanted to climb up'

(33) (M 3:09)
> Eran   las tres y ya   venían   los coches
> be-PAST-IMPERF the three and already come-PAST-IMPERF the cars
> 'It was 3 o'clock and the cars were already coming..'

However, there are also a few cases of imperfective past tense forms which make reference to real events. In the first example, M. is looking for a toy horse in the sand and in the second for pieces of a jigsaw puzzle:

(34)   (M 2:10)
   Estaba   aquí
   be-PAST-IMPERF here
   'It was here'

(35)   (M 3:04)
   Estaban   las dos lunas   pero ya   se me han   perdido
   be-PAST-IMPERF the two moons but   already REFL   AUX lost-PART
   'The two moons were here but I've already lost them'

In these cases, the correlation between state verbs and imperfective past tense forms is clear.

When the perfective past forms *pretérito indefinido* emerge at the age of 2:08, they are first applied to *ready-made* expressions like:

(36)   (M 2:08)
   Se   acabó   el   cuento
   REFL finish-PAST-PERF the story
   'The story finished (That's the end of the story)'

From age 3, these forms become more frequent. On the one hand, they refer to the same kind of instantaneous actions without any temporal distance from Speech Time as the present perfect forms referred to in examples (19)–(24), in a very similar way to that described by Jacobsen (1986) for Peruvian Spanish:

(37)   (M 3:02)
   Se   cayó
   REFL fall-PAST-PERF
   'It fell down'

(38)   (M 3:05)
   La paré
   it stop-PAST-PERF
   'I stopped it' [a ball]

(39)   (M 3:10)
   Este se   mató
   this REFL kill-PAST-PERF
   'This one killed himself' [an aeroplane that crashed]

Some examples of these perfective past tense forms , however, do contain temporal references to real actions in the past (near or remote):

(40)   (M 3:01)
Yo lo pinté
I   it paint-PAST-PERF
'I painted it'

(41)   (M 3:05)
Pu-pues ayer   fui   a — esto
We-ell   yesterday go-PAST-PERF to — this
'We-ell yesterday I went to — this'

(42)   (M 3:11)
A mi me dijo   que no
to me DAT say-PAST-PERF REL no
'He said no to me'

Although a correlation inherent semantics-verb forms in fact is maintained between perfective past tense forms and types of verbs, a much more important factor seems to be discourse context. M. maintains a fairly clear distribution of his past tense forms: the imperfective forms are related to imaginary activities, whereas the perfective forms (less frequent) refer to real events.

11.   Past tense morphology in Basque in the bilingual child's productions

In Basque, on the contrary, there are very few examples of past tense verb forms referring to pretence activities in the adult input. In fact, before the emergence of past tense forms in M.'s corpus at the age of 2:10, only 2 or 3 examples are attested in the adult input: *Hemen zegoen garajea* 'Here was the garage'; *Hau itxasoa zala, bale?* 'So this was the sea, OK?'. References to real events in the past appear regularly in the input from session 14 (age 1:11), although they are totally absent in sessions 6, 8 and 10. M. follows the same pattern, producing perfective past forms with references to real events, just as the great majority of the examples of past tense forms in adult-guided conversations:

(43)   (M 2:10)
I: Baina nun   ikusi   zenuen   ba?
     but   where see-PERF AUX-TRANS-PAST eh
     Nun   ikusi   zenuen?
     where see-PERF AUX-TRANS-PAST
     'But where did you see (him) then? Where did you see (him)?'

M: Baina ez nintzen   joan   mendira,   e!
But   not AUX-INTRANS-PAST go-PERF mountain-to-the, eh!
'But I didn't go to the mountain'

(44)   (M 2:10)
Egun baten, apurtu   zuen   gizon bat(ek)
one   day   break-PERF AUX-TRANS-PAST man   one(-ERG)
'One day, a man broke it'

(45)   (M 3:01)
Hau kotxie erosi   oztan   aitaxok
this car   buy-PERF AUX-TRANS-PAST-DAT daddy
'Daddy bought me this car.'

(46)   (M 3:05)
Eta atzo   aittittekin   joan   giñen
and yesterday grandfather-with go-PERF AUX-INTRANS-PAST
'And yesterday we went with grandfather'

(47)   (M 3:08)
Ba,   bizikletaz joan   zana
well, bike-by   go-PERF AUX-INTRANS-PAST-REL
'Well, the one who went by bike'

The imperfective past tense forms produced during the same period are very few, only six tokens in all, and they do not seem to respond to a determined discourse context. On the one hand, they are applied to real events in the past:

(48)   (M 3:05)
Baine edaten   zuten   ura   asko, egiteko   haundiak
but   drink-IMPERF AUX-TRANS-PAST water a.lot become.to big
'But they drank/were drinking lots of water in order to grow'

On the other hand, as we can see below in (53) they are also applied to story-telling contexts and to pretence activities. Now, when it comes to imaginary play situations and story-telling, these references emerge 9 months later in Basque than in Spanish and their use is established around 3:06, that is, a year later than in Spanish. Quite a few of them have to do with children's tales that M. has heard (or watched the video version of) at school. At this age, M. also starts applying past tense forms to his own imaginary games and pretence activities. In this context some synthetic past tense forms emerge, as in the following case, when M. is handling an object as if it were a plate:

(49) (M 3:07)
      Ba   hau zen.   Hau zen
      well this be-SYNT-PAST this be-SYNT-PAST
      'Well this was (it). This was (it)'

(50) (M 3:07)
      Bai z(erg)atik hor   zego(e)n   gainean
      yes because   there be-SYNT-PAST on.top
      'Yes because there it was on top'

But at the same time, perfective past tense forms of lexical verbs also appear for the same purpose:

(51) (M 3:07)
      Ikusi! Mahaia egon   zan   hemen
      look   table-the be-PERF AUX-INTRANS-PAST here
      'Look! The table was here'

Somewhat later, all three Basque past tense forms, i.e. the synthetic forms, as well as perfective and imperfective forms of lexical verbs, appear in this context of imaginary play:

(52) (M 3:11)
      Gordinflon joan   zen   eskolara
      fatty   go-PERF AUX-INTRANS-PAST school.to
      'Fatty went to school'

(53) (M 3:11)
      Eske   hau joaten   zen   kotxen   bila
      because this go-IMPERF AUX-INTRANS-PAST car.the.for get
      'Because this one went to get the car'

(54) (M 3:11)
      Hau zen   kapotie. Hor barruan ertzainak   egon
      this be-SYNT-PAST boot-the there inside policemen-the be-PERF
      ziren
      AUX-INTRANS-PAST
      'This was the boot. In there were the policemen'

In these utterances, the child does not seem to establish a very clear limit concerning the use of past tense forms in imaginary actitivites. This may in part be due to language specific features. Other studies have indicated that the perfective past forms are the most frequent in all discourse contexts in Basque (Dolz *et al.* 1988; Bonnotte, Kaifer, Fayol and Idiazabal 1993; Bronckart 1996). But more interesting in this case is undoubtedly the fact that adult input characteristics seem to have determined to a great extent the frequency of use in the child's productions. The imperfective past forms in Spanish for imaginary play situations were used by M.'s father on every occasion when their conversational exchanges were video-taped, whereas M.'s mother almost exclusively uses the Basque tense forms for references to real past events. In fact, only 3 examples of pretence activities were recorded in the Basque input, and this fact seems to have been reflected by the child.

12. Past tense morphology in Basque in the monolingual child's productions

In the adult input directed to the Basque-speaking monolingual little girl, no examples of past tense forms referring to pretence activities are found. All past tense forms used by the adults make references to real events in the past. This fact is also reflected in the child's productions: the first utterances containing perfective past tense forms, produced at the age of 2:06, all contain references to real events. Some of them also include temporal adverbs:

(55) (B 2:06)
Hau ya   erori   zen
this already fall-PERF AUX-INTRANS-PAST
'This one already fell down'

(56) (B 2:07)
Niri   x oparitu   zuten   hori atzo
To.me x give-PERF AUX-TRANS-PAST that yesterday
'They gave it to me yesterday'

(57) (B 2:09)
Atzo   Naiarak erosi   zuen
Yesterday Naiara   buy-PERF AUX-TRANS-PAST
'Yesterday Naiara bought (it)'

(58) (B 2:11)
Atzo   bie(k) dutxatu   ginen
Yesterday both   have.shower-PERF AUX-INTRANS-PAST
'Yesterday both (of us) had a shower'

The imperfective past tense forms emerge with a time lag of a few months and contain a mixture of references to real events, to picture stories and comments on (non-past) activities (61). As can be seen, the temporal value of them is doubtful. The first example even contains the progressive particle *ari* and is produced when B. sees snow in a picture-story book:

(59) (B 2:09)
Ni elurren zapa(l)tzen   ari   nintzen
I   snow.in tread-IMPERF PROG AUX-INTRANS-PAST
'I was treading the snow'

(60) (B 2:11)
Nola egiten zen ba?[1]
how do-IMP AUX-INTRANS-PAST then?
'How was this done, then?'

(61) (B 3:00)
Bitu nii . . . nola ibiltzen nintzan
look me . . . how do-IMP AUX-INTRANS-PAST
'Look I . . . what I was doing'

The few examples of synthetic past forms seem to respond to a sort of *thinking aloud* about the little girl's own activities, as in the following case when she doesn't find a cloth:

(62) (B 2:10)
Nun zen trapua?
where be-SYNT-PAST cloth
'Where was the cloth?'

There are, however, some utterances containing synthetic past tense forms that do refer to real events, as in the following case, when B. is talking about her own birthday:

(63)   (B 3:00)
     Nire zorionak ziren   ta
     my   birthday be-SYNT-PAST because
     'Because it was my birthday'

It seems equally difficult to find a correlation between inherent semantics and perfective and imperfective past tense forms in the productions of B. as in M.'s productions in Basque, where perfective forms are much more abundant with all semantic classes. It is true, however, that the first steps in the acquisition and use of the Basque past tense forms are very similar in both children. In fact, we believe there is enough evidence to give support to the hypothesis that bilingual children develop their languages much in the same way as monolinguals.

13. Discussion

Before going into a discussion of the data offered, a brief summary of the different verb forms produced by the two children and their contexts of appearance might be helpful (Table 1).

The main difference between the two children is the fact that there are no examples of the use of past tense verb forms for pretence activities in the corpus of B. As we have seen, these do appear in M.'s corpus in Basque, although much later than in Spanish. We can think of two possible explanations. In the first place, the characteristics of the adult input, which gives very few examples of this use in the case of M. and does not provide B. with this kind of discursive context at all. As a second reason, it is important to point out here that B. was a year younger than M. when data collecting stopped, and although she had already acquired a very rich morphology, her discourse capacity may still not have developed to the same degree as M.'s.

It is true that Spanish past tense imperfective forms are correlated to state verbs (*estaba, era* 'was', 'were') or non resultative activity verbs to a certain extent. The perfective forms, on the other hand, mainly emerge with achievement verbs (*cayó* 'fell', *paré* 'stopped'). In Basque, however, perfective forms are extended to all kinds of verbs, and although the imperfective forms mainly appear with activity verbs, 'Aktionsart' does not seem to be of equal relevance in the contexts we have analysed.

Table 1. Distribution of past tense perfective, imperfective and synthetic forms

Mikel Spanish	Imperfective	79	**Perfective**	23	**Total**	102
(1:07–4:00)	Pretence	71	Pretence	5		
	Real events	8	Real events	18		
Mikel Basque	Imperfective	6	**Perfective**	142	**Total**	156
(1:07–4:00)	Pretence Imp.	4	Pretence	5(17)*		
	Real events Imp.	2	Real events	120		
	Synthetic	8				
Bianditz Basque	Imperfective	6	**Perfective**	22	**Total**	38
(1:06–3:00)	Real events Imp.	6	Real events	22		
	Pretence Imp.	–	Pretence	–		
	Synthetic	10				

*In this case, the number of tokens is not relevant. M. repeats the same verb form (joan zen 'he went') 17 times.

Discourse context and specific features of adult input, however, have had a strong influence on the productions of these children. M. has been exposed to imperfective past tense forms in Spanish for the purpose of imaginary play or pretence activities from the very start of our data collection, and this is also what he reproduces. In Basque, both children have been exposed to perfective past forms for references to real past events during practically all our video-taped sessions, and this is also exactly what they first produce.

When M. starts to produce his past verb forms for pretence activities in Basque, the question of linguistic transfer (Müller 1998) regains interest. Nevertheless, it is difficult to argue in favour of a *direct* transfer of linguistic structures in this case, since the use of exclusively imperfective past tense forms for this purpose is not transferred to Basque. As we have seen, M. makes use of the three different past tense forms in Basque, without a clearly discernible pattern. The reason why past tense verb forms for pretence activities appear later in M.'s productions in Basque can only partly be explained by input habits. We believe, however, that this is a subject for future investigations.

Notes

*   Financial support from the DGES (PB98–0239) is gratefully acknowledged.

1. An impersonal construction in Basque, not really a passive sentence.

CHAPTER 6

Finding first words in the input[*]

Evidence from a bilingual child

Elena Nicoladis

1. Introduction

Children acquire language with remarkable speed, leaving little doubt that the human mind is biased in some way so that children are exceptional language learners. How exactly the mind is biased is extremely controversial among researchers. Suggestions have ranged from Universal Grammar to a universal avoidance of homonymy (Chomsky 1965; Ullman 1963). This chapter is focused on the question: how might the mind be biased in order to find the first words in the input? While a number of different cognitive biases have been proposed (see Tardif, Shatz and Naigles 1997, for a recent review), I will concentrate on two: noun bias and perceptual salience of the ends of utterances.

One of most popular hypotheses for possible biases for finding first words is the noun-bias, or natural partitioning, hypothesis (Au, Dapretto and Song 1994; Gentner 1982; Markman 1990). According to this hypothesis, children have a bias to find nouns easier to learn than other kinds of words. This bias is thought to be due to the fact that nouns name objects and objects are thought to be more easily available to children's minds than actions or states. Reasons for thinking that objects are easier for children have included: (1) objects are perceptually obvious, (2) objects are semantically easier than predicates and (3) the object category is innate (Caselli, Bates, Casadio, Fenson, Fenson, Sanderl and Weir 1995; Gentner 1982; Golinkoff, Mervis and Hirsh-Pasek 1994; Macnamara 1982; Markman 1990). While many researchers have shown that words other than nouns occur in children's early vocabularies (Bloom, Tinker and Margulis 1993; Dromi 1987; Iverson, Capirici and Caselli 1994; Nelson 1973), the noun-bias hypothesis suggests that nouns will occur more frequently than other kinds of words. Indeed, while there are exceptions, it has been shown to be true more often than not that children have a large number of nouns in their early vocabularies in a variety of languages (Au *et al.* 1994; Bassano 1996; Bates, Marchman, Thal, Fenson, Dale, Reznick, Reilly and Hartung 1994; Caselli *et al.* 1995; Cohen 1969; Descoeudres 1930; Dromi 1987; Iverson *et al.* 1994; Gentner 1982; Goldfield 1993; Sakurai 1999). For example, Gentner (1982) showed that children learning Chinese, Japanese, Kaluli, German, English and Turkish had more nouns in their vocabularies than predicates. A similar study in Korean supported the noun-bias hypothesis, showing that not only did Korean children have more nouns than verbs in their early vocabularies but the proportion was even greater than adult child-directed speech (which had about equal numbers of noun and verb types; Au *et al.* 1994).

There are a number of difficulties with the noun-bias hypothesis. One difficulty in interpreting studies on the noun bias hypothesis is the different definitions of *noun* and *verb* that have been used across studies. Most studies on the noun bias hypothesis have implied that *noun* and *verb* refer to semantic categories (i.e., objects and actions respectively, Dromi 1987). Others have argued that the terms *noun* and *verb* refer to syntactic categories requiring all characteristics of the adult categories (e.g., Maratsos 1988). Still others have agreed that lexical categories are syntactic categories but have argued that they need not have all the characteristics of the adult categories (e.g., Ninio 1988). For much (but not all) of the work on the noun bias, the semantic definition has been implied, so that children's words for objects are thought to occur earlier in development or are acquired more easily than predicating words (see Nelson, Hampson and Shaw 1993).

A more serious criticism of the research on children's noun bias is the assumption that children can choose their words on the basis of lexical category. In fact, children may not initially display evidence of knowledge of lexical categories in their production. For example, after carefully examining the referents of her child's words in the one-word stage, Dromi (1987) found that until the child knew about 40 words, most of the referents of her words were not clearly categorizable. That is, most of the child's words referred to multiple or unclear semantic categories. For example, her word for 'hot' was used as an object word (to refer to heaters and ovens) as well as a modifying word (to refer to the property of being hot or cold). Similarly, Ninio and Snow (1996) have argued that children's first words are embedded in a pragmatic context and (by implication) they have no lexical categories (see also Dore 1985; Nelson and Lucariello 1985, for similar arguments). The lack of evidence for lexical categories in children's production appears to be limited to their early words. Nelson *et al.* (1993) showed that by 1;8 (years; months) children are quite accurate at semantic categorization of their words. Occasional mis-categorizations of words occur in older children; for example, Egger (1879) reported that a twenty-eight-month-old French-speaking child thought the expression *beau habit* 'beautiful outfit' referred to the action of going out. Mis-categorizations of lexical category are, however, rarely reported in children beyond the one-word stage. In sum, while children clearly know lexical cat-egories later in development, it is not clear that they know these categories when they first begin to use language.

Given the problems in interpreting the evidence as unambiguously in support of the noun-bias hypothesis, some researchers have offered alternative explanations for the preponderance of nouns in many children's early vocabu-lary. The rest of this review will focus on the possibility of perceptual salience in the input, although there are many other possible alternative explanations. To illustrate something of the range of possible alternative explanations, I shall briefly mention two. One alternative explanation comes from Dromi (1987), who suggested that nouns are generally less inflected than verbs so they are easier to pick out of the speech stream. This explained why her Hebrew-speaking daughter produced action words early on, but no adult verbs (see also Gentner 1982). A second alternative explanation is that pragmatics may play a major role in how children acquire their early words. Children growing up in contexts in which actions are favored over naming games may learn many verbs early on (Choi and Gopnik 1995; de León 1999; Goldfield 1993; Tardif *et al.* 1997).

The purpose of this chapter is to examine the importance of yet another possible explanation for the preponderance of nouns in children's early vocabularies: perceptual salience in the input. Au *et al.* (1994), for example, point out that both the beginning and the ends of utterances are thought to be highly perceptually salient (see also Cohen 1969, for similar speculation on the role of input). Children might then pick their early words from one or the other (or both) of these places (Goldfield 1993; Tardif *et al.* 1997). Newport, Gleitman and Gleitman (1977) found that the initial position of parents' utterances was related to children's acquisition of auxiliary verbs. Tardif *et al.* (1997) argue that while this might be so, the final position might be impor-tant, particularly in acquiring early words. This explanation could account for why children do not seem to be constrained by lexical categories in their early production. This explanation could also account for results with Korean- and Chinese-speaking children who are exposed to languages in which verbs frequently appear at the ends of utterances. Choi and Gopnik (1995) found that 9 Korean-speaking children generally showed a verb bias in their early vocabularies while English-speaking children showed a noun bias (cf. Au *et al.* 1994). Tardif (1996) found that nine out of ten Mandarin-speaking children had more verbs than nouns in their early vocabularies.

The argument that the ends of utterances might be perceptually salient for children who are acquiring their early words has usually been posed *post hoc*. That is, only after finding cross-linguistic differences in vocabulary composition do researchers suggest that the final position might be important. Because the explanation is usually proposed *post hoc*, it has not been spelled out exactly how children might use the ends of utterances. Do they sample randomly from the ends of utterances in choosing their early vocabulary words? This possibility seems unlikely, since children often seem convinced that their early words are meaningful (Westbury and Nicoladis 1998; cf. Clark 1993). Nevertheless, the purpose of this study was to ask: Do children sample randomly from the ends of utterances? By asking this question, I hope to refine the hypothesis of how children might use the ends of utterances.

This study focused on the early vocabulary acquisition of an English-Portuguese bilingual child in a one parent-one language home. Using data from bilingual children can be a powerful test of proposed universals in language acquisition because bilingual children can act as a small crosslinguistic experiment of their own. To the extent that a proposed universal is in fact universal, it should appear regardless of the children's level of proficiency in that language and/or should act on the input in the same way regardless of the input characteristics are presented in either language (see Nicoladis, Mayberry and Genesee 1999, for an illustration of this methodology).

In this case, if children universally attend to the ends of utterances to find their early lexical items, then bilingual children should pick their words from the ends of utterances, regardless of language-specific differences in ending utterances with different parts of speech. In English child-directed speech, many nouns have been shown to appear at the ends of utterances relative to verbs (Tardif *et al.* 1997). While I know of no studies on Portuguese, it is possible that it will show a different pattern of word types at the ends of utterances, since a similar language (Italian) has been shown to have a more equal distribution of nouns and verbs at the ends of utterances than English (Tardif *et al.* 1997). If the two languages differ in the ratio of nouns and verbs that appear at the ends of utterances, then it becomes interesting to look at the distribution of nouns and verbs in the child's two languages. By looking at a bilingual child acquiring languages that differ on the distribution of word types at the ends of utterances, we can see if perceptual salience is indeed playing an important role in his acquisition of both languages.

To answer the larger question of whether children sample randomly from the ends of utterances, this study will address three smaller questions. (1) Were there more nouns or verbs at ends of input utterances in English or Portuguese? As discussed above, we can expect the English-speaking mother to use many more nouns than verbs at the ends of utterances. We have no way of predicting what will happen in Portuguese, but it is possible that the Portuguese-speaking father might use about equal numbers of nouns and verbs at the ends of utterances if Portuguese follows a similar pattern of use as Italian. (2) Were there more nouns or verbs in the child's English or Portuguese? If the child uses the ends of utterances to choose his early vocabulary words, we would expect to find a large number of nouns in his English vocabulary and very few verbs. The word types in his Portuguese vocabulary should mirror the number of nouns and verbs appearing at the end of his father's utterances. In contrast, if the child is interested in finding nouns in the input, we should find a high proportion of nouns in both languages regardless of how the parents' utterances end. (3) Did the child's words come from any particular place in the input utterances? If the ends of utterances are particularly salient for the child, we might expect his early words to have occurred in final position of his parents' utterances more often than in any other position. Because we have longitudinal data over a period of six months, it is possible to look back and see if the words that the child chose were more likely to occur in any particular position in the parents' utterances.

2.   Method

This study involved one bilingual boy in a one parent-one language home in the United States. His father addressed the child primarily in Brazilian Portuguese and his mother primarily in English. Mario was an only child throughout the course of this study. The mother was the child's primary caregiver, working only occasionally outside the home. When she worked, she left Mario in the care of an English-speaking neighbor. The father worked full-time outside the home at a white-collar job. Both parents had postgraduate degrees in domains that were not related to language or cognition.

It should be noted that Mario spent most of his time in English and most of his acquaintances spoke primarily English. Nobody but the father spoke to

Mario regularly in Portuguese. On the basis of exposure time alone, it seems likely that Mario would use more words in English. The justification of this conjecture is that previous research has shown correlations between the time bilingual children are exposed to each of their languages and their vocabulary size in each language (Pearson, Fernández, Lewedeg and Oller 1997).

The family was followed from the time Mario was 1;0.14 (when he had a productive vocabulary of seven words) until he was 1;6.6 and had just started to produce an occasional two-word utterance. Mario's cumulative productive vocabulary at 1;6.6 was about 100 words (i.e., 87 words that could be positively verified through parental report or videotaped production plus, after the child was 1;5, at least 35 words the parents reported were produced but could not be positively verified). The main reason for stopping at this age was because we could no longer be as certain we had a valid measure of the child's entire vocabulary. Within a week or two of the last session, the parents reported that the child was now learning so many new words that they no longer felt they could accurately report his new ones. More details on collecting data on the child's vocabulary are reported below.

The family was filmed in free play interactions twice a week: once with the father and child alone and once with the mother and child alone. The mother was often present in the house when the father was filmed with Mario and occasionally in the same room. In the sessions with the mother and child alone, the father was never present. Each session was 15 minutes long and there was a total of 23 sessions with each parent across the six-month period, giving a total of almost 12 hours of interaction in total. The sessions with the father were filmed by a native speaker of Brazilian Portuguese whose English proficiency was limited at the start of the study but improved rapidly over these six months and the sessions with the mother were filmed by the author who speaks only a few words of Portuguese. Across the six-month period, the Portuguese-speaking observer used 363 utterances that were recorded on videotape; 349 (96.1 per cent) of these were in Portuguese only. Similarly, across the six-month period, the English-speaking observer used 303 utterances on videotape, 302 (99.6 per cent) of which were in English only.

These sessions were transcribed according to the CHAT system (MacWhinney 1991). The parents' and the child's utterances were coded for language (i.e., Portuguese-only, English-only, mixed, either language, or uncodable) and addressee (e.g., mother, father, toy, etc.). The language code was defined according to standard dictionary entries of Brazilian Portuguese and American English with a few exceptions described below. A mixed utterance was defined as a word that contained at least one morpheme from both Portuguese and English. The *either* language category consisted of words that could belong to either Portuguese or English, such as proper nouns and some interjections (see Genesee, Nicoladis and Paradis 1995). *Mommy* and *Daddy* were counted as part of either language until session 15 when Mario learned the Portuguese translation of the latter word, *Papai*. This was done on the basis of findings from other studies showing that bilingual children sometimes have only one proper noun per referent in the early stages (see Genesee *et al.* 1995). At session 15, both *Mommy* and *Daddy* were counted as English words. The only other words counted as either language were the child's name and the word *yea* (meaning 'hooray'). Uncodable utterances were utterances that could be transcribed phonetically but could not be assigned a clear language category. Most of the child's utterances across this age were coded as uncodable. An average of 60 per cent (SD=16.6) of the utterances addressed to the mother and 56 per cent (SD=20.0) of the utterances addressed to the father were categorized as uncodable. To check inter-rater reliability, the child's utterances in ten randomly chosen sessions were independently transcribed by the observer who was not present at the filming session. The coding agreement was 88 per cent. Differences were resolved by discussion.

In order to make language-coding judgments on a standard basis, the child's utterances were transcribed in broad phonetic transcription. Some prosodic dimensions of the child's utterances (i.e., the number of syllables and whether or not a syllable was open or closed) were particularly useful in making judgments about the language of a child's utterance. For example, the child's production of the Portuguese word *bola* was a two-syllable word with open syllables and his English word *ball* was a one-syllable word.

To get as complete as possible a measure of the child's productive vocabulary, the child's vocabulary was determined both from weekly parental reports and from the videotaped sessions. The parents reported that they felt that they could give fairly accurate recall of the child's new words over the course of a week until the last few weeks of the study when the child learned a lot of new words in a single week. A conservative definition of a word was used in counting the child's vocabulary (see Vihman and McCune 1994, for discussion of this issue): only words based on clear adult targets were included. Several reliably-produced, child-invented forms were thus excluded. These were excluded because they could not be coded as belonging to either English or Portuguese and thus were not relevant to the issues under examination here.

Also, the interjections *hmm*, *mm* and *oh* were excluded from all analyses on the intuition that they were less word-like than other words. Finally, words were included in the vocabulary count only when the child produced them spontaneously and at least several times within a day or two.

To assess the agreement of the researchers' and the parents' judgments of the child's words as part of his productive vocabulary, we compared the reports of the parents to the transcriptions for the child's first 50 words. 48 of the child's first 50 words as reported by the parents also appeared on video-tape; this figure suggests that the parents were using a similar definition to the researchers in identifying the child's words. There was only one word of the first 50 words that appeared on videotape that the parents did not report as a new word for the child. Naturally, even with such high agreement between parents and researchers about what constitutes a word, it is still possible that we do not have a complete measure of the child's early production vocabulary. It is possible that the parents forgot to report words or that the researchers failed to detect a target word for the child in an *uncodable utterance*. Table 1 shows the number of words in the child's cumulative vocabulary in each language across the six months as counted by our measures. As can be seen in this table, his English vocabulary was consistently greater than his Portuguese vocabulary, as would have been predicted by his relative exposure time to the two languages.

To classify the words used by both parents as nouns, verbs, etc., the syntactic frame of the parents' utterances was used. Because the child was in the one-word stage, his utterances did not contain syntactic cues for which lexical category his words might belong to. To classify his words, I used two pieces of evidence: (1) a judgment of the most frequent category of that word in the input and (2) how the child used the word himself. For example, the word *shut* could be either a verb or an adjective; the child used it after shutting a plastic container. This word was classified as being neither a verb nor a noun. In another example, the child recited all the English vowels in a row *aeiou* when his mother asked him to. While the vowels could be considered a noun, the child did not seem to relate them to anything concrete in the environment, so they were also classified as neither nouns nor verbs (see Tables 3 and 4 for a list of all of the child's words and how they were classified).

Before turning to the results, a word about how word types in the input were counted is in order. Any count of word types makes assumptions about how children perceive words in the input. While we cannot know if these assumptions are justified, we can at least use some consistency across studies.

To count types of nouns, singular and plural forms were counted as a single type in both English and Portuguese (e.g., both *egg* and *eggs* were counted as a single type, as were *vez* and *vezes*). Diminutive forms were counted as different types in both languages (e.g., *dog* and *doggie* were counted as different types, as were *livro* and *livrinho*). As for verbs, in English the -ing and the third person -s were counted as instances of the same type as the bare verb (e.g., *drink* and *drinking* were counted as a single type, as were *go* and *goes*). In Portuguese, all verb forms were counted as different types (e.g., *chegou* and *chegamos* were counted as different types), with the exception of the child's production of *abre* and *abrir*, which were difficult to distinguish. For words

Table 1. Number of words in child's cumulative vocabulary by session and language

Session	Child's age at recording session with		Number of words in cumulative vocabulary		
	Mother	Father	Portuguese	English	Either
1	1;0.17	1;0.14	1	7	2
2	1;0.24	1;0.21	1	10	3
3	1;1.1	1;0.28	2	12	3
4	1;1.8	1;1.9	2	14	3
5	1;1.15	1;1.12	3	14	3
6	1;1.22	1;1.20	4	20	3
7	1;1.29	1;1.27	4	21	3
8	1;2.5	1;2.3	4	21	3
9	1;2.12	1;2.11	5	23	3
10	1;2.19	1;2.18	5	23	3
Family holidays/illness					
11	1;3.10	1;3.11	6	27	3
12	1;3.17	1;3.16	6	32	3
13	1;3.24	1;3.21	8	33	3
14	1;4.0	1;3.28	8	33	3
15	1;4.7	1;4.4	9	38	1*
16	1;4.14	1;4.13	9	38	1
17	1;4.21	1;4.18	9	41	1
18	1;4.28	1;4.25	9	43	1
19	1;5.6	1;5.3	12	46	1
20	1;5.13	1;5.11	14	48	1
21	1;5.20	1;5.18	16	51	2
22	1;5.25	1;5.24	17	59	2
23	1;6.6	1;6.4	19	66	2

*As explained in the text, in session 15, Mario's words *Mommy* and *Daddy* were reclassified as English words because he started using the Portuguese equivalent of *Daddy*, *Papai*

classified as *other* (i.e., neither nouns nor verbs), both the masculine and feminine forms were counted as a single type (e.g., *sujo* and *suja* were counted as one type) as well as singular and plural forms.

3.   Results and discussion

The first question we are interested in answering is whether or not English and Portuguese show different input characteristics with regard to nouns and verbs at the ends of utterances. Figure 1 shows the percentage of tokens and types of nouns and verbs at the ends of the mother's English utterances and the father's Portuguese utterances totaled across all sessions. The percentages for tokens are based on a total of 3,450 utterances by the mother and 4,260 utterances by the father. The percentages for types are based on a total of 476 different types at the ends of utterances by the mother and 597 different types by the father. The scale of the tokens and types is different, with both parents using fewer noun and verb tokens than types; this suggests that the most frequent category of words to occur at the ends of utterances is neither nouns nor verbs in both languages. While the scale is different, the ratio of nouns to verbs in terms of types or tokens is virtually identical. While the percentage of noun and verb tokens is smaller than types, the relative ratio of nouns and verbs remains the

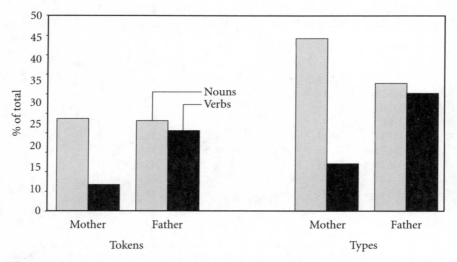

Figure 1.

same whether tokens or types are counted. So the mother used 3.5 noun tokens for every verb token and 3.6 noun types for every verb type. Similarly, the father used 1.1 noun tokens for every verb token and 1.1 noun type for every verb type.

The relative proportion of nouns and verbs in English and Portuguese shown in Figure 1 are similar here as those reported elsewhere for similar languages (compare English and Italian in Tardif *et al.* 1997). Here (as in other reports), the majority of utterances end in words other than nouns or verbs. However, there is a greater proportion of nouns than verbs in English and approximately equal proportion of nouns and verbs in Portuguese. If Mario were sampling randomly from the ends of utterances, his Portuguese vocabulary would include approximately equal numbers of nouns and verbs and his English vocabulary would include more nouns than verbs.

Table 2 summarizes the number and percentage of the child's vocabulary in common nouns, verbs and other kinds of words in English and Portuguese. Proper nouns were excluded from the category of *common nouns* for two reasons: (1) as discussed above, it is not always clear that proper nouns belong to two separate languages for bilingual children and (2) the noun bias hypothesis has usually been concerned with object words and proper nouns do not usually refer to objects (see Tardif 1996). As can be seen in Table 2, the relative proportion of nouns and verbs is virtually identical in both languages and there is no significant difference between the two languages by lexical category, $\chi^2 (2) = 0.11$, n.s. This finding suggests that the child did not choose his vocabulary words randomly from the ends of utterances presented to him in the input.

While he did not choose his words randomly, the child could still have found the ends of utterances particularly useful in vocabulary acquisition. Because we have such good longitudinal data from this family, it is possible to look at the parents' use of particular words before they entered the child's productive vocabulary. To do this, I looked at the position in the utterance (i.e., initial, medial, final, or alone) in which the word occurred in all sessions

Table 2. Distribution of child's cumulative vocabulary by language and lexical category

	Noun	Verb	Other
English	27 (41%)	3 (5%)	36 (55%)
Portuguese	7 (37%)	1 (5%)	11 (58%)

prior to the appearance of that word in the child's vocabulary. The initial position referred to the first word in an utterance, the final position to the last word, and the medial position to any words that occurred between the first and last words. The sessions prior to the apperance of that word in the child's vocabulary were defined as all parental uses of that word prior to the session in which the child started using that word. For example, the word *cheese* appeared in the child's vocabulary in session 6 so I counted the number of times in which the mother had used the word *cheese* in sessions 1 to 5. One consequence from this methodology is that for the child's earliest words, we necessarily have very little data of parental use before the child produced the world. In contrast, for the child's later words, we sometimes have access to a lot of tokens of those words in the input. For example, the child already knew the word *Mommy* when the study started, so we have no way of knowing how the mother used that word before the child started using it. In contrast, the word *no* was learned in session 19, so we had 18 previous sessions to examine. It is therefore important to look for similarities in parental usage across different word types.

Table 3 summarizes the English data. While the numbers here are small, there is a high proportion of nouns that the child used that occurred primarily in final position of input utterances. The same is true of the other words with the notable exception of *no* which was more likely to occur initially or alone. The verbs that the child learned were marginally more likely to occur at the ends of utterances than in any other position, although they also frequently occurred medially.

Table 3. Where child's English vocabulary words occurred in the input before he produced them spontaneously

	Session	Beginning	Middle	End	Alone
Nouns					
apple	1	–	–	–	–
banana	1	–	–	–	–
ball	6	0	0	3	0
cheese	6	0	0	1	0
key	6	–	–	–	–
birdie	7	–	–	–	–
e@l	9	–	–	–	–
hat	9	0	0	1	0
flower	11	–	–	–	–
light	11	0	2	5	0
baby	12	0	0	1	0

doggie	12	–	–	–	–
kitty	12	–	–	–	–
snow	12	0	1	0	0
cookie	15	0	1	4	1
eye	15	0	0	2	0
cereal	17	0	3	1	0
cracker	17	–	–	–	–
shoe	18	0	0	1	0
shower	19	–	–	–	–
pie	21	–	–	–	–
potato	22	–	–	–	–
puppy	22	0	0	2	0
moon	22	0	0	1	0
eggs	22	–	–	–	–
burp	23	–	–	–	–
door	23	0	0	2	0
pickle	23	–	–	–	–
TOTAL nouns		0	7	18	1
Verbs					
kick	4	–	–	–	–
help	18	0	0	2	0
go	22	4	35	36	0
TOTAL verbs		4	35	38	0
Other					
byebye	1	–	–	–	–
Daddy	1	–	–	–	–
dirty	1	–	–	–	–
Mommy	1	–	–	–	–
more	1	–	–	–	–
numnum	1	–	–	–	–
up	1	–	–	–	–
down	2	0	1	1	0
thank+you	2	0	0	2	4
yeah	2	1	0	2	15
this	3	0	1	5	0
shut	3	–	–	–	–
no+no	4	0	0	0	2
hi	6	0	0	3	3
peekaboo	6	–	–	–	–
please	6	–	–	–	–
Santa	11	–	–	–	–
wow	11	0	0	0	4
here	12	4	0	8	4
abc	13	–	–	–	–
uhoh	15	2	0	0	22

done	17	0	2	1	2
yes	19	2	0	2	4
no	19	71	6	3	106
gone	20	0	1	3	0
aeiou	20	–	–	–	–
sure	21	1	3	2	0
upside+down	21	0	2	3	0
nice	22	2	9	8	0
outside	22	0	1	3	0
out	22	0	18	13	1
Grandma	23	0	0	1	0
Granny	23	–	–	–	–
beepbeep	23	–	–	–	–
achoo	23	–	–	–	–
TOTAL		83	44	60	167

Table 4 summarizes the father's use of Portuguese words that figured in the child's vocabulary before he used those words productively. At a first glance, it would look as if the child favored a medial position for his choice of Portuguese words. However, the father used a lot of tag questions which might mean that the word prior to the tag question would be salient. The father almost always had a slight but noticeable pause before adding on these questions. In parentheses in Table 4 the numbers are shown if the following tag questions are ignored: *hein, né, ahn, mm, dá, tá, e, quer, ja, vem*, and the child's name. Most of these tag questions are interjections. If the tag questions are ignored, the results look quite similar to English, with the child favoring the final position for his choice of nouns and other words (with the notable exception of *não*). The few instances of the father's use of the one verb in the child's vocabulary were in medial position.

4. Conclusion

This study has shown that this child's early words were likely to come from ends of utterances, but they were not randomly chosen from ends of utterances. Because English and Portuguese show different ratios of nouns and verbs at the ends of utterances, if the child had been sampling randomly from the final position he should have used more nouns than verbs in English and about equal numbers of nouns and verbs in Portuguese. The results showed, however, that the child used more nouns than verbs in both English and

Table 4. Where child's Portuguese vocabulary words occurred in the input before he produced them spontaneously

	Session	Beginning	Middle	End	Alone
Nouns					
bola	5	0 (0)	6 (3)	10 (13)	0 (0)
água	6	0 (0)	5 (3)	0 (2)	0 (0)
nariz	9	–	–	–	–
banho	11	0 (0)	13 (8)	7 (12)	1 (1)
leite	13	3 (3)	5 (2)	11 (13)	8 (9)
chave	21	–	–	–	–
batata	22	0 (0)	1 (1)	0 (0)	0 (0)
Total nouns		3 (3)	30 (17)	28 (40)	9 (10)
Verbs					
abre/abrir	23	1 (1)	5 (5)	0 (0)	0 (0)
Total verbs		1(1)	5 (5)	0 (0)	0 (0)
Other					
sete	1	–	–	–	–
não	3	23 (23)	16 (15)	10 (8)	11 (14)
aiaiai	13	1 (1)	0 (0)	1 (1)	1 (1)
Papai	15	0 (0)	27 (16)	17 (27)	0 (1)
oi	19	0 (0)	0 (0)	0 (0)	1 (1)
tchau(tchau)	19	1 (1)	0 (0)	3 (3)	3 (3)
Mamãe	19	3 (3)	22 (13)	25 (34)	3 (3)
alô	20	–	–	–	–
mais	20	2 (2)	55 (48)	53 (60)	5 (5)
auau	21	0 (0)	3 (3)	9(9)	13 (13)
fora	23	0 (0)	3 (3)	1 (4)	0 (0)
Total other		30 (30)	126 (95)	119 (146)	37 (41)

Note: Numbers in parentheses indicate the numbers of times these words were produced in each position if tag questions are ignored

Portuguese and the difference between the two languages was not significant. However, when we looked back at where the child's productive vocabulary words were likely to have occurred in the input, the final position was the most likely position, particularly for nouns.

These results suggest that while the perceptual salience of the ends of utterances may be very important for locating words, children are choosing only some of the words they can locate to be part of their productive vocabularies. Therefore, as many researchers have suggested, meaning (in terms of semantics or pragmatics or both) certainly plays an important role in vocabulary acquisition (e.g., Bloom 1970; Clark 1987, 1993; Goldfield 1993; Golinkoff *et al.* 1994; Markman 1990; McCune-Nicolich 1981; Nelson 1973; Tomasello, Strosber and Akhtar 1996; Tomasello and Merriman 1995). For example, it is possible to argue on the basis of the data presented here that children do have an innate noun bias that guides children's choice of words once they have used the ends of utterances to find word boundaries.

It is important to note that the conclusion presented here is based on analyses of relatively small numbers of words used within one family. To test the generalizability of the findings, it is important to collect longitudinal data on more families, perhaps even starting before children use any conventional words at all. The results could also be further strengthened by having longer observation sessions at each time period. Another interesting way to extend the present results would be to examine languages with radically different input characteristics, say more verbs than nouns at the ends of utterances.

By examining a variety of different languages and language combinations, we can be more certain about how children are using the input to learn language. Furthermore, by examining data from bilingual children, it is possible to understand the relative importance of various cues in early lexical acquisition. Cues that are hypothesized to be universal should certainly hold true in both languages of a bilingual child, even when the input characteristics of those two languages are different. For example, if it is correct that children attend to the ends of utterances, then Korean-English bilingual children should acquire more verbs in Korean and more nouns in English. Alternatively, if it is correct that language acquisition is guided by easy access to words for objects, then Korean-English bilingual children might acquire more nouns in Korean than monolingual children. Furthermore, proposed universal biases in language acquisition must hold true even when bilingual children show mismatches in the proficiency of their two languages, a not uncommon occurrence among simultaneous bilingual first language acquirers (see Nicoladis and Genesee 1997a).

In sum, the take-home message of this chapter is that children most likely use a variety of strategies to learn their early words (see also Tardif *et al.* 1997). As this chapter has shown, they may be biased to focus on the ends of utterances to find their early words, but they must also use other strategies to choose among the words presented to them at the ends of utterances. In doing so, we have seen that data from bilingual children can be used as a powerful test of proposed universal biases in language acquisition.

Notes

* I would like to thank Mario and his family for their patience and enthusiasm in participating in this study for so long and so consistently. Giovanni Secco videotaped and transcribed all the Portuguese sessions and made interrater checks on transcription. An earlier version of this paper was presented at the Eighteenth International Congress for the Study of Child Language in San Sebastian, Basque Country/Spain in July 1999. Johanne Paradis and Chris Westbury were kind enough to give me feedback on an earlier version of this chapter.

CHAPTER 7

Managing linguistic boundaries in early trilingual development[*]

Suzanne Quay

1. Introduction

Much progress has been made in research on third language acquisition and trilingualism in recent years. This is evident in the publication of edited volumes on this topic by Cenoz and Genesee (1998) and Cenoz and Jessner (2000). A special issue on trilingualism edited by Cenoz, Hufeisen and Jessner (2000) has also appeared in an electronic journal. Another indication of a burgeoning interest in this area is the number of research presentations at the first International Conference on Third Language Acquisition and Trilingualism, which took place at the University of Innsbruck, Austria in September 1999 (55 abstracts can be found on the conference homepage at http://www.spz.tu-darmstadt.de/projekt_L3). Much of this research so far has focused on learning a third language at school or in adulthood, and on educational systems providing support for trilingual competence. This is an encouraging sign in a world that is becoming increasingly more multilingual due in part to the exigencies of globalization (resulting in more and more families living and working abroad), in part to intercultural marriages (resulting in linguistically mixed families), and in part to the political and economical value attached to multilingual ability. Unfortunately, we know very little about raising multilingual children as work on trilingual families and early trilingual development is still in its infancy.

Since multilingualism is becoming widespread in the world, studying multilingual children can help us, as Levy (1985: 552) has pointed out for bilingual children, to "establish the boundaries within which the process of language acquisition must unfold" and can thus be "theoretically, extremely informative". Cases of multilingual development can show, for example, the nature of the influence of input languages in linguistic development more obviously than cases of monolingual development where the input is more homogeneous. Snow (1995: 187) writes that "most children clearly receive more input than is strictly necessary to support normal language acquisition, as shown by the fact that input can be distributed over two or three languages with the result that the child is a fully bilingual or trilingual speaker". How such children become bilingual and trilingual is the subject of ongoing research. A fair amount of literature can now be found on bilingual children's language choice as a reflection of input factors, but no systematic studies (of which I am aware) have been done in the same way for early trilingual acquisition. So what we do know about multilingual development at present comes mainly from studies of young children who are exposed to two rather than three or more languages from birth. (The contents of the other chapters in this volume further supports this statement.)

1.1 Studies of early bilingual acquisition

A central issue in many bilingual studies has been whether or not bilingual children separate the two linguistic systems exemplified in their input during the initial stages of speech production. The available evidence from recent studies of language choice in bilinguals under age two suggests that children do separate the two systems relatively early from the beginning stages of acquisition. This is attested in their ability to choose the appropriate language for a given interlocutor and context. In a study by Genesee, Nicoladis, and Paradis (1995), five French-English bilingual children ranging in age from 1;10 to 2;2 (year;month) were all — including the youngest — able to use more English with their English-speaking mother than their French-speaking fathers, and more French with their fathers than their mothers in spite of the fact that four of the five children were considered to be *dominant* in either English or French. Findings from another four French-English bilingual children between the ages of 1;7 and 3;0 are reported in Nicoladis and Genesee (1996). While there was an initial period when the children did not use the appropriate language with each parent, the ability to do so emerged at ages varying from 1;9 to 2;4. In a study of three German–French bilinguals, Köppe (1997) reports that *mixing* rates decreased sharply at about age two for one child, Ivar, and between ages 1;8 and 1;10 for the other two children, Annika and Pascal. The fact that utterances that did not match the language context became less frequent at the particular ages mentioned above is an indication of the children's developing ability to make appropriate language choices. What is implied in these studies is that the separation of the input by the parents (where the child receives one source language from the father and the other from the mother) helps developing bilinguals to differentiate early on between the two languages they hear.

Deuchar and Quay (2000), however, present a case where the child's bilingual input alternated from the same sources according to the location of the interaction and to the presence of monolingual speakers. Spanish was used by both parents to address their daughter in the home environment unless monolingual English speakers were also present, in which case both parents would address their child in English. Outside the home, particularly on the campus of a British university where the mother worked and where the child attended a university crèche, the child would be addressed in English by her mother. Yet, in the absence of input separation according to person, evidence of contextually appropriate language choice emerged in this study as early as around age 1;7 (probably because this study investigated language choice much earlier, between ages 1;3 and 1;9, than the studies mentioned above). Quay (1995) has suggested that language differentiation is not evident at earlier points in development because the infant does not have the lexical resources to demonstrate language choice. So rather than focusing on the question of one vs. two systems in infant bilingualism (that is, whether children acquiring two languages simultaneously start out with one linguistic system that later develops into two, or whether they have two systems from the very beginning), it may be more fruitful to investigate how and when language differentiation occurs.

With regard to the role of parental input, separation of the input according to person does not appear absolutely necessary for bilingual development and is moreover impractical from a social and pragmatic point of view in situations where monolinguals or even multilinguals who share only one of the bilingual child's languages are present. Bhatia and Ritchie (1999: 588) have even argued that separating the input to the child in the case of a *one-parent–one-language* approach as described in many bilingual studies "may create a socially unnatural setting for language use, which can lead to a failure to acquire pragmatic competence on the part of bilingual children". What all researchers should be able to agree on is that children need to receive sufficient and consistent input and need sufficient and consistent interaction in each language to be socialized into the appropriate use of two (or more) languages. What is *sufficient*, however, in terms of input and interaction has not yet been established.

1.2 Parental discourse strategies in bilingual development

Many bilingual studies have shown in addition that it is not just the amount but also the *kind* of input that is important. For example, when parents code-mix, children do so as well (Goodz 1989; Nicoladis and Genesee 1997b; Kasuya 1998). In particular, parental discourse strategies seem to have an effect on child bilingual production. Döpke (1992: 103), in a study of six German–English bilingual children living in Australia (aged 2;4 or 2;8 at the onset of the study), found that the children were "more likely to make active use of the minority language, German, if the interaction between child and German-speaking parent was equally or more child centred than the interaction between child and English-speaking parent". A child centred mode of interaction is described as one where the adult maintains topics introduced by the child and is generally responsive to the child's contributions. That parental input provides rich information about children's linguistic behaviors — particularly where code-mixing occurs in the bilingual child's speech — is clearly shown by Lanza (1997). The language choice of the two Norwegian-English two-year-old children she studied was influenced by whether their parents negotiated a bilingual context where they accepted utterances by their child in both languages or a monolingual context where they accepted utterances from only one language. The child was more likely to use words from both languages in the same interaction in a bilingual rather than in a monolingual context. In a study of four Japanese-English families, Kasuya (1998) notes additionally that parents who made their preference for the use of the minority language, Japanese, quite explicit (thus negotiating a monolingual context) had the highest success rate in relation to the child's subsequent choice of Japanese in interactions. Although Nicoladis and Genesee (1998) conclude that parental discourse and response affect bilingual children's code-mixing, they found in their quantitative analyses of data from five French-English developing bilinguals in Montreal a negative correlation between parental response and the children's code-mixing. They therefore question Lanza's parental discourse hypothesis for code-mixing and suggest that other factors may be in play like, for example, sociolinguistic differences, unequal language proficiency or the participants' inability to comprehend parental strategies for directing language use. Lanza (1998b) has responded to that study by stating that data aggregated for quantitative analyses can mask important developmental trends and has suggested that qualitative as well as quantitative approaches should be implemented.

1.3   The literature on trilingual development in childhood

Unfortunately, we know very little about the nature of input and language choice in multilingual acquisition from the available literature on early trilingual development. By *early trilingual development*, I am referring to the case of children who are exposed to three languages regularly before their first words. Hoffmann (1985: 480) has previously differentiated between *infant* trilingual and *child* trilingual by using the arbitrary point of age three as set by McLaughlin (1978). Her son who acquired German, Spanish and English before age three was thus categorized as an *infant trilingual* while his sister was referred to as an infant bilingual who acquired German and Spanish from birth but as a *child trilingual* who acquired English after age three. What is of importance is not so much the terminological distinctions but how early children are exposed to their three languages. I am particularly interested in those cases where children have been exposed to three languages before or near the onset of speech.

Although descriptions of young children who are exposed to three languages exist in several books for parents of bilingual children (de Jong 1986; Harding and Riley 1986; Arnberg 1987), studies that actually examine the speech data from trilingual children are few and far between. Table 1 lists six such studies of trilingual children that could be obtained. A recent announcement (in June 2000) was made though of the addition of the first CHILDES (The Child Language Data Exchange System: MacWhinney 1995) corpus on trilingual acquisition based on data collected for a doctoral dissertation at the University of Veszprém, Hungary (Navracsics 1999; this corpus can be accessed at http://childes.psy.cmu.edu). The dissertation focused primarily on the later development of Hungarian by a pair of siblings, Nasim and Nabil. They were exposed to English and Persian from birth in Canada before their family moved to Hungary where the children started attending a monolingual Hungarian nursery school at aged three and two respectively. It was found that within a year and a half, Hungarian became the children's dominant language.

1.3.1   *Input factors and types of childhood trilingualism*

If we turn to the studies in Table 1, we see that only four children have clearly been exposed to three languages before the onset of speech — three children, Vuk, Uva, and Egon, in the study by Mikès (1990) and the child, Robin, in the study by Hoffmann and Widdicombe (1999). The child Marina described in Kazazis (1970) and the siblings E and M in Stavans (1992) could possibly

Table 1. The literature on trilingual children

Author	Subject(s)	Ages of children during period of study	Input Languages	Country of residence (city, when indicated by authors)	Data collection method	Main issue
Kazazis (1970)	Marina	4;7–4;9	· Swedish from mother · Greek from father · English* from community	USA (Chicago)	No indication	Code-mixing specifically in Greek possessive genitive
Oksaar (1978)	Sven	3;11–5;8	· Estonian · Swedish · German from 3;11 from community	Germany (Hamburg)	No indication (except that "data were obtained almost every day in various communicative acts" — p. 129)	Code-switching and interference
Hoffmann (1985)	Cristina (C) Pascual (P)	to age 8 to age 5	· Spanish from father · German from mother · English from 2;9 (C) and from infancy* (P) from community	UK	Notes, diary** (recorded by both parents), recordings** (presumably, audio), vocabulary recall tests	Patterns of trilingual acquisition at different linguistic levels

Table 1. (cont.)

Author	Subject(s)	Ages of children during period of study	Input Languages	Country of residence (city, when indicated by authors)	Data collection method	Main issue
Mikès (1990)	Vuk Uva Egon	0;10–1;11	• Hungarian from mother • Serbocroatian from father and community • German* from maternal grandmother	former Yugoslavia (Novi Sad)	Diary (daily on weekdays) and audio recordings**	Lexical development and lexical differentiation
Stavans (1992)	E M	5;5–6;8 2;6–3;9	• Spanish from father • Hebrew from mother • English* from community	USA	Audio recordings** (sessions of 45–60 mins. over a period of 15 months)	Code-switching
Hoffmann and Widdicombe (1999)	Robin	4;4–4;5	• Italian from father • English from mother • French from community	France (Paris)	Audio recordings (10 hours mainly of mother-child interactions)	Code-switching, coining and interference

* no indication of exact age of exposure to language
** no indication of how often recordings were made

belong to this same category but the age of their actual exposure to English, the language of the community in the United States where their families live, has not been specified. Pascual, one of the two children in the study by Hoffmann (1985), is referred to as an *infant* trilingual but there is no clear indication that he was exposed to his third language before the onset of speech since age three was chosen to distinguish *infant* from *child* trilingual in that study. Two children in Table 1, viz. Cristina in Hoffmann (1985) and Sven in Oksaar (1978), were exposed to their third language after age three when their first two languages were already well-established like Nasim in Navracsics (1999).

Kazazis (1970) does not actually qualify as a case study of trilingual development as it deals specifically with just two examples of the treatment of the Greek possessive genitive in the speech of a trilingual girl at ages 4;7 and 4;9. There is no information on how or whether any other data were collected. Kazazis (1970) was included in Table 1 only because there is such a dearth of studies devoted to childhood trilingual acquisition that it seems interesting just to note that Swedish, Greek and English are the language combinations for a child living in the United States.

In all but the study by Mikès (1990), the children have been exposed to one language from each parent and to the third language from the community — specifically, playmates in Kazazis (1970); home helpers, visitors, playmates, television and radio in Oksaar (1978); playmates, school friends, some television in Hoffmann (1985); daycare, friends and visitors to home in Stavans (1992); crèche from three months of age, then nursery school, then school in Hoffmann and Widdicombe (1999). Mikès (1990) is the only study in Table 1 where the children (who are also exposed to one language from each parent) are exposed to the third language from another family member, specifically the maternal grandmother, rather than from outsiders, institutions or media in their country of residence.

1.3.2 *Limitations of trilingual studies reviewed*
Basic information on language input (in terms of who talks to the child, when, for how long, and in what linguistic form) is given in the most detail in Hoffmann (1985) and Mikès (1990). Input descriptions are insufficiently informative (very informal or anecdotal) in the other studies listed in Table 1. Moreover, most of the studies give minimal, if any, information about their data collection methods (outlined in the penultimate column of Table 1). Hoffmann and Widdicombe (1999), unlike the other studies, do indicate that ten hours of audio recordings were collected over a short period of time at

ages 4;4 to 4;5 when the child interacted mainly with his English-speaking mother. Although Mikès (1990) states that diary data were collected daily on weekdays, there is no mention of frequency of audio recordings. Hoffmann (1985) and Stavans (1992), like Mikès (1990), claim to have made audio recordings but do not indicate how often such recordings were made, whether they were transcribed, and how many, if any, of such recordings were used for their discussions and interpretations (the main issue of each study is indicated in the last column of Table 1 and will be discussed further in the next section).

These methodological flaws have been highlighted here to show: (1) that none of the studies deals systematically with early trilingual development and (2) that we should proceed with caution in evaluating the results from these studies.

1.3.3 *Some insights into trilingual development and behavior*

In spite of the lack of methodological depth required for conclusive statements and the fact that many of the studies are narrowly focused (particularly Kazazis 1970), the studies do seem to indicate some trends, particularly with regard to code-switching. For example, Stavans (1992) and Hoffmann and Widdicombe (1999) have both noted that code-switching involves mainly two languages even when trilingual switching could have been possible as in settings with trilingual parents. Code-switching by trilingual children also appears to be affected by factors such as participants, topics, availability of lexical resources and emphatic function:

a. *Participants*: Whether or not participants are monolingual, bilingual or trilingual affects which language or languages trilingual children will use. The children, E and M, in Stavans (1992) code-switched more with trilingual interlocutors than with bilingual ones. Negligible or no code-switching would occur in multilingual children's speech when they interacted with monolingual interlocutors (Oksaar 1978; Stavans 1992).

b. *Topics*: Some topics used to convey messages about their environment are either culturally bound (Stavans 1992) or bound to the location (Oksaar 1978). For example, a topic on food items may be culturally bound to one of the three languages and reference to those items would always be in that particular language regardless of language context (Stavans 1992). Some topics are bound to the location where one language is usually employed. For example, when speaking Estonian, Sven in Oksaar (1978) would code-switch to Swedish for topics referring to the activities at home that are carried out by the Swedish house helper or for topics referring to his Swedish playmates and their environment.

c. *Lexical resources*: Not surprisingly, code-switching is also affected by a lack of lexical resources (Hoffmann and Widdicombe 1999). Moreover, some lexical resources tend to be more easily and quickly available in one language than in another (Hoffmann 1985; Mikès 1990).

d. *Emphatic function*: Mikès (1990: 114) gives four examples occurring between ages 1;8.19 and 1;9.26 (examples 7 to 10) where utterances contain equivalent words in two and even one example of three languages (the word *more* in German, Serbocroatian and Hungarian) as the child attempts to obtain something or to reinforce requests. When Sven was bilingual between ages 2;4 and 2;10 (he was not exposed to his third language until age 3;11), Oksaar (1978: 132) mentions that he would code-switch to Swedish to strengthen arguments uttered in Estonian when his parents did not react to his requests.

When code-switching occurs, it seems to proceed in the direction of the dominant language.[1] Hoffmann (1985) found that interference and mixing occurred in the same direction, from strongest to weaker languages, in her two children according to their language dominance at particular points of development. Although both children started out with Spanish as their dominant language, this changed according to changes in their language input conditions. Once Cristina started primary school at age 4;9, her English quickly overtook her German and Spanish so that when code-switching occurred, it would usually be the insertion of English items into otherwise German or Spanish utterances. Pascual's language dominance changed twice. His German became stronger than his Spanish between ages 2;5 and 3;3 due to the presence of a German *au-pair* who gave Pascual a great deal of attention and stimulus (the implication here is that during this period, the quantity and quality of Pascual's exposure to German increased and resulted in a change in language dominance).[2] English became Pascual's strongest language when he started attending an English-speaking playschool at age 3;6. In explaining why their subject, Robin, used French for code-switching with his parents in the home context (where French was rarely used) instead of using the other home language, Hoffmann and Widdicombe (1999: 56) propose that "this preference for French as a medium for switching, when either English or Italian was being used as the base language, indicates that French is emerging as the child's dominant, or preferred, language". (We need to keep in mind though that the authors do not actually have adequate data of the child interacting with his Italian-speaking father so it is premature to make conclusions about the child's code-switching in an Italian-language context at this point.)

Mikès (1990) is the only study in Table 1 that addresses the issue of lexical acquisition in three languages in any detail. She concludes that her three grandchildren Vuk, Uva and Egon developed three lexical systems from the very beginning because they had acquired equivalent pairs and triplets within their first fifty words.[3] However, in work on bilingual acquisition, Johnson and Lancaster (1998) and Deuchar and Quay (2000: 64) have argued that the availability of translation equivalents is not a sufficient condition to indicate lexical differentiation. The ability to use such words in appropriate language contexts is also required and Mikès (1990) cannot demonstrate this in the absence of data collected in three separate language contexts (cf. Deuchar and Quay 2000: 91 on criteria for the systematic study of language choice). The early lexical productions of Vuk, Uva, and Egon, however, serve as an indication of the complex interaction between input from the environment and vocabulary learning. After all, the children would not have equivalent pairs and triplets had they not been exposed to such words in their environment.

1.4 Language practices of trilingual families

Through the use of questionnaires, Barron-Hauwaert (2000) has been able to study more trilingual families and their children than would be possible through the longitudinal case-study approach. Ten trilingual families with children ranging in age from two to twelve years, living mainly in Europe, have responded to how the three languages were acquired (Barron-Hauwaert 2000).[4] All the parents speak their own language to their children from birth and live in a third language country (much like the case studies in Table 1 with the exception of Mikès 1990). Strikingly, half of the parents report that they considered the local language as their children's first language (L1) in terms of proficiency while the other half had children who spoke a parental language as a first language. Besides the actual languages addressed to the children, the children appeared also to be aware that the language spoken between the parents could function as a *lingua franca* in the families, to the extent that a *prestigious* language could threaten the survival of a parental language with a *minority* status.

The responses to the questionnaire reveal that the age of the children affected which language they could use the best. Three children aged two to three and a half were most proficient in their mother's language, reflecting the fact that they probably spent most of their day at home with their mothers. Two children over the age of three or four were reported to use their father's language as their L1. Of children in primary school (aged six and older), the local language was used the most proficiently by four out of five because of greater exposure at school. The fifth child, aged nine, has his father's language, Italian, as his L1 probably because he had attended school in Italy until age six. Two families having children around age three were also found to use the local language as their L1. This has been attributed to early childcare in the local language. In general, the parental reports from this study suggest that language proficiency, in terms of strongest (L1) to weakest (L3) language, is affected by amount of input.

1.5 Aims of a project on trilingual development before age two

In the rest of this chapter, an ongoing project on early trilingual development will be introduced. I aim to show systematically and more comprehensively than has previously been done the relationship between language exposure in context and an infant's demonstrated language capacities. This case features German, English and the non Indo-European language Japanese as the languages in combination for a family residing in Japan during the period of study. Bhatia and Ritchie (1999: 603) have pointed out that most bilingual acquisition studies and, I should add, most of the trilingual ones listed in Table 1, are "overwhelmingly devoted to the Indo-European languages of Western Europe", so that "more diversified research in terms of input languages and regions" are still needed. This new study is a first step towards meeting this need.

Is early trilingual development the same or distinct from early bilingual development? How are the two connected by the theme of multilingual language use? It has not yet been established in the literature on bilingual acquisition what the minimum input requirements are for language production in two languages nor what the effects are of different ages of exposure (as in simultaneous vs. early sequential) for early bilingualism. In my case study of trilingual language acquisition before age two, I will explore these issues by looking at input conditions such as:

a. *Input quantity*: the relationship between the amount of input in each language and acquisition patterns;
b. *Input quality*: the relationship between parental discourse and patterns of interaction;
c. *Input delay*: the relationship between later vs. earlier regular exposure of language and subsequent linguistic production.

This chapter will focus predominantly on the data that have been collected in the home (although data have also been collected in a daycare environment where the child was being exposed to the local language of the community). The home environment is the one where two languages have been heard from birth. As linguistic environments are potentially very changeable and did in fact change when my subject entered a third language daycare environment at age 0;11, one question that will be asked is whether there is any correlation between *input quantity* for each language at particular points in time and the child's ability to understand and produce items from three languages. In terms of *input quality*, what role do parents play in their children's acquisition of the ability to make appropriate language choices in ongoing interactions? Since the infant was exposed to two languages from birth and a third from age 0;11 onwards, is there a *delay* in the development of the language to which he receives later exposure? These questions will be answered based on empirical evidence from a naturalistic longitudinal case study of one trilingual family and their infant son between the ages 0;11 to 1;10.

2. Methodology

2.1 The trilingual family

The subject of this study, Freddy, was born on April 24th 1997 in Tokyo, Japan to a German father and an American mother. From birth, Freddy heard German from his father, a landscape architect with a Masters in Engineering, and English from his mother, a university professor with a doctorate in Sociology. Freddy's parents spoke primarily German to each other and to the child when all three were alone together. Both parents were also competent in speaking Japanese, the main language of the local community, and they code-switched according to the language spoken by interlocutors. For example, they spoke Japanese when interacting with Japanese speakers and English when interacting with English speakers.

Freddy can be described as a sociable infant. He had a ready smile for all those who came into contact with him, making him a favorite not only among adults but also among the monolingual Japanese children at the daycare that he attended from age 0;11 onwards for six hours each weekday.[5] Of the eight other children at the daycare, seven were older than Freddy with the oldest boy being a year and nine months older. The youngest, a girl, was only two months and two weeks younger than Freddy. Four boys (including Freddy) and five girls were in the infant section of the daycare. Freddy's best friends seemed to be the two children closest in age to him, a boy one month and twelve days older than him and the youngest child already mentioned. All the staff at the daycare were monolingual Japanese speakers.

2.2 Language exposure patterns

Freddy lived in Japan for the period of this study until age 1;10.9 (year;month. day). Although he spent his first twenty-two months in Tokyo, his family visited relatives in Germany for two weeks when he was only two and a half months old. During a six-week period in the summer of his second year (between ages 1;2.24 and 1;4.4), the family spent three weeks in the United States and two weeks in Germany, followed by an additional week back in the States.

Table 2 shows the estimated frequency of language exposure that Freddy received from his parents, caregivers, peers, and visitors based on a questionnaire completed by Freddy's mother at age 1;0, at age 1;5 and again at age 1;9. The questionnaire focused on the child's social background (described in the previous section) and changing language exposure patterns. Until 11 months of age, Freddy heard English 70 per cent of the time and German 30 per cent of the time (see Table 2). On entering the daycare one month before his first birthday, the proportions changed with a distribution of 50 per cent English, 20 per cent German, and 30 per cent Japanese heard by the infant. Most of the people who came into contact with the infant in his first year of life spoke English. In terms of visitors and people visited, 85 per cent spoke English, 10 per cent spoke Japanese and 5 per cent spoke German (the family had some visitors from Germany staying in their home shortly before Freddy's first birthday). He did have a babysitter who was a native Twi speaker from Ghana who would sometimes sing in Twi to him (amounting to less than 1 per cent of the time) but otherwise addressed him in English during the six to seven

Table 2. Language exposure patterns

Age	% English	% German	% Japanese
birth to 0;11	70	30	n/a
0;11 to 1;0	50	20	30
1;0 to 1;5	43	23	34
1;5 to 1;9	45	10	45

hours that she spent with him each week until age 0;11. Of his peers outside the daycare, 95 per cent spoke English. The daycare supervisor, in an interview which took place after Freddy had been in the daycare about four weeks, reported that Freddy could not yet understand any Japanese the way other Japanese children his age could.

In his second year of life (cf. the last two rows of Table 2), the amount of input from each language changed again. From age 1;0 to 1;5, Freddy's exposure to English decreased to 43 per cent of the time, with corresponding slight increases to 23 per cent of the time for German and 34 per cent of the time for Japanese. We need to keep in mind though that within this four-month period, Freddy's family spent six weeks abroad in Germany and in the United States so there was no exposure at all to Japanese for part of that time. In the next four-month period from age 1;5 to 1;9, Freddy's exposure to German fell to 10 per cent due to his father's busy work schedule as well as to the absence of his father for part of the time as the family prepared for a major move to Germany which took place when Freddy was aged 1;10. Both English and Japanese were heard equally about 45 per cent of the time during this last period in Japan. The increase in exposure to Japanese was also due in part to the fact that Freddy enjoyed watching Japanese children's television programs for one hour to one and a half hours each day. Some of the programs were bilingual Japanese-English shows. The mother also reported that around this period, she started taking Freddy to the park or to the nearby McDonald's play area. At these places, she and her son would spend one hour once or twice a week in a Japanese language environment with other mothers and their children. Freddy's main playmate outside of the daycare was also Japanese and he would see this boy twice a week for one to one and a half hours.

Freddy clearly heard Japanese from a larger segment of society — adults and children of all ages — than he did English or German. Between ages 1;0 and 1;5, he had some contact about once a week for one hour with two English-speaking children of about his age. However, most of the time he heard English and German spoken mainly by adults, with German being spoken by a much smaller number of adults than English.

2.3 Data collection

Data collection began when the child entered the Japanese daycare at age 11 months and produced his first word shortly after. Besides using a parental questionnaire (mentioned above), data were also collected regularly through various methods such as interviews, MacArthur Communicative Development Inventories, diary records, and video recordings, all of which will be described further below.

2.3.1 *Questionnaire and interviews*

In conjunction with using the parental questionnaire to establish the social background and language exposure patterns for the child, interviews were conducted with the parent(s) and at the daycare at ages 1;0, 1;5 and 1;9. In the interviews, parent(s) and daycare staff were asked questions about the child's general behavior, understanding and use of particular words and gestures, knowledge of specific games, preferences for certain toys and whether imaginative play occurred. Such information gave the researcher a better overall *feel* for the child's sociopsychological as well as linguistic development.

2.3.2 *MacArthur Communicative Development Inventory*

The MacArthur Communicative Development Inventory (hereafter, called the MCDI) is a type of parental report that has been used to assess children's understanding or understanding with production of common vocabulary items. Every three to four weeks, the mother completed the English version of the MCDI — the infant short form from ages 1;0 to 1;4 and the toddler short form from ages 1;4 to 1;9 (details about the short form versions of the MCDI are in Fenson, Pethick and Cox 1994). The mother, without being asked, also indicated on the form when her son understood English words but produced the words understood in English in either German or Japanese (the MCDI was of course designed to assess monolingual children and does not take into account the language variations that may occur in terms of understanding with production in multilingual children). Because a German version of the MCDI was not available, the German-speaking father was asked to consider, also every three to four weeks, whether the items on the English version of the parental report were applicable in a German language context (basically, translate the English items into German and report on whether the child understood or produced these words in German).[6] The Japanese version was a full MCDI form adapted into Japanese by Ogura and her colleagues at Kobe University (Ogura 1998; Ogura, Yamashita and Murase 1998). The Japanese MCDI was used to interview various members of the daycare staff (more than one staff member and different volunteer caregivers were present each day) when Freddy was aged 1;0, 1;5 and 1;9 to obtain an idea of Freddy's receptive and expressive vocabulary in that language environment. It was not possible to ask any one daycare staff member to complete the checklist on a more regular basis than during the interviews.

The MCDI has not been used in this study for its original normative purposes but to determine the number of words the child understood and produced in each of the three languages he heard. Pearson (1998: 356) has pointed out for bilingual acquisition research that these parental checklists are designed for the assessment of lexical growth in monolinguals and cautions that "as with all tests, the application of monolingual norms to bilinguals should be avoided whenever possible" (see Pearson 1998 for further discussion of the MCDI).

2.3.3 *Diaries*

Because the MCDI does not provide exhaustive inventories, the mother was asked to keep a diary of words her child understood (in addition to those noted on the MCDI) as well as words produced. The mother's diary noted her son's production of lexical items in English, German and Japanese from ages 0;10.25 to 1;10.1. For the words her child understood, she listed them in her diary roughly once a month. For the words he produced, they were listed on average every two weeks.[7] Although the infant short version of the MCDI focuses on vocabulary comprehension (with an additional column for indicating understanding with production) up to age 1;4, the toddler short form is limited to vocabulary production. The developers, according to Fenson, Pethick and Cox (1994: 11), felt that "parents were unlikely to be able to keep track of words comprehended beyond 16 months". This is supported by the fact that the mother (without having been told this) stopped listing other words recognized by her son by age 1;4. She did continue to make some general notes in the diary up until Freddy was about age 1;6 such as: "he understands most all commands now directed at objects common to his everyday environment", but finally writes around age 1;7 that "we stopped recording words recognized because he seems to understand so much".

Diary records from Freddy's daycare were also used for this project to supplement the Japanese MCDI. In Japan, it is common practice for daily diaries to be kept for each child each day that he or she is in attendance at a daycare so that parents can be informed about their child's day. Members of the daycare staff were thus requested from the beginning to note Freddy's linguistic progress in addition to their usual entries about the child's behavior and activities.

2.3.4 *Video recordings*

Video recordings were made every week (when possible) in the home, once with the mother addressing the child in English (considered to be an English language context situation) and once with the father addressing the child in German (considered to be a German language context situation). Video recordings were also made each week in the daycare, a Japanese language environment. A Sony Handycam Hi8 Video Camera Recorder (CCD-TRV85 NTSC) was used in all three separate language contexts. One video camera was left with the parents to use on a tripod as this created an environment whereby the child could in fact draw specifically on his knowledge from one or the other of his two home languages in interactions with either his English-speaking mother or with his German-speaking father without interference from a camera operator who could possibly affect the child's language choice. A second video camera was used by the Japanese-speaking research assistant who was sent into the daycare each week to videotape Freddy playing at the daycare or at different parks near the daycare.[8] Seventy-seven sessions (each mostly thirty minutes in length though several home recordings were forty to sixty minutes long) were recorded in total — thirty sessions in the Japanese daycare, twenty-nine sessions with the mother speaking English and eighteen sessions with the father speaking German.

Full transcripts in the CHAT format of CHILDES (MacWhinney 1995; see also Sokolov and Snow 1993) are being made for thirty minutes of video-recorded sessions in the German, English, and Japanese language contexts (please note that all reference to *contexts* is based only on the main language used by the child's interlocutors and does not imply that the infant is aware of having the three languages).[9] Due to the on-going nature of this time-consuming task, this chapter reports on a small part of the data and focuses, moreover, only on the video recordings made in the home in order to address the issue of *parental* input and language choice. Table 3 shows the six pairs of

Table 3. Video recordings analyzed

Pairs of recordings	English context	(Duration)	German context	(Duration)
1	1;1.0ENG	(30 min)	1;1.0GER	(22 min)
2	1;2.22ENG	(20 min)	1;2.22GER	(28.5 min)
3	1;4.29ENG	(30 min)	1;5.5GER	(30 min)
4	1;6.26ENG	(30 min)	1;6.24GER	(30 min)
5	1;8.22ENG	(30 min)	1;8.22GER	(30min)
6	1;10ENG	(30 min)	1;9.30GER	(30 min)

video recordings selected (mainly because complete transcripts have been done and checked by this investigator) from sessions where the child interacted with one or the other of his parents. His mother addressed him in English in the English context sessions and his father addressed him in German in the German context sessions. The mother was also present for some of the time and was speaking German in session 1;1.0GER. This would not be unusual as the parents report that they spoke German with each other in the home. The six pairs of recordings are spaced at approximately six- to eight-week intervals between ages 1;1 and 1;10. Each pair of English and German context sessions was usually recorded on the same day or within one or two days of each other, with the exception of the third pair in Table 1 where the German session was recorded six days after the English one. Only three recordings are shorter than thirty minutes in length — 1;1.0GER at 22 minutes, 1;2.22ENG at 20 minutes and 1;2.22GER at 28.5 minutes. It was not always possible to continue recording for 30 minutes in these early sessions when Freddy was, for example, sleepy or needed his diaper changed.

Coding of utterances. In order to investigate the child's language choice patterns, it was necessary to code his utterances as English, German, or Japanese. The identification of Freddy's early utterances was not an easy task. The phonetic transcriptions of the child's utterances in PHONASCII (MacWhinney 1995: 82–5) along with information on the child's actions and the adult's responses in the transcripts aided in the coding of utterances. In most cases, coding relied on the phonetic resemblance of the utterance to an adult source word in English, German or Japanese, but phonetically simple versions of adult source words were also accepted. For utterances that clearly resembled adult source words, the child's reference or use also had to be similar or match the adult's or the child's own use in other situations. Coding was also made easier when previous occurrences of the particular utterance had already been noted in other sources (diaries, MCDIs, interviews) thus providing further evidence of the child's consistent use of a word for a particular meaning.[10]

Utterances coded as ENG, GER or JAP could be clearly identified as coming from an English, German or Japanese source respectively. However, many of the child's utterances were categorized as OTHER because they were: (i) *non language-specific* utterances such as unintelligible speech, onomatopoeia and sound effects; (ii) *ambiguous* between English and German (such as *here/hier* and *yeah/ja*), between English and Japanese (such as *bye/bai*), between German and Japanese (such as *ne/ne*, roughly meaning 'no' in German and 'isn't it?'/'right?' in Japanese) or between all three languages (such as *teddy/ Teddy/tedii* to refer to bears in general); (iii) *imitations* of immediately preceding adult utterances or within 10 seconds of the preceding adult utterance; or (iv) *proper names* (such as *mama, papa, Daichan,* etc.), including names of characters from television programs or in books.[11]

2.4 Limitations and strengths of methods used in this study

Although five different methods of data collection have been presented above, only two — the MCDI and the video recordings — are considered to be the main sources of data for this project. The questionnaire, interviews and diaries (which supplement the main data sources) are different forms of parental reports that have been criticized for their validity and reliability (a discussion of disadvantages and limitations of parental reports can be found in Berglund 1999).[12] Some of the problems with such parental reports have been dealt with by the development of the MCDI. Since the instruments are checklists, parents are relying on their *recognition memory* rather than their *recall memory* when they report on children's present rather than past behavior. Such checklists are felt to increase the validity of parental reports. While the validity of various aspects of the MCDI has been ascertained in several studies (Thal and Bates 1988; Bates, Thal, Whitesell, Fenson and Oakes 1989; Pine, Lieven and Rowland 1996; Robinson and Mervis 1999), Naka, Miyata and Nisisawa (1999) found the checklist to be unreliable because the caregivers in their study tended to overgeneralize in word identification. The caregivers' abilities in completing the J-CDI (Japanese version of the MCDI) varied according to their concentration. In comparisons with tape recordings made by the investigators, mistakes were found to be made in the reports due to errors in memory.

Video recordings, on the other hand, can give information that the MCDI cannot provide on pragmatic skills, parental communication, and the nature of interaction and non-verbal communication beyond simple gestures. Video recordings are considered to leave less room than parental reports for overgeneralization, error and bias. Genesee (1989) has warned that parental information cannot be totally reliable when it concerns parents' own speech. Research by Goodz (1989) and Kasuya (1998) on bilingual families has found that parents claiming to use only the *one parent–one language* approach or to use mainly one language did not model such speech, thus showing a discrepancy between reported language use and actual production. This, of course, does not preclude that parents are still the best sources for estimates about their children's early exposure patterns and for descriptions of sociolinguistic background (De Houwer 1995:224–5 and Kasuya 1998:331 also defend the usefulness of certain types of parental information).

Video recordings, however, also have limitations as they provide a particular sampling that may not be typical of language production during the rest of a day when no recording is being made. The activities recorded in the home where useful language samples could be obtained were of the child playing with his toys or looking at books. Recordings were not made, for instance, during the daily diaper-changing event but his mother reported in the diary that the English word, *down*, was produced at age 1;5.15 when Freddy wanted to be lifted down from his changing table. Similarly, *up-down* was used at age 1;8.13 in the morning when he wanted his mother to get up and take him downstairs. Such utterances never appear in the recordings because they are not appropriate to the situations or activities being recorded. From the English version of the MCDI infant short form completed for Freddy at age 1;3 by the mother, we find that he understands the item *night night*, but actually says *ne ne* (*nenne* is the Japanese baby word for 'sleep'). He understands the items *finish* and *all gone* on the MCDI but actually produces *all done* for both concepts. None of these items appears on the video recordings analyzed because they are not needed during the play activities recorded. However, these examples from the diary and MCDI indicate that parental reports can complement the particular sampling limitations of video recordings.

I believe that the different methods in combination contribute to the strengths of this case study. The MCDI supplemented by the diaries and interviews will be used to determine the composition of the early lexicon in terms of vocabulary comprehension and production in the three languages. The video recordings collected in separate language contexts will be used to examine the child's language choice in terms of parental input. Only through the systematic analyses of data collected through a combination of methods can I expect to make reliable inferences about the child's language knowledge.

3. Results of quantitative analyses

3.1 Results from the parental and daycare reports

The data obtained from the diaries and interviews were combined with the data from the MCDI from the three language contexts to determine the number of new word types in each of the three languages in terms of words understood up to age 1;4 and in terms of words produced up to age 1;9. Any items that did not have a clearly identifiable language source (that is, items which were ambiguous between two or all three of the languages) were excluded from analysis.

3.1.1 *Comprehension*

Figure 1 shows that in terms of vocabulary comprehension, Freddy appears to understand more English words than German or Japanese ones from ages 1;0 to 1;4. According to parental and daycare reports from the checklists and diary, he could understand 15 English words and no German nor Japanese ones at age 1;0. At age 1;1, he understood only one Japanese item compared to 6 more English words. At age 1;2, there was no change to his ability to understand German or Japanese words but he could now understand 27 English items. At age 1;3, there was still no indication of any comprehension of German but he could now understand 2 Japanese words and 40 English ones. By age 1;4, Freddy's parents indicate that he can understand 29 German words. His comprehension of Japanese remains the same at 2 words and his English comprehension increases to 52 items understood.

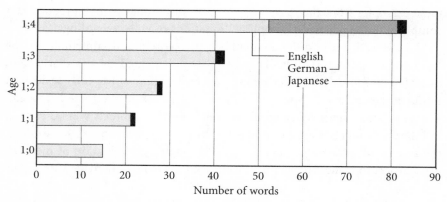

Figure 1. Words understood in each language (based on the MCDI, diaries and interviews)

3.1.2 *Production*

Figure 2 shows the number of words produced in each language from ages 1;0 to 1;9 according to parental and daycare reports (based again on the MCDI, diaries and interviews). The number of English word types increases steadily with, on average, about four words added each month until age 1;8. The sharpest increase occurs between ages 1;8 and 1;9 with the production of eighteen new English words reported. Thus, a total of fifty English words have been produced by age 1;9. The number of Japanese words produced is minimal until age 1;6. Ten additional new words are produced then, followed by five more at age 1;7, two more at age 1;8 and another spurt of nine new words by age 1;9, resulting in a total of 30 Japanese words by that age. The growth of German vocabulary is low throughout with only eight German words reported to have been produced by 1;9. The greatest vocabulary growth for Freddy occurs after age 1;5 so that by age 1;9, he has a total of 88 different vocabulary types in his lexicon from three language sources.

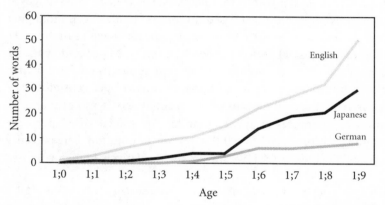

Figure 2. Words produced in each language (based on the MCDI, diaries and interviews)

3.2 Results from video recordings done in the home environment

Table 4 shows the number of types (T) and tokens (t) that were assigned to the categories ENG, GER, JAP and OTHER for each of the six pairs of video recordings analyzed. As mentioned earlier, many of his utterances could not be identified with any particular language source. In terms of total *tokens* of utterances for all twelve sessions investigated, 15 per cent (N=267) could be coded as ENG, GER or JAP and the remaining 85 per cent (N=1477) were classified as OTHER (percentages are calculated from the results displayed in Table 4). One reason for mentioning here the large extent of utterances classified as OTHER is to show that the child was very vocal in the video recordings. Besides the words excluded for a study of language choice (because they are imitations, proper names, or ambiguous between two or more languages), there were many non language-specific utterances that appeared to be the child's own language. Hoffmann (1985: 484) has mentioned the same phenomenon for her son, Pascual, who "had a lot of 'own language' (i.e. language which did not resemble either German or Spanish or English), which was difficult to understand for us". In a longitudinal study of 42 normally developing monolingual English-speaking children, Hart and Risley (1999) found that the amount of nonword utterances (called *non language-specific utterances* in my study) produced by the children exceeded the amount of recognizable words until around age 1;7. From the data given in Hart and Risley (1999: 277), it was possible to calculate the average percentage of nonword utterances produced (also based on tokens) by the 42 monolingual children for each month up to age 1;10 to be: 96 per cent at age 11 months; 94 per cent at age 12 months; 90 per cent at age 13 months; 88 per cent at age 14 months; 82 per cent at age 15 months; 74 per cent at age 16 months; 65 per cent at age 17 months; 58 per cent at age 18 months; 46 per cent at age 19 months; 44 per cent at age 20 months; 36 per cent at age 21 months; and 31 per cent nonword utterances at age 22 months. An average of 67 per cent nonword utterances is produced for all the months in question. The percentage of utterances classified as OTHER for Freddy is relatively higher at 85 per

Table 4. The number of types (T) and tokens (t) in each category (ENG, GER, JAP, OTHER) for the twelve sessions

Session	Eng T (t)	Ger T (t)	Jap T (t)	Other T (t)
1;1.0ENG	1 (1)	1 (1)	1 (1)	38 (69)
1;1.0GER	0 (0)	2 (2)	4 (7)	55 (92)
1;2.22ENG	0 (0)	0 (0)	0 (0)	22 (35)
1;2.22GER	1 (1)	2 (9)	6 (28)	105 (149)
1;4.29ENG	0 (0)	1 (1)	5 (7)	154 (175)
1;5.5GER	1 (1)	4 (16)	5 (27)	70 (89)
1;6.26ENG	1 (1)	1 (1)	2 (3)	139 (155)
1;6.24GER	2 (2)	2 (2)	10 (25)	132 (160)
1;8.22ENG	5 (11)	1 (2)	7 (15)	114 (147)
1;8.22GER	2 (2)	3 (3)	5 (35)	162 (215)
1;10.0ENG	1 (1)	0 (0)	6 (7)	46 (51)
1;9.30GER	1 (1)	0 (0)	7 (54)	121 (140)
TOTAL	15 (21)	17 (37)	58 (209)	1,158 (1,477)

Note: the six pairs of recordings are listed with ENG preceding GER for each pair.

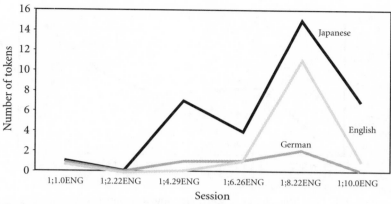

Figure 3. Language choice in English context sessions

cent for all data conflated up to age 1;10 but not unusually so because the category OTHER includes not only the unrecognizable utterances but also those meaningful items that are being excluded for the purpose of investigating the child's language choice (as mentioned above).

Figures 3 and 4 show the number of tokens produced in the English context and the German context sessions respectively. Freddy appears to be producing mainly Japanese utterances in both contexts, but more so in the German (Figure 4) than in the English context (Figure 3). The number of English and German tokens is too small to determine any clear patterns of distribution in the two contexts.

The results are unexpected, given the earlier overview of Freddy's comprehension and production in three languages as shown in Figures 1 and 2 respectively. Based on the data obtained from the MCDI, diaries and interviews, we would have expected Freddy to produce more English words than German or Japanese ones. Contrary to our expectations, in both the English context sessions shown in Figure 3 and the German context sessions shown in Figure 4, Freddy consistently produces more Japanese tokens.

Because the numbers are small, the data will be conflated across all six pairs of recordings regardless of language context. Out of all the data that could be identified as having a language-specific source, 78 per cent (N=209) are Japanese utterances (in terms of tokens; as shown in the last row of Table 4). Only 8 per cent (N=21) are English utterances in spite of the fact that the MCDI and diaries report that Freddy produced the most English utterances by age 1;9 (cf. Figure 2). German, which the parents were not sure

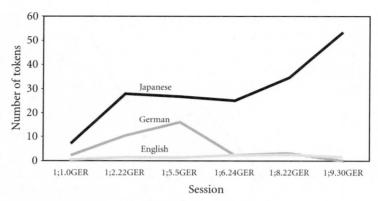

Figure 4. Language choice in German context sessions

that Freddy understood until after age 1;4, was produced slightly more often than English as such utterances made up 14 per cent (N=37) of his total language-identifiable production.

4. Discussion

In order to interpret the results from the quantitative analyses, I will examine all data collected qualitatively in the discussions that follow on input and the child's language use.

4.1 Trilingual input and early comprehension

There is no indication in Figure 1 that Freddy understood any German words until age 1;4. After spending two weeks in Germany when Freddy was aged 1;3.11 to 1;3.27, his mother writes in the diary that while in Germany:

> [Freddy] shocked us with how much he understood in German when spoken to by the extended family. We hadn't any indication up until now that he understood anything more than our gestures. About Aug. 6–7, after just a few days in Germany, when his grandmother instructed him (he was standing in front of a bird cage in the yard) to go see the bunnies (at a point further away in the yard) he looked at her and immediately took off for the bunny cage. We were all really surprised. My in-laws felt he understood normally for a German child his age and even found him to be advanced.

As mentioned earlier, the German MCDI was adapted from the American one and may not have been a reliable measure (see footnote 6) of Freddy's German ability. The father who was responsible for completing the German checklist may also have been conservative in his assessments of his son's German comprehension. Evidence, subtle rather than blatant, could be found in the transcripts as early as age 1;1 shown in (1) that Freddy (FRE) understood German. The infant, however, demonstrated his German comprehension by responding with a Japanese utterance that had the same semantic content as his father's (FAT) preceding German utterance. (Please note that all examples shown are from the author's own unpublished data. Although the original transcripts are in full CHAT format, dependent tiers, including all phonetic transcriptions of the child's utterances, have been eliminated from the examples presented in this chapter unless they were felt to be necessary for clarity such as English translations, %eng, or explanations of language use, %exp. For more details, please refer to the CHAT Symbol Summary in MacWhinney 1995: 126–9.)

(1)   Excerpt from 1;1.0GER:

    *FAT: komm!
    %eng: come on
    *FAT: bleib hier.
    %eng: stay here
    *FRE: koko?
    %exp: Japanese utterance
    %eng: here
    *FAT: bleib hier, du Kleiner.
    %eng: stay here little one

The daycare staff, much as the parents had reported for German, found little indication of Freddy's Japanese comprehension. In an interview with several staff members at the daycare when Freddy was 1;5.25 of age, it was discovered that none of them was sure whether Freddy really understood any Japanese as he often seemed to follow what everyone else did and was almost always the last one to do things (like going outside, putting on his jacket, or having a drink). Therefore, the daycare staff members interviewed were not certain if this was due to the fact that he did not want to stop what he was doing or that he did not understand their instructions in Japanese and was simply following the actions of the other children. They felt that Freddy's personality made it difficult to assess his vocabulary comprehension. He reportedly had a strong will so that they were uncertain as to whether his lack of response was due to a lack of comprehension or to a lack of interest in activities other than the one he was already engaged in. This is corroborated by Freddy's mother in an interview when Freddy was age 1;9 when she reported that since age one, Freddy had been demonstrating a very strong will and would ignore anything his parents said if he was already immersed in something of interest to him. Such behavior made it difficult for the parents as well as for the daycare staff to assess Freddy's comprehension, and his parents were not even aware of his ability to understand German until after they had spent two weeks in Germany in an all German language environment.

With regard to the relationship between input quantity and acquisition patterns in terms of comprehension, the quantitative results shown in Figure 1 seem to correlate somewhat with the fact that from birth until age 1;4, Freddy had heard English the most in his environment and therefore understood this language the most, followed by German which he had also heard from birth but to a lesser degree. He had only heard Japanese since age 0;11 and his comprehension of this language seems to be very limited at least as reported by the daycare. Example (1) from the video recordings and the discussion above suggest that parental and daycare reports of German and Japanese comprehension respectively may have been confounded by the child's personality. Hence no conclusive statements can be made about the effect of trilingual input on the child's ability to understand each of the three languages in his environment.

What can be inferred, however, is that the assessment of comprehension when three languages are involved poses more difficulties than if one language is involved as the number of possible interpretations increases with each additional language. The daycare staff who were aware that Freddy heard English and German at home from birth tended to assume that he understood those languages better than Japanese. They seemed subconsciously to excuse the child from understanding Japanese or to lower their expectations of what he should understand. Moreover, only when the family was in a strictly monolingual German environment (thus eliminating the two other language environments as factors) could they witness Freddy's understanding of German.

4.2 Trilingual input and vocabulary production from ages 1;0 to 1;9

The parents and daycare staff, not surprisingly, found it easier to report on Freddy's production than on his comprehension. In terms of vocabulary production as indicated in the MCDI, diaries and interviews, the amount of growth in each language follows closely on the parents' estimates of the amount of language the child was hearing (cf. Table 2 and Figure 2). He produced the greatest number of new English word types over time in the language he heard the most since birth and hears 45 per cent of the time between ages 1;5 and 1;9. Since age 0;11 he has heard more Japanese than German and produces more new Japanese word types than German ones. His production of new German word types is the lowest and is reflected by the fact that he heard German only 10 per cent of the time in the period between ages 1;5 and 1;9. A bilingual study by Pearson, Fernández, Lewedag and Oller (1997) used the MCDI in English and in Spanish to examine different patterns of exposure in 25 English–Spanish bilingual infants between ages 0;8 and 2;6. Like my results from the MCDI, they also found a substantial correlation between the quantity of input in a given language and the amount of vocabulary learning in that language during the second year of life.

Unlike the results for comprehension in the three languages, the results for production based on parental and daycare reports show an acquisition pattern that corresponds to the amount of input. If we look at the first words produced by the child, we see that the first clear Japanese utterance is produced quite early on as the eighth word in the child's lexical repertoire.

1. *mama* (E/G) 0;11.3
2. *papa* (E/G) 0;11.3
3. *kitty* (ENG) 0;11.5
4. *hallo* (E/G) 1;0.13
5. *doggy* (ENG) 1;0.22
6. *up-down* (ENG) 1;1.16
7. *teddy* (E/G/J) 1;1.23
8. *dame* (JAP=*no*) 1;1.24

The first two words he produced as well as the fourth and seventh items have not been included in the quantitative analyses because they are ambiguous between two or all three languages. A more complete investigation of lexical acquisition in this trilingual child is beyond the scope of this chapter as the construction of Freddy's cumulative lexicon from all available sources is still in progress. The results in Table 4 show that the first Japanese utterances may be earlier than indicated in the parental/daycare reports as a total of five Japanese types (eight tokens) were produced in the English and German sessions recorded at age 1;1.

The results obtained so far on Freddy's vocabulary production suggest not only that the amount of input received from each language is important for that language to be produced (as evident in the vocabulary acquired in each language) but also that the delayed exposure to Japanese at age 0;11 has not greatly affected the development of that language. From age 1;1 onwards in Figure 2, the child is shown to produce more Japanese words than German ones (although he has heard German from birth). Of course, a possible factor here is that the number of early words ambiguous between English and German may have caused a corresponding decrease in what could be coded as clearly German vocabulary. This would, however, not change the fact that Japanese utterances were produced quite early and noted by the mother as well as by the daycare staff soon after the onset of speech despite a shorter exposure to the language.

4.3 Language choice in the home

Figures 3 and 4 indicate that Freddy has a preference for speaking Japanese more than his other two home languages even in interactions with his English-speaking mother and German-speaking father. This case does not show developing contextual sensitivity as predicted by the studies of bilingual development reviewed earlier. Because Freddy produces mainly Japanese tokens even when addressed in English or in German, the small number of English and German tokens produced cannot be used to demonstrate that more English than German is being produced in the English context nor more German than English in the German context. What then do the results show? This case actually provides evidence that trilingual development is distinct from bilingual development. In a bilingual situation, one can expect the child to produce either more or less of one language than the other. In the trilingual case, the number of possibilities has increased manifold. Freddy could have shown contextual sensitivity in his language choice, no contextual sensitivity or a marked preference for any one or two of his three languages.

The fact that he shows a marked preference for using Japanese instead of his home languages even in the home environment confirms the conclusion reached earlier from looking at his vocabulary production (based on the MCDI, interviews and diaries) that later exposure to Japanese from age 0;11 onwards has not affected his ability to produce the language. Table 5 lists the English, German and Japanese types (with corresponding number of tokens in decreasing order) that appeared across the six pairs of video recordings from ages 1;1 to 1;10. Like the trilingual grandchildren in Mikès (1990), Freddy has produced equivalent pairs and triplets. He has two English/German equivalent pairs (*oh/ach* and *oink-oink/Buu Wuu*), two German/Japanese pairs (*guck-mal/mite* 'look' and *Wau Wau/wanwan* 'woof woof' or 'dog'), and two English/German/Japanese equivalent triplets (*there/da/atta* and *no/noe/dame*). Because the number of tokens produced for these equivalent terms is small, no lexical differentiation has been or could be demonstrated. The results, in general, suggest that Freddy was not using his trilingual vocabulary in contextually appropriate ways at any point up to age 1;10. One can see in Table 5 though that the child's vocabulary in all three languages is composed mainly of functional rather than referential (content) words. For example, the child appears to have compensated for having few specific nouns in Japanese by the frequent use (49 tokens) of the functional deictic, *kore* 'this'. The Japanese words are mainly interactional in nature with items like *hai* 'yes' or 'here', *dame* 'no' or 'don't' and *yatte* 'do-it'. Please note that Freddy did produce what can be considered as the equivalent triplet *yeah/ja/hai* 'yes' but *yeah/ja* were excluded from the language choice analysis for being ambiguous between English and German.

The fact that Freddy produced Japanese vocabulary that could be used in a wide range of interactions early in and throughout his linguistic development up to age 1;10 has implications for terminological distinctions regarding different patterns of childhood bi- or multi-lingualism. As mentioned earlier, Hoffmann (1985) adopted the criterion of the third birthday as the determining point for the distinction between simultaneous and successive language acquisition (*infant* vs. *child trilingual* in her terms) arbitrarily set by McLaughlin (1978). De Houwer (1995) has been more stringent by rejecting the term *simultaneous* in favor of Meisel's (1989) term *Bilingual First Language Acquisition* (BFLA) to refer to the process of acquisition in a child exposed to two languages within the first month of birth. She proposed the use of *Bilingual Second Language Acquisition* (BSLA) for situations where exposure to a second language starts "no earlier than one month after birth, but before age two" (De Houwer 1995: 223). My case study provides no empirical support for the one-month-after-birth distinction. Contrary to expectations that the child would be able to produce more of the two languages he heard from birth, he is producing (according to video data) the language he hears from age 0;11 with the first clear Japanese utterances appearing as early as age 1;1 in the earliest video recordings shown in Table 4 (since earlier recordings still await transcription, there is a possibility that at a later stage when all videotapes have been transcribed, an even earlier occurrence may exist). The column of Japanese types produced in Table 5 shows that Freddy had sufficient lexical resources in Japanese not only for interactions with peers at the daycare but

Table 5. Types (with number of tokens in parenthesis) appearing across 6 pairs of video sessions up to age 1;10

English	German	Translation	Japanese	Translation
there (5)	da (17)	*there*	hai (74)	*yes or here*
oh (5)	ach (12)	*oh*	kore (49)	*this*
oink-oink (3)	guck-mal (3)	*look*	uwa (23)	*JAP exclamation of surprise*
that (2)	Wau Wau (2)	*woof woof*	wanwan (15)	*doggie or woof woof*
out (1)	ich-kann (1)	*I-can*	dame (7)	*no/don't*
uh-oh (1)	noe (1)	*no/not*	koko (4)	*here*
this (1)	Buu Wuu (1)	*oink-oink*	are (4)	*that (one)*
no (1)			yatte (4)	*do-it*
cheese (1)			(inai) baa (3)	*(peek-a-)boo*
moon (1)			nani (3)	*what*
			bubu (2)	*car*
			mite (2)	*look*
			nja (nja) (2)	*kitty*
			atta (2)	*there it is*
			kocchi (2)	*this way/come along*
			yada (2)	*no (I don't want...)*
			ei (1)	*JAP exclamation when throwing something aimed at someone*
			ara (1)	*strange or what's this?*
			gakko (1)	*school*
			nande (1)	*why*
			oshi (1)	*let's go, said to oneself*
			owari (1)	*finished*
			haitta (1)	*[it's] got in*
			ooi (1)	*hello (for calling someone who is far from you)*
			hora (1)	*look/see*
			gocha-gocha (1)	*mess*
			ichi (1)	*one*
T=10, t=21	T=7, t=37		T=27, t=209	

also with his trilingual parents (to be discussed further in the section on parental discourse styles).

The results of my case study provide empirical evidence for the suggestion that what I earlier defined as *early trilingual development* when children are exposed to three languages regularly before their first words can also be termed *Trilingual First Language Acquisition*. The language to which Freddy is exposed at age 0;11 just before the onset of speech is the one that he prefers to use more often than the two languages to which he was exposed from birth.

Thus this case suggests that delayed input for one language up until the onset of speech does not necessarily make the acquisition of that language different from the acquisition of language(s) where input is from birth. Rather than stating an age to distinguish first language(s) from successive language acquisition, I have used the onset of speech as the criterion to distinguish simultaneous from successive acquisition. Similarly, Bhatia and Ritchie (1999: 585) use the one-word stage as their criterion in reference to bilingual acquisition. However, I prefer the *onset of speech* to the *one-word stage* as a criterion because there have been reports of children producing two- or multi-word utterances from the onset of speech (for example, Damon in Clark (1993: 25) began producing multi-word utterances from age 1;1.29). If my case can be accepted as one of trilingual first language acquisition, then we can probably also consider bilingual first language acquisition to occur when exposure to two languages occurs before or near the onset of speech. Because this is a case study of one child, I would call for more studies of multilingual children with different ages of exposure to different languages before the onset of speech to verify the distinction between simultaneous and successive acquisition established by the empirical data from this study.

4.4 Factors affecting language choice in video-recorded sessions

The bilingual and trilingual literature reviewed earlier indicates that many factors pertaining to the input can affect children's language choices. In this section, I will examine in detail the speech of Freddy's parents as well as evaluate other possible factors that could have encouraged Freddy to produce Japanese more often than his other two home languages. The six pairs of video recordings used in the quantitative analyses will be examined qualitatively in the discussions that follow.

4.4.1 *Parental discourse styles*

Although studies like Döpke (1992), Lanza (1997) and Kasuya (1998) refer to *parental discourse strategies* (my emphasis), I prefer the term *style* to *strategy* in referring to the parents' discourse in my own study as the latter term can imply that parents are consciously speaking in a certain way. I do not want to suggest at all that Freddy's parents were making a conscious effort to speak in a particular manner to their infant son. It is possible, of course, that parents of older children above age two as in the studies by Döpke (1992) and Kasuya (1998) may intentionally use particular strategies to ensure that their children use more of one language than another. This was not the case in the interactions between Freddy and his parents. At the beginning stages of language acquisition examined, his parents were happy with any intelligible utterances he made regardless of the language of the utterance.

Lanza (1988) has pointed out, however, that one aspect of linguistic input is metalinguistic in nature. *Metalinguistic input* is defined as a cue that parents can provide to a child that "his utterance was in some way insufficient, unacceptable, inappropriate or incomprehensible to the native speaker or adult" (Lanza 1988: 70). Out of the five parental strategies toward child language mixes proposed by Lanza (1997), the first two, *minimal grasp* and *expressed guess*, which were considered to create a monolingual context, were never used by Freddy's parents in response to Freddy's inappropriate language choice.[13] Freddy's mother (MOT) did *repeat* the content of Freddy's Japanese utterance in English (the third strategy) as shown in (2):

(2)   Excerpt from 1;10ENG:

     *MOT: you know what's in there?
     *FRE: wan wan.
     %eng: dog
     %exp: Japanese child language
     *MOT: no, not a dog.

Example (3) shows the father repeating the content of Freddy's English utterance in German:

(3)   Excerpt from 1;9.30GER:

     *FRE: xxx, moon.
     *FAT: ja, ja.
     %eng: yes, yes
     *FAT: das ist der Mond.
     %eng: that is the moon

The mother also tended to imitate her son's utterances without repeating the content in English. She would incorporate her son's inappropriate lexical choice into her own utterances, similar but not exactly as described for Lanza's fifth strategy, *code-switching*, considered to create the most bilingual context. According to Lanza's definition, *code-switching* also occurs when the adult switches into the other language after the child's inappropriate language choice but this situation was not found in any of the transcripts examined. Unlike the parents in Lanza (1997) and Kasuya (1998), Freddy's mother often imitated her

son's utterances in his other two languages, thus showing her easy acceptance
of lexical items from any three of his languages. In (4) and (5) from the same
English context session at age 1;6.26, the mother accepts her son's utterances in
German and Japanese respectively (shown in bold). In (4), Freddy's mother
repeats the German utterance and picks up the figure for him:

(4)   *MOT: oh.
        %exp: FRE has just dropped a toy figure
        *FRE: **da.**
        %eng: there
        %exp: German utterance
        *MOT: **da.**
        %act: gets up, picks up the piece FRE threw, sits back on her side,
             starts building

In (5), she repeats her son's use of the Japanese version of the game of peek-a-
boo and comments on the fact that he produces the Japanese version even
though she uses the English version ('...' indicates that intervening material
has been omitted):

(5)   *MOT: I can't [//] I can just see your eye ⟨right there⟩ [⟩].
        *FRE: **ba.**
        %eng: boo
        *MOT: **ba.**
        *MOT: you want to play "**ba**" with that?
        %exp: "ba" is a Japanese game, "inai inai ba", like "peek-a-boo"
        . . .
        *MOT: aah +..
        *MOT: peek-a-boo!
        *MOT: aah +..
        *FRE: **ba ba ba ba.**
        %act: covers both eyes with hands
        *MOT: peek-a-boo.
        *FRE: 0.
        %act: removes hands from eyes
        *MOT: you still do "ba".
        . . .
        *MOT: even though I say "peek-a-boo".
Note that in (6) from session 1;8.22ENG when the mother is looking at a book

with her son, the mother not only repeats her son's Japanese baby words for *cat* and *dog* (for which he actually had English equivalents according to the MCDI and diary data) but she also praises him for having used the Japanese lexical items, thus rendering the quantitative results favoring Japanese production in the home less surprising.

(6)   *MOT: what's that?
       *FRE: **nya.**
       %eng: cat
       %exp: Japanese baby word for 'cat'
       *MOT: **nya nya.**
       *MOT: **that's right.**
       . . .
       *MOT: how (a)bout that?
       *FRE: **wan wan.**
       %eng: dog
       %exp: Japanese baby word for 'dog'
       *MOT: **wan wan.**
       *MOT: **that's right.**

The father had a slightly different discourse style from the mother. He did not imitate his son's use of Japanese or English but seemed to use Lanza's (1997) fourth strategy, *move on*, in his interactions with Freddy as shown in (7). Basically, he continues the conversation and show that he has understood the child's Japanese.

(7)   Excerpt from 1;6.24GER:
       *FAT: wer ist das?
       %eng: who is it
       *FRE: hai.[14]
       %eng: here you are
       %exp: Japanese utterance
       %act: gives toy dinosaur to FAT
       *FAT: danke schoen.
       %eng: thank you

Of the six types of parental discourse strategies outlined by Kasuya (1998: 344–5), only three are different from the ones already suggested by Lanza (1997) — Kasuya's two explicit strategies, *instruction* (instructing a child to say something by using an explicit word such as *say* or *tell* or telling the child that the adult does not understand) and *correction* (correcting the child's utterance by giving the correct equivalent and telling the child he is wrong), and one implicit strategy not mentioned by Lanza (1997), *translation* (giving the same information in both languages). No examples could be found of Freddy's parents using correction or translation in their interactions with Freddy but incidences of instruction, as defined by Kasuya (1998), did occur. Freddy's father, in particular, had a more explicit style than his mother in the interactions as the father often asked his son in many of the German language sessions, *was sagst du? ich verstehe dich nicht* 'what are you saying? I do not understand you'. Both parents also explicitly tried to ask Freddy to *say* certain words for them (highlighted in bold) as in the two examples below. In (8), the mother and son are looking at a book.

(8) Excerpt from 1;4.29ENG:

    *MOT: a duckling.
    %act: looks at FRE
    *MOT: can you say ⟨'duck'⟩ [⟩]?
    %act: looks at FRE
    *FRE: ⟨yyy⟩ [⟨].
    %pho: (g) u t t u k u i e [?]
    %act: points at a picture of a horse

Example (9) is typical of several attempts that the father has already made in earlier sessions to *teach* Freddy to say *Ball* (note that the German *Ball* and the English *ball* would be very similar in pronunciation and even had Freddy produced this word spontaneously, it would have been coded as OTHER because of the ambiguous language source).

(9) Excerpt from 1;8.22GER:

    *FAT: sag mal "Ball".
    %eng: say "ball"
    *FAT: Freddy.
    *FAT: Ball.
    %eng: ball
    *FRE: 0.
    %act: takes the ball from FAT's hand

While explicit instruction appears to have had no effect on Freddy, Kasuya (1998) does find that instructing a child to say something in Japanese worked with her older subjects (aged 2;10, 3;5 and 4;1 at her three data collection points) and promoted the use of the minority language in the home (her subjects were living in the United States). Kasuya (1998) reports that while an explicit strategy encouraged the children to speak more Japanese in her study, she admits that most parents chose to use an implicit strategy the most often by continuing in Japanese even when the child produced English utterances. She writes that the "primary goal of the interaction appears to be to encourage language behavior irrespective of its form. In monolingual families, this motivation is shown by the parents' tolerance of a variety of linguistic errors" (Kasuya 1998:342). The monolingual English-speaking grandmother in Deuchar and Quay (2000:105) and the monolingual English-speaking grandmother of Siri in Lanza (1997:258) accepted Spanish and Norwegian words respectively spoken by their bilingual granddaughters. Adults, whether monolingual (like the grandmothers just mentioned) or trilingual (like Freddy's parents), accept words in a language other than the one they are using in order for the conversation to progress and for breakdown to be avoided. Barron-Hauwaert (2000), in her questionnaire, asked parents about their reactions to children's inappropriate language choice. In 90 per cent of the families, the parents repeated the *right* word (*repeat* the content of the child's utterance in the appropriate language) or continued the conversation (*moved on*). Barron-Hauwaert (2000) inferred from this that the parents noticed the error but accepted it as normal in trilingual families.

4.4.2 *Parental code-switching*
As mentioned above, the type of code-switching described by Lanza (1997) and Kasuya (1998) where the adult switches into the other language *after* the child's inappropriate language choice was not found in any of the transcripts examined.

Lexical borrowing. The most typical type of code-switching demonstrated by the mother involved *lexical borrowing* from Japanese. She would insert Japanese lexical items (shown in bold) that she knew her son had acquired at the daycare into otherwise English utterances as in (10), (11) and (12).

(10)   Excerpt from 1;6.26ENG:

    *MOT: that's what you play with in the park all the time, is acorns.
    *FRE: 0.
    %act: grabs the "tree-on-wheels" toy and starts taking it apart
    *MOT: you're the **donguri** king.
    %exp: 'donguri' is Japanese for acorn

Examples (11) and (12) show that her lexical borrowing is mainly confined to

Japanese baby words or Japanese child language items:

(11) Excerpt from 1;8.22ENG:
      [while looking at a picture book]
      *MOT: but that's a **bu bu**.
      *MOT: that's a car!
      %exp: "bu bu" is the *Japanese* baby word for 'car'
      *MOT: you like the car?
      . . .
      [while working on a puzzle]
      *MOT: now, how (a)bout if the doggie chases the kitty?
      %act: picks up dog piece
      *MOT: **wan wan wan wan wan, wan wan wan wan wan.**
      %act: brings dog to cat, as if dog is barking in *Japanese* way at cat;
             picks up cat
      *MOT: **nya nya nya.**
      %exp: MOT is making the sound a cat makes in *Japanese*
      *MOT: **wan wan wan wan.**
      *MOT: **nya nya nya.**
      *FRE: 0.
      %act: takes dog piece from MOT and fits it into the puzzle board
      *MOT: put that doggie back.
      *MOT: he's being a menace.

(12) Excerpt from 1;10ENG:
      *MOT: you know what you were gonna do.
      *MOT: you were gonna go to see a **zou-san**.
      %exp: "zou-san" is *Japanese* child language for 'elephant'
      *MOT: yeah, you were gonna go see ⟨a **zou-san**⟩ [⟩].
      *FRE: ⟨yyy⟩ [⟨].
      %pho: o o

Example (13) shows Freddy's mother actually initiating a code-switch into Japanese (shown in bold) that results in one of only three occurrences of code-mixing within the same utterance by the child. The mother tells her son that dogs bark by saying *woof, wan wan* and *bow wow*, which not only demonstrates her own acceptance of synonyms across languages and within one language but also encourages her child to produce such equivalents in his speech.

(13) Excerpt from 1;8.22ENG:

*MOT: those are doggies.
*MOT: woof woof, woof.
*FRE: 0.
%act: no response
*MOT: **wan wan!**
%exp: Japanese child language for dog
*FRE: **wan** woof.
%exp: code mixes Japanese with English
*FRE: **wan wan wan.**
%eng: woof woof woof
*MOT: bow wow, that's right.
*MOT: it says both "**wan wan**" and "bow wow".

Spontaneous code-switching. Another type of code-switching more typical of the father than of the mother in the transcripts examined is that of *spontaneous* code-switching (not triggered by the child's language choice). Example (14) shows the father switching to Japanese (shown in bold) just before turning off the video camera and after having spoken German throughout the session:

(14)   Excerpt from 1;2.22GER:

    *FRE: 0.
    %act: picks up two rings from the floor
    *FAT: **chotto matte.**
    %eng: wait a minute
    %exp: Japanese utterance
    *FAT: Fred.
    *FAT: **chotto matte.**
    %act: turns off camera

In (15), the father switches to English several times within the same session:

(15)   Excerpt from **1;5.5GER**

    *FAT: 0.
    %act: puts down his pen and turns around
    *FRE: yyy.
    %pho: h u h u a i e
    %act: picks up a toy
    *FAT: **what?**
    *FRE: guck mal.

%eng: look
%exp: German utterance
%act: gives the toy to FAT

. . .

*FAT: ich schlag mal eine neue Seite # auf.
%eng: I will turn to a new page
*FAT: hn?
*FAT: wollen wir eine andere, aaaa.
%eng: do we want another
%act: turns the page
*FAT: **look at this.**
*FAT: der ist der "**Ducky**".
%eng: it is the duck
%act: points to a picture

Overheard speech. As mentioned earlier, besides their regular pattern of
language use within the family, the parents would speak Japanese with Japanese speakers, and English with English speakers. They rarely had the opportunity to speak German with others in Japan. Nevertheless, Freddy could often
overhear his parents using languages other than the one that they regularly
used with him. This would occur when his parents spoke with visitors or on
the phone as, for example, in session 1;6.26ENG when the phone rang while
the mother and Freddy were playing with Lego figures. She had to code-switch
to Japanese and Freddy actually stopped playing and looked at his mother
when she switches from English to Japanese (shown in bold) in (16).

(16) *MOT: 0.
      %act: completes her new Lego figure, puts it next to the big dinosaur
      %exp: the phone rings
      *FRE: 0.
      %act: looks around, reacting to the phone
      *MOT: 0.
      %act: looks at her watch, gets up
      *MOT: I think I have to change your diaper.
      *FRE: 0.
      %act: holding his figure, turns around 180 degrees, stretches out to
               touch the young woman in the big box-shaped Lego
      *MOT: hello.
      %act: she answers the phone

*MOT: **a sumimasen.**
%eng: oh, I'm sorry.
*MOT: **daredesuka?**
%eng: who is this?
*FRE: 0.
%act: **stops playing with the Lego pieces, looks at MOT,** looks into space
*MOT: **hai.**
%eng: yes

In their daily life in Japan, it is not practical for the parents to hide their trilingual ability from their son so there are many occasions like in (16) when Freddy could overhear his parents speaking languages other than the one they usually used with him. He would actually also be addressed in, for example, English, by the father if English visitors were also present in the home. Freddy's parents were thus inadvertently socializing him into proper trilingual pragmatic behavior.

4.4.3 *Participants, topic, lexical resources and activity*

Stavans (1992) has pointed out that the *participant's* perceived linguistic capability and the speaker's own linguistic ability affects the speaker's language choice. It would seem from the examples given that Freddy is exposed to the fact that his parents understand all three languages. Thus, his more frequent use of Japanese than German with the German-speaking father and of Japanese than English with the English-speaking mother does not impede conversations at all. The discourse styles of both parents seem to create a trilingual context that encourages the child to use his available *lexical resources* from any of his languages. Without realizing it (because both were aware of being their son's only models for German within the home with the mother being the main model for English), the parents were accommodating to their child's preference for producing utterances in Japanese (cf. examples (5)–(7), (10)–(14)). While Oksaar (1978) and Stavans (1992) found that *topic* influenced the code-switching done by their older subjects, *activity* rather than topic seems to be affecting Freddy's language choice as Freddy was too young yet to initiate the discussion of particular topics. In the daycare each day, he played with toys or looked at books. For the most part in the video recordings with his parents, he also played with toys and looked at books. Perhaps in this situation, Japanese is the appropriate language on the whole to use for these activities. When I looked again at the mother's diary, I found that when Freddy produced English utterances, it was not when playing with toys or looking at books but during diverse activities such as riding on his mother's bicycle, eating, toilet training, getting up and ready in the mornings, and so on.

4.4.4 *Emphatic function*

Another factor brought up in the trilingual acquisition literature (cf. Mikès 1990) is that code-switching can be used in an emphatic function to reinforce requests. As mentioned for example (13), there were only three occurrences of code-mixing (code-switches within the same utterance) by the child. Example (17) is one of those three where Freddy was trying to show his father something in a picture book. Because his father did not respond to him, his code-mixed utterance (shown in bold) seemed to be used for emphatic effect to get his father's attention.

(17)   Excerpt from 1;2.22GER:

       *FRE: da da da!
       %eng: there
       %exp: German utterance; wants to show FAT something in a picture book
       *FAT: Freddy.
       *FAT: komm hier, Freddy.
       %eng: come (over) here Freddy
       *FAT: Freddy.
       %act: sits down next to FRE on the floor
       *FAT: komm hier.
       %eng: come here
       *FRE: **there there da!**
       %exp: code-mixed English and German for 'there'; still trying to show FAT something

While no other such examples could be found in the six pairs of transcripts for Freddy, (18) shows the father using code-switching to strengthen his request that Freddy should stop throwing things.

(18)   Excerpt from 1;6.24GER

       *FRE: ei.
       %eng: Japanese exclamation when throwing something aiming at someone
       %act: throws Pooh-Bear at FAT

*FAT:	ach wer ist das?
%eng:	oh who is it
*FRE:	0.
%act:	throws a boy figurine away violently
*FAT:	ach, Freddy, **don't**.
%exp:	FAT codeswitches to English
*FAT:	nicht werfen, noe?
%eng:	don't throw, no

4.4.5 *Personality and sociopsychological factors*

Hoffmann and Widdicombe's (1999) subject, Robin at age four, is the most similar in terms of pattern of language exposure to Freddy. Robin heard Italian only from his father, English from his mother, and attended a French crèche when he was only a few months old, followed by a nursery school on a fairly full-time basis in Paris where the family lived. His parents reported that Robin was "equally proficient in all three [languages] with no clear signs of one language being favoured over, or being stronger than, the other two" (Hoffmann and Widdicombe 1999: 55), but the researchers found that Robin's code-switches favored the local language, French. Similarly, although Freddy's parents (and the daycare staff) reported vocabulary production in the three languages that correlated somewhat with the amount of input the child received from each language, the video recordings done in the home showed that he favored the local language, Japanese.

Two of the studies in Table 1 reviewed earlier address the issue of language choice anecdotally (without empirical data) but conclude that personality and sociopsychological factors may play a role in trilingual children's language choice. Hoffmann (1985) found that while her daughter at age eight was willing to use "the appropriate language to each parent quite consistently, irrespective of whether English-speaking children are present or not" (Hoffmann 1985: 489–90), her son at age five often addressed his parents in English. Hoffmann (1985) suggests that her trilingual children's language choice is a reflection of their personality. She reports that "Christina is more sensitive, thoughtful and reserved than Pascual" (ibid.: 489) and is therefore willing to accommodate to the language used by each parent while Pascual "has just not got the time and patience to stop and think about how he is going to put what he wants to say" (ibid.: 490). In Hoffmann and Widdicombe (1999: 58), the child's choice of French over his two home languages for code-switching is thought possibly to "indicate that the language he uses with his peers is more important to him psycholinguistically and qualitatively than the languages he uses with his parents (adults); or ... it may be that the effect of the community language, which in his environment he can perceive as being the lingua franca, could be more heavily weighted in the child's mind than the languages he uses at home". Freddy before age two already seemed to have a personality like Hoffmann's (1985) son, Pascual, who although he could speak all three of his languages preferred to speak in English, the local language, even when addressed in Italian or German. Freddy preferred the daycare language, Japanese, to his home languages, English and German. Perhaps, as suggested for Robin, Freddy may find the language of his daycare peers to be more important psycholinguistically and qualitatively than the languages he uses with his parents. Freddy may also find Japanese to be more appropriate or better suited in most situations with respect to the participants he encounters in his community. Most are monolingual Japanese speakers and those like his parents who are multilingual tend also to know Japanese. Could he have some cognitive awareness that he can only get what he wants in the daycare when he uses Japanese? When he is in the home, he can still get what he wants by using Japanese because his parents will always respond to him. Hence there is less of a need for him to produce German or English words to get what he wants, particularly at home. His preference for using Japanese thus makes sense in his overall interactional domain.

4.5 Active vs. passive trilingualism

Since this investigation stops when Freddy is age 1;10, it is too early yet to categorize him as being trilingual. He is definitely a *developing trilingual* in terms of being exposed to three different languages in his daily life. Freddy shows no indication of using his languages in contextually appropriate ways in the video recordings due in part to different amounts of input from each language resulting in different amounts of lexical resources available for each language, and in part to all the factors mentioned earlier. Although he seemed mainly to be producing Japanese utterances in the recordings examined, Freddy had *passive* competence (or receptive knowledge) of the parental languages, German and English — enough for him to understand his parents and respond in Japanese! He has chosen for the most part to speak Japanese and to understand rather than speak English and German (at least in the video recordings examined). Although the daycare recordings have not been discussed in this chapter, a preliminary examination shows that almost all identifiable utterances made in the daycare were in Japanese. Some English and German items were produced in the home recordings and their low incidence may be attributed partly to the fact that items ambiguous between English and German were excluded for the language choice analyses. While investigating the E/G utterances is beyond the scope of this chapter, the possibility remains that the child may have employed many such utterances as a compromise system to manage his three languages effectively (this would be an interesting topic of investigation for future research of bilingual or trilingual children exposed to lexically cognate languages). Even passive competence is valuable as the potential exists for his two weaker languages to be activated and used more actively later on (for a discussion of aspects of production that indicate a weak language, see Schlyter 1994). The status of strong and weak languages can change over the course of the child's life. Identifying the factors that can make a child's language performance stronger or weaker should be of great interest to researchers for its educational implications. Even having a weaker language can benefit children as a study by Yelland, Pollard and Mercuri (1993) on *marginal bilingual* children four to six years of age (who have a less well-developed second language) suggests that such children have an advantage over monolingual peers in terms of thinking and reading acquisition when they start formal schooling.

5.   Summary and conclusion

Faced with three languages in his environment, the child manages to function within the realms of all three by *choosing* the language that works in the most cases. For Freddy, Japanese can be used in the daycare and at the playground with monolingual Japanese adults and children as well as in the home with his trilingual parents. Receptive competence in English and German appears to be enough for successful interactions with his parents. In other words, English and German are necessary for comprehending and participating in conversations with his parents but are not necessary for him to use with his parents to be understood.

As to whether there is any correlation between *input quantity* for each language at particular points in time and the child's ability to understand and produce items from three languages, no correlation was found in the video data but some indication of a correlation could be found in the parental report data. Freddy is obviously receiving the critical input necessary for understanding speech in all three languages. However, his actual language choice in production seems not to be affected by the amount of development reported for each of his three languages. According to parental report, English was the language for which he had the largest lexical resources. Yet, he produced English the least in the video data. The high incidence of Japanese utterances produced by Freddy in the video-recorded sessions can be attributed in part to parental discourse styles:

a. The parents consistently accept utterances in Japanese without indicating non-comprehension and thus create a trilingual context in their interactions with the child.
b. Their son can overhear them speaking Japanese either on the phone, with visitors or with others outside the home.
c. The mother often inserts Japanese lexical items, borrowed particularly from Japanese child language that she knows her son uses at the daycare, into otherwise English conversations.
d. The father sometimes code-switches into Japanese in otherwise German interactions with his son.

However, especially in the earlier sessions, the parents did not always understand their son's utterances. Since a large number of utterances could not be identified as having a particular language source (considered to be *nonword* utterances in Hart and Risley 1999), they may also have become accustomed to continuing the conversation whether or not they clearly understood their son's utterances. For this reason, it is not surprising that they would thus be willing to accept their son's utterances in any of the three languages regardless of the language context of the conversation. The *quality of the input* could thus be said to be different at home than at the daycare in that the trilingual parents tried to understand and accepted all the child's productions in all three languages, while at the daycare the monolingual staff could only respond to the Japanese utterances they could understand.

No differences were found between later exposure to Japanese at age 0;11 and earlier exposure to English and German from birth in the child's linguistic production in the video recordings. In spite of *input delay* with regard to Japanese, there was no delay in the development of Japanese evident in his production. As already discussed, this calls into question distinctions between *simultaneous* and *successive* acquisition based on differences in age of exposure that is earlier than the onset of speech as established in this study.

The relationship between input and production is certainly complex and one that needs to be further explored. It is difficult to isolate crucial variables because they are confounded by sociopsychological factors. How much of the child's language behavior can be attributed to motivation? That is, is the child driven by motivation to be understood by as many interlocutors as possible in his language choice? Is it learning in context as in interactions with his parents who accept all his utterances? Is it simply the frequency of practice as in, for example, the occurrence of routines in the daycare with a wider variety of interlocutors that leads to a preference for using Japanese over the two home languages? Or is the input from daycare peers at a level more appropriate for language development? Adequate input is not enough to explain language choice in a developing trilingual infant. The results obtained in this study suggest that the parental discourse styles have more effect than actual language input provided in the home. If language dominance can be defined as the greater use of one language over two others to which a child is exposed, then Freddy appears to be dominant in Japanese in spite of his later exposure to this language than to his other two and in spite of fewer one-on-one interactions at the daycare where exposure to Japanese is in group situations. Based on an analysis of code-switching in their subject, Robin, at age 4;4 and 4;5, Hoffmann and Widdicombe (1999: 58) claim to have "established that language dominance does not apparently depend on length of exposure, but may depend on the people, context or topic habitually associated with a particular language". The same could be claimed for Freddy. Nevertheless, the importance of the linguistic environment is undeniable as the proficiency between the three languages of the trilingual child can be altered with changes in exposure patterns. While much more remains to be learned about how trilingual children's competence in three languages changes as a result of adaptations to new acquisition contexts, the study of trilingual children with careful identification of factors relevant to acquisition can reveal how children adapt their language(s) to new language environments and new language situations.

Tangential to my initial aims, but nevertheless important, the difference in the results obtained from the video recordings from the results obtained from the MCDI, diaries and interviews indicates that different methods of data collection produces different results. This suggests that we must be cautious about making conclusions about children's language development based on one method alone. Ideally, converging evidence across multiple methods would be the most powerful approach to hypothesis testing corroboration regarding what does and does not occur in the linguistic competence of a child. In this case study, a more comprehensive picture of a child's development in three languages than has previously been available could be provided because of the combination of different methods used.

Although there is currently little research on early trilingual development or trilingual first language acquisition, it is evident that being trilingual is not the same as being bilingual as the three languages can be manifested in production in more ways than two languages. The three can never be equally distributed as could occur in bilingual situations and the need to use each of three languages would usually occur less often than perhaps the need to use two different languages. The subject of this study, Freddy, has shown himself more than capable of managing linguistic boundaries in his early trilingual input. This case study is a step towards gaining deeper insights into the process of language development in trilingual children and provides not only directions for future investigations of early trilingual development but also implications concerning methodological requirements for studies of child language.

Notes

* I gratefully acknowledge a grant from the Matsushita International Foundation and the time, generous cooperation and active participation of Freddy's parents, the daycare staff and Freddy himself on this project. My thanks to Petra Bernardini, Ute Bohnacker, Jonas Granfeldt, Regina Köppe and Suzanne Schlyter for their discussion of a preliminary version of this chapter as well as to the participants of four seminars on various aspects of this project at Nagoya Gakuin, Concordia, McGill and Lund Universities as their questions and comments have helped my thoughts on this topic to mature and to evolve. Thanks are also due to the two editors of this volume, Jasone Cenoz and Fred Genesee, for their helpful comments. I alone am responsible for any shortcomings in this work.

1. Kazazis (1970) also suggests that the reason why Marina at age 4;7 and 4;9 extended the possessive genitive construction found in English and Swedish to her Greek grammar is due to the fact that English was used with the most people in her environment (and is thus her dominant language) and that Swedish agreed with the English grammar on that particular point.

2. Mikès (1990) also reports that there was a delay in Egon's acquisition of German lexical equivalents for Serbocroatian and Hungarian words until his German input was increased at age 1;6 from a few hours a week to four or five hours per day four times a week with his German-speaking grandmother. Then, the child quickly made up for the missing German equivalents.

3. Vuk at 1;5 used twelve equivalent pairs (four Serbocroatian–Hungarian, five Serbocroatian–German and three Hungarian–German). Uva from 1;9 to 1;11 produced a total of 13 equivalent pairs (eight Serbocroatian–Hungarian, two Serbocroatian–German and 3

Hungarian–German) as well as five Serbocroatian–Hungarian–German equivalent triplets. Egon from 1;4 to 1;6 used 15 equivalent pairs (ten Serbocroatian–Hungarian, two Serbocroatian–German, three Hungarian–German) and four Serbocroatian–Hungarian–German equivalent triplets (Mikès 1990: 112–13).

4. Three families live in Belgium and three in Switzerland with the remaining four families in France, Germany, England and Nepal respectively.

5. Please note, however, that in terms of exposure to Japanese, the child was not awake for the full six hours as he took naps at the daycare ranging anywhere from two to three hours each day.

6. Because no modifications were made to accommodate differences between English and German, the adapted German MCDI is less reliable than desired. I am aware that lexical and grammatical items differ in several respects as a result of language and culture so that merely translating an American instrument to the German language renders the instrument insufficiently accurate for use in the German language context. However, since the German version of the MCDI was not yet being released to researchers world-wide when inquiries were made, my adapted version was a stopgap measure. Recently, I have come across a reference to the German MCDI by Grimm, Doil, Müller and Wilde (1996) which may be of help to others doing such research.

7. The fact that the diary entries were made once a month for words understood and fortnightly for words produced is not a serious methodological drawback as the mother's diary was never meant to be the main source of data for analysis but only a supplement to the MCDI which, as mentioned, is not an exhaustive vocabulary list. I am very grateful to the mother for her efforts with the diary (and the English MCDI) in spite of heavy work and family commitments.

8. I am grateful to Ayako Inoue, Noriko Tamura and Junko Ogawa who took turns video recording Freddy in the daycare. My thanks also to all three and Yuki Takai for their translation work and clerical assistance on this project.

9. I am grateful to Ayako Kuwabara, Junko Ogawa, Kyoko Okamura, Natsumi Sakurai, Yoko Sato, Bettina Shimazu and Sayaka Yoshida for their work on transcribing the data.

10. For descriptions of word identification in other studies, see Deuchar and Quay (2000: 95), and Golinkoff and Hirsh-Pasek (1999: 93–4).

11. It has been brought to my attention that, if I had the time in the future, it would be interesting to calculate how many of the ambiguous utterances from among the total utterances classified as OTHER were from the cognate languages German and English. It is true that the category OTHER is large because many utterances were ambiguous. However, they were not only ambiguous between German and English. An inordinate amount of *ne* was produced which is ambiguous between Japanese (meaning 'isn't it?/right?') and German (meaning 'no').

12. Note, however, that in my study, not only the parents but daycare staff also made such reports in the diaries and interviews. This often provided converging evidence that corroborated the separate reports of each.

13. A minimal grasp occurs when an adult conveys a meta-communicative message to the

child as in *this is a context in which to speak language A only* by not indicating comprehension and requesting clarification. An expressed guess occurs when the adult indicates comprehension of the child's use of the other language but requests clarification (Lanza 1997).

14. Freddy's use of the Japanese word, *hai*, to mean 'here you are' in (7) is just one of two common uses of the term. *Hai* is also used to indicate agreement with 'yes' as its English equivalent. Although it was clear that Freddy used this term in two different ways, occurrences of *hai* has been counted only once as a single utterance type in the results reported earlier in Table 4.

Chapter 8

Bilingual first language acquisition[*]

A discourse perspective on language contact in parent–child interaction

Elizabeth Lanza

1. Introduction

The impact of language input on language acquisition has received increasingly more attention in studies of bilingual first language acquisition (De Houwer 1995) although the notion of language input, or for that matter context, is often too vague in current studies. In order to critically investigate the young bilingual child's output, particularly in regard to language contact, we need to come to grips with the input the child receives. Such an investigation warrants a focus on the micro-level of interaction in bilingual acquisition through a discourse perspective on language contact in parent–child (caregiver–child) interaction. Indeed it is important to examine the micro-level of interaction in investigating *any* level of linguistic development by bilingual children, that is, even if the focus of the study is not on interaction, even if we are not looking at language choice *per se* (cf. Lanza 1998a). However, the focus of this chapter will be on the issue of language contact and language choice in conversations between children acquiring two languages simultaneously in families in which each parent speaks a different language to the child.

All children, monolingual as well as bilingual, are *socialized* into community norms for language use and language choice through everyday interactions. The child is not only a little linguist trying to figure out the intricacies of the structure of the language(s) in his or her environment but is also at the same time trying to figure out the basis for the evident variation in language use, particularly in bilingual contexts. Although we can look at the actual forms used in interaction with bilingual children, I would like to argue that we need to examine the indexical value this input can convey, or signal, in interaction. In order to do this, we need to anchor the child's bilingual first language acquisition within a language socialization framework. There is a need for a theoretical framework for analyzing the bilingual child's language input and for relating it to the bilingual child's acquisition and use of his or her two (or more) languages. Levinson (1983: 284) has claimed that conversation is the "matrix for language acquisition". And Cook-Gumperz (1986: 54) has so succinctly stated: "Children's language socialization occurs as part of the continuing history of conversational exchanges that make up daily life". Hence a developmental discourse perspective on language contact in parent–child interaction can provide insight into the child's acquisition of two or more languages from infancy.

A conversationally oriented approach is needed in studies of bilingual acquisition, and the theoretical framework of language socialization as developed in the work of Ochs and Schieffelin (Ochs 1988; Schieffelin 1990; Ochs and Schieffelin 1995) can provide such an approach. According to Schieffelin and Ochs (1986: 163), language socialization refers to "socialization through the use of language" and "socialization to use language". In other words, the processing of linguistic knowledge occurs simultaneously with the processing of social knowledge, with language socialization beginning as soon as an infant has social contact. Through the process of language socialization, the child constructs a social identity and this occurs within interactional contexts, as socialization is an *interactive* process (Schieffelin 1990). The child is thus an active participant in the socialization process.

This chapter will address theoretical and methodological issues involved in the investigation of the micro-level of interaction in bilingual first language acquisition. The chapter will be divided up in the following manner: First, I will present an overview of discourse analytic approaches to the study of linguistic activity and particularly how this has been applied to the study of conversational code-switching, a bilingual activity. The study of bilingual first language acquisition has much to gain from this work as language mixing is an important aspect of bilingual acquisition. Then I will outline how I have applied a conversationally oriented approach within the theoretical framework of language socialization in my own work. This framework anchors itself onto the same theories underlying the study of conversational discourse.

Although I will present examples from other studies of bilingual first language acquisition, the data for my analyses come principally from a longitudinal study of a 2-year-old girl acquiring Norwegian and English in Norway with an American mother and Norwegian father. The parents claimed to use the one person — one language strategy of interaction with their daughter. Audio-taped conversations in dyadic and triadic interactions from just prior to the child's second birthday until the age of 2;7 form the main database supplemented by a parental diary, visits by the researcher, and interviews with the parents (see Lanza 1997). Finally, I highlight some other recent studies of bilingual parent–child interaction and bring up some methodological implications relevant for the study of bilingual acquisition. I want to stress the importance of taking a critical stance to the underlying assumptions in our analytical approaches to examining the child's simultaneous acquisition of two languages in interaction. I wish to argue that what we need is a pragmatic/discourse analytic approach to investigating situated meaning in conversation and the indexical value that discourse strategies convey in conversation between caregivers and bilingual children as they are socialized into the use of two languages.

2.   Discourse analytic approaches to linguistic activity

The language socialization approach is inherently sociolinguistic. Schiffrin (1994: 416) outlines some sociolinguistic assumptions which essentially underly various approaches to discourse that view language as social interaction, including interactional sociolinguistics and conversation analysis. An important initial assumption in this approach is that the analysis of discourse is empirical. Hence we need actual transcripts of face-to-face interaction in order to seriously address the issue of context, not just notes of recorded speech such as diaries of children's language development. Despite the intrinsic value of such records for documenting children's utterances, actual recorded speech is essential for investigating the contextual dimensions of conversational interaction.

The key words that I would like to highlight in regards to the sociolinguistic assumptions of discourse analysis are *contextualization, interactional achievement,* and *sequentiality.* These concepts will figure in the analyses of the data presented below. Context is interactionally achieved, not something that is predetermined (Duranti and Goodwin 1992). In other words, situation is not a predetermined set of norms functioning solely as a constraint on linguistic performance. Participants in conversational interaction continually produce frames for subsequent activities, which in turn create new frames. Participants in an interaction jointly achieve a conversational context. Sequentiality is a key concept here as we trace this achievement in discourse. As for early bilingualism, we may ask how a caregiver and child negotiate across turns a context for language choice in ongoing conversational discourse. Conceptually, this calls into question any claim that a particular interaction is a context for one language or another, before an analysis of the interaction is actually made.

Auer (1984, 1995, 1998), building on Gumperz's (1982) notion of contextualization, has especially contributed to a discourse analytic approach to code-switching or language alternation in the application of conversation analytic principles to bilingual interaction. A contextualization cue can be any aspect of linguistic form which provides a metacommunicative message concerning the relationship between the speakers, signalling the participants' orientation to each other (see Gumperz 1982: Chapter 6). The notion of contextualization cues rests upon sociolinguistic assumptions of discourse analysis. Gumperz's work, moreover, builds on the theories that underly the theoretical framework of language socialization, namely theoretical approaches from symbolic interactionism (Mead 1934) and more recent phenomenological approaches to the study of society (e.g. Berger and Luckman 1966; see Schieffelin and Ochs 1986).

Auer's work, however, represents a somewhat different development of Gumperz's interactional paradigm as he criticizes the taxonomic approach to the functions of code-switching. He argues convincingly for a sequential approach to analysing language alternation as it is only through a sequential analysis that we can unveil the situated meaning of the alternation. As Auer (1995: 123) states so clearly, "The same cue may receive a different interpretation on different occasions", hence we must examine the cue within the conversational context. This is an important point to which we will return in the analyses below. Thus the analyst needs to focus on the sequential development of interaction, since the meanings of contextualization cues unfold as interaction takes its course, and cannot be discussed without reference to the conversational context. Recently, Shin and Milroy (2000) employed Auer's model in their detailed qualitative analysis of the use of code-switching among Korean-English bilingual children in a classroom (see also Li Wei and Milroy 1995).

Within Auer's framework, a useful distinction is drawn between participant-related switching and discourse-related switching. The former is motivated by a need to negotiate the appropriate language for the interaction, taking into account the language preference or competence of the interactants. On the other hand, discourse-related switching occurs "where the new language prototypically evokes a new *frame* or *footing* for the interaction which is then shared by all participants" (Auer 1998: 8). Or as Shin and Milroy

(2000: 370) state, it "can be seen to organize and structure the ongoing conversation with respect to such procedures as turn-taking, topical cohesion, sequencing of activities and repair". Participant-related switching and discourse-related switching are not strictly separated.

The discourse functions of code-switching have received considerable attention in the literature (see Myers-Scotton 1993: Chapter 3, for a review) compared to the processes of language negotiation in participant-related switching, which is the focus of this chapter. Auer (1998: 9) presents a schematization of a language negotiation sequence, as illustrated in Figure 1.

```
. . .
A1
A2        A=language of interaction (convergent choices)
A1
    B2   ← language (re)negotiation starts
    A1
    B2   negotiation sequence (divergent choices)
    A1
    B2
    . . .
    B1   ← language (re)negotiation stops
    B2
    B1   B=language of interaction (convergent choices)
    . . .
```

Figure 1. Language negotiation sequence from Auer (1998: 9)

In the conversational sequence in Figure 1, speakers 1 and 2 are bilingual in languages A and B. In the first three turns we see that speaker 1 and speaker 2 employ convergent language choices, namely that of language A. In other words, both speakers use language A. In the fourth turn, speaker 2 switches over to language B thus opening a language negotiation sequence which continues over the immediately following turns in which speaker 1 and speaker 2 employ divergent language choices, that is, different languages in the interaction. That is, speaker 1 continues using language A while speaker 2 has gone over to language B. Finally, speaker 1 adopts language B thereby making a convergent choice with speaker 2 who had initially opened the language negotiation sequence.

The reasons for the choice of one language or another may relate to greater socio-cultural parameters for the interaction. But as Li Wei (1998: 163) points out, the *why* questions of language alternation can only be addressed after the *how* questions. A focus on the micro-level of interaction does not exclude reference to macro-level phenomena such as social structure or ideology. As Auer (1998: 12–13) claims, "a sequential approach to code-switching does not exclude linking microscopic aspects of conversational organisation to ethnographically documented wider (macroscopic) structures, but rather serves to ground the former in the latter".

What is of interest within a language socialization perspective in bilingual first language acquisition is the negotiation sequence that ensues once the young child presents a divergent language choice. By observing the parent's reaction to the child's mixing, we may unveil the parent's attitudes towards this mixing and hence how the parent socializes the child linguistically. These attitudes may relate to norms within the larger community or even the smaller social unit of the family. In other words, from a language socialization perspective we see that the child's alternation of languages will be met by different reactions depending upon the more mature interlocutor's preferences. The adult socializes the child into a particular interpretation of such an alternation — either as more or less acceptable or as something to be avoided. It is the parent's reactions that may be considered contextualization cues within a language socialization perspective, that serve to contextualize the child's language alternation. Certain responses will become conventionalized as the parent develops a particular interactional style with the child. A discourse perspective to interaction can provide a means for studying the language socialization of bilingual children, for coming to grips with linguistic input, in investigating the social processes in bilingual caregiver–child interactions. The question now is, how can we apply this to bilingual first language acquisition data?

3. Language socialization in the discourse of bilingual first language acquisition

A focus always found in language socialization studies is on language praxis (Duranti 1988). As Ochs (1996: 408) states, "a prevailing perspective in language socialization research is that language practices are socially organized and that, as novices recurrently engage in these practices with more expert members of society, they develop an understanding of social actions, events, emotions, esthetics, knowledgeability, statuses, relationships, and other sociocultural phenomena". Hence the bilingual child is socialized to use his or her languages appropriately, whether this may be a clear separation of languages or language contact through code-switching. Speaking is a continuous process of contextualization (Duranti 1997) and parental responses to mixing function as contextualization cues, signalling whether the interactional context is to be more monolingual or more bilingual in nature. Furthermore, the parent's role as a monolingual or bilingual is contextualized in interaction through his or her responses to the child's mixing (Lanza 1992, 1997). Drawing on Goffman's (1981) theatre metaphor in the presentation of self, we may ask which of the parent's roles as a monolingual or bilingual is on the front stage while the other remains on the backstage revealing itself to various degrees.

I now turn to some examples of language contact, or language mixing, in bilingual first language acquisition and present a discourse perspective for analyzing this mixing. Before analyzing longer stretches of discourse from the data on Siri, I first present various types of shorter focused language negotiation sequences in parent–child conversations, sequences which are initiated by the child's mixing. By *mixing* I refer to the child's use of both languages in discourse. This may be through the use of mixed utterances or through the use of utterances in the other language within the discourse, as illustrated in examples (1) and (2) below.[1]

(1) [Siri (2;3) and her father are changing her doll (Lanza 1997: 264)[2]]

      SIRI   FATHER

→ sånn/ og ny **diaper**/
   'like that/ and new **diaper**'

                                   Og så en ny bleie
                                   'And then a new diaper'

→ **clothes**?/

(2) [Siri (2;0) and her mother are looking at a book (Lanza 1997: 263)]

      SIRI   MOTHER

→ **tiss**?/
   'pee?'

                                     Aw, is he peeing?

   yeah/

Drawing on my own data on bilingual 2-year-olds and other examples in the literature, I have proposed a continuum of discourse strategies or potential contextualization cues on the part of the parent in response to the child's mixing (in Lanza 1992, 1997). These strategies can serve to signal a more or less monolingual or bilingual interactional context. Furthermore, these cues indicate the degree to which the child is compelled by the adult to maintain

Table 1. Parental discourse strategies towards child language mixing (Lanza 1997)

1. *Minimal Grasp Strategy* (Ochs 1988):
   Adult indicates no comprehension of the child's language choice.
2. *Expressed Guess Strategy* (Ochs 1988):
   Adult asks a yes-no question using the other language.
3. Adult Repetition of the content of the child's utterance, using the other language.
4. *A Move On Strategy*: the conversation merely continues.
5. Adult Code Switches.

the use of the one language or the other in conversation. Table 1 lists the parental discourse strategies that can serve to propose a more or less monolingual or bilingual context once a language negotiation sequence is initiated.

As discussed in Lanza (1997: 260–1), the notion of strategy may imply active calculation on the part of the parent. Some discourse strategies may in fact constitute a conscious plan for communication; however, not all discourse strategies are always consciously used. Schiffrin (1984) points out two interpretations of the term *strategy*. On the one hand, "discourse strategies are akin to cognitive or perceptual strategies: models, below the level of awareness, for receiving, organizing, and processing information" (Schiffrin 1984: 956). On the other hand, discourse strategies may be interpreted as "plans to achieve particular goals, analogous to strategies for winning a game (cf. Goffman 1969)".

Studies of conversational code-switching, a particular type of discourse strategy, have indeed shown that even adult bilinguals may be unaware of what language they are using as they are so immersed in the interaction. An analogy can be drawn with the use of discourse strategies in general. Discourse strategies may thus at times operate below the level of consciousness and playback techniques may even surprise the individual of his or her own language use. Therefore, although there may be degrees of consciousness with which the parents employed various discourse strategies, what is of particular interest is the children's response to these strategies, and the discourse the parent and child co-construct and over time the interactional style they create. The child's response to these strategies may indicate the child's perception of the context. The child's degree of mixing can thus be evaluated in relation to the extent to which the parent creates a monolingual or bilingual context with the child, that is, to the extent to which the parent highlights his or her role of a monolingual or a bilingual.

The strategies listed in Figure 2 can be placed on a continuum indicating their potential for making a bid for a monolingual or bilingual context once the child has opened negotiations for a bilingual context through mixing. Note

Monolingual					Bilingual
Context					Context
Minimal grasp	Expressed guess	Adult repetition	Move on strategy	Code-switching	

Figure 2. Parental strategies toward child language mixes (Lanza 1997)

that I employ the word *open*, as negotiations are indeed an interactional process and must be sequentially analyzed.

Let us now consider some examples of these parental strategies in bilingual parent–child interaction. Before presenting language negotiation sequences from my own data, I present examples of each strategy in (3)–(7) from other studies in order to illustrate the applicability of these strategies. In (3) below we find two examples of the minimal grasp as the parent provides minimal support for the child's utterance through a request for clarification, leaving him or her to reformulate the utterance. Döpke (1992) noted in her study that only those bilingual children who were met with so-called high-constraint insisting strategies such as the minimal grasp actively used the minority language.

In the first example we note the effect of the repeated sequencing of the mother's minimal grasp which eventually results in the child's switching to German, the language choice of the mother. This excerpt illustrates quite clearly the need to examine units of relevant discourse. A mere quantification of the child's mixing in the conversation and the parent's response would miss this cumulative effect of the parent's strategy, which is important from a language socialization perspective. In both examples in (3), the parents react verbally to the child's mix. Note that also a non-verbal cue such as silence indicating a lack of comprehension can function as a minimal grasp.

Minimal Grasp Strategy

(3) a. [Giula (2;4): Mother speaks German, Father speaks Italian. They live in Rome. (Taeschner 1983: 201)]
 G: Mami aple.
  'Mommy open'
 → M: Wie bitte?
  'What, please?'
 G: Mami aple.
 → M: Wie bitte?
 G: Mami aple.
 → M: Wie?

G: APLEEEEEEE!!!!
→   M: [covers her ears] Wie bitte?
G: Aufmachen?
'Open?'

b.   [Daniel (2;4) is bilingual in Finnish and Swedish and lives in Sweden. He is talking to his Finnish-speaking mother. (Huss 1991: 120)]
M: mikä tuolla on?
'What is that?'
D: yks **fägel**.
'A **bird**'
→   M: mikä?
'What?'
D: lintu tiinä [pro *siinä*]
'bird there'

In (4) the mother repeats in German with a questioning intonation the content of the child's mix in English. Siri's mother's reply in (2) above is also an example of an expressed guess. With an expressed guess the child can either confirm or disconfirm the guess. Note that with the expressed guess the parent subtly reveals his or her role as a bilingual through the translation of the child's mix.

Expressed Guess Strategy

(4)   [Jacob (2;8) is bilingual in German and English and lives in Australia. He is talking with his German-speaking mother. (Döpke 1992: 95)]
J: do it again
→   M: noch mal?
'again?'
J: yeah.

With a repetition the parent repeats the child's meaning using the other language in a non-question form. (5) below, as well as Siri's father's response in (1), are examples of the repetition strategy.

Adult Repetition

(5)   [MAT (ca. 2;0), bilingual in French and English, lives in Montreal. He is speaking to his French-speaking father. (Nicoladis 1994: 114)]
M: [holds a puzzle piece in the air] plane!
→   F: avion!
'plane'

Note that since a non-question form is used in a repetition, no answer is required of the child. The question/answer pair forms an adjacency pair, a sequentially constrained pair of turns at talk. With such pairs, the occurrence of a first pair-part creates a slot for the occurrence of the second pair-part; a non-occurrence of the second pair-part is recognized as an absence/violation. Evidence for this type of constraint is found in the fact that when a non-occurrence takes place, the first pair-part is repeated. Hence the repetition strategy places less of an interactional demand on the child than the express guess and the minimal grasp.

With the move on strategy the caregiver merely continues the conversation thereby implicitly indicating comprehension and acceptance of the child's mixing. The conversational excerpt in (6) illustrates this strategy.

Move on strategy

(6) [Ken (2;8) tries to ask mother to go and get a ball for him. (Mishina 1997: 101); transcription rendered in CHILDES format)]
    1   K: I want ge:t!
    2   K: I want &g-,
→ 3   M: **jibunde otrinasai.**
    4   'get it by yourself'
    5   K: I want # ge:t.

Finally, with code-switching the parent either switches over completely to the other language as in (7) or employs intra-sentential code-switching.

Code-switching

(7) [Tomas (2;0) and his mother have just finished reading a book. (Lanza 1997: 267)]

TOMAS	MOTHER
	O. K. Are we finished? You wanna go downstairs and have dinner? Are you hungry?
ikke nå/ 'not now'	
→	**Ikke nå? Du, skal vi ned og spise mat?** 'Hey, shall we go downstairs and eat?'

Note that a discourse analysis of language contact in parent–child interaction using these strategies is not an analysis of speech acts as done in Nicoladis and Genesee (1998). Each one of the surface forms delineated in the descriptions of the strategies, and not just code-switching, could in fact be used to perform a multitude of speech acts. In other words, the focus of the analysis is how these response patterns or strategies function in discourse in language negotiation sequences.

4.   A case study of a 2-year-old bilingual child

In Lanza (1997) I traced the bilingual development of a young girl I have named Siri. As noted above, Siri's mother was American and her father, Norwegian. During the period in which I documented her bilingual development, from just prior to her second birthday until she was 2;7, she lived in Norway. An examination of the structure of Siri's mixed utterances revealed that Siri was more or less dominant in Norwegian throughout the entire study. This evaluation was also supported by evidence of her preference for that language, her problems in accessing English lexical items particularly towards the end of the study, and her general grammatical development which was more advanced in Norwegian than English. Her parents also stated that she seemed *stronger* in Norwegian. Despite this, her English developed although her mother was her more or less sole input in that language. Siri mixed grammatically and to a certain extent lexically with her mother while she only mixed lexically with her father. Her grammatical mixing has been analyzed in terms of her dominance in Norwegian (see Lanza 1993, 1997, 2000).

From the age of 2;2, Siri mixed lexically more often with her father than with her mother despite her dominance in Norwegian, the language of her father. For understanding Siri's lexical mixing, a discourse perspective was necessary. Both parents claimed to practice the one-person–one-language strategy of interaction with their child; however, upon closer inspection of the interactional data, I noted that the father employed strategies closer to the bilingual end of the continuum in Figure 2 in response to Siri's lexical mixing while her mother started using those more towards the monolingual end from the time Siri was 2;1. Consider examples (8) and (9) below.

(8)   [Siri (2;2) and her mother are in the kitchen. Her mother is cooking. Siri
is drawing and has prior to this excerpt been singing to herself.]

SIRI	MOTHER
1 mer↑≠mer↑≠mer≠ mer↑≠mer?/ 'more'	
2	More?
3 mer paper/ 'more'	
4	More paper?
5 //yeah]/	//I think] —
6	I think it's in or (.) maybe we don't have any, Siri.
7 (p) no/	
8	(p) No.
9	Well, go to your room and see if you can find it'
10 Mama finde/[3]	
11	Siri run and find it.
12 yeah/	
13	Mama's standin' right here.
14 //Mama løpe]/ 'run'	Mama's got to look//after the food].
15 Mama løpe/ Mama løpe/ Mama løpe/	
16	'What do you want Mama to do?
17 run/	
18	Run.
19 Mama run/	
20	Mama run. OK.

[Siri's mother goes off to get paper.]

Siri's repeated use of the Norwegian function word *mer* 'more' opens the
interaction between Siri who had been singing to herself and her mother who
had been busy cooking dinner. Although the analysis focuses on lexical
mixing, we may note that in lines 2 and 4 the mother responds to Siri's grammatical mixing by an expressed guess strategy, and once Siri confirms in line 5,

the conversation moves on with a convergent language choice. Siri's mother then expands Siri's grammatically mixed utterance in line 11. In line 14 Siri issues a lexical mix which opens a language negotiation sequence. She initially overlaps with her mother's utterance in line 14, and continues repeating her mix in line 15 once she has gained the floor. In line 16 her mother responds with a minimal grasp strategy issued with a high rise intonation pattern. Siri then responds in 17 with the English equivalent of her mix and the conversation continues once again with a convergent language choice. The recurrence of the word *run* serves the discourse function of emphasis of the English item.

Let us now look at an interaction between Siri and her father. Although the interaction in (8) involves free play as opposed to a book-reading interaction in (9), the two interactions are nonetheless comparable as they are typical for the parents' interactional styles.

(9)   [Siri (2;0) and her father are looking at picture books.]

	SIRI	FATHER
1		Hvilken skal du lese da?
		'Which one are you going to read then?'
2	Um:/hm:/**hug**/ **hug**	
3		Å, bamsen får en kos, eller en **hug**, ja.
		'Oh, the teddy bear gets a hug, or a **hug**, yes.'
4		Se, der får bamsen en kos. Ja.
		'Look, the teddy bear gets a hug there. Yes.'
5		Bamsen er rømt hjemmifra.
		'The teddy bear has run away from home.'
6		Det er ingen som vil=
		'There is no one who wants='
7	=det≠det/= 'that'	
8		= leke med den.
		'to play with it.'
9	det / det↑/ 'that'	
10		Ja, så kommer han til en snill pike.
		'Yes, then he comes to a nice girl.'
11		Og så får han en <u>kos</u>.
		'And then he gets a <u>hug</u>.'

12 **hug**↑
13   Mm. En **hug**. En kos.
              'A **hug**. A hug.'
14   Hun vasker bamsen, óg.
              'She's washing the teddy bear, too.'
15   Bamsen er skitten.
              'The teddy bear is dirty.'
16 ja/
    'yes'
17   Mm.
18 skitten↑/
    'dirty'
19   Skitten, ja.
              'Dirty, yes.'

In line 2 Siri makes a divergent language choice and her father initially responds with a repetition of the item in Norwegian. However, he follows up with a reinforcement of the English item. The conversation continues and once again, Siri recycles the English lexical item in line 12. In line 13 her father this time repeats the English approvingly and follows up with the Norwegian equivalent. And once again the conversation continues with convergent language choices. Note that the repetition of each item in the other language by the father may also be considered examples of discourse-related switching for emphasis.

With her mother Siri makes divergent choices which are not accepted. With her father, on the other hand, her divergent choices are integrated in the father's language choice. In (8) Siri's mother responded to Siri's lexical mix with a minimal grasp. In (9) Siri's father responded to the child's mixes with a repetition, yet he also repeated the English equivalent hence signalling the appropriacy of that item. Often he would model the correct adult English pronunciation of Siri's attempted English words in addition to providing the Norwegian equivalent in a repetition. Siri's mother, on the other hand, would not provide such modelling. Micro-analyses of parent–child interaction in Siri's home revealed that Siri's parents had different approaches to their daughter's language socialization. While her father was more open for the use of English throughout the study, her mother followed an English only approach especially from 2;2 as she feared that Siri would lose her English in competition with Norwegian, as noted in her diary on Siri's development.

Important to point out is the fact that each parent used his or her respective language in addressing Siri. Any mix was rather in response to Siri's mixing as noted in (9) above.

The discourse analysis required a developmental perspective as well as sensitivity to the type of mixing. For example, Siri's mother's discourse strategies seemed to vary according to the age of the child and the type of lexical mixing as well. Until Siri was 2;2 her mother modelled the English equivalents of Siri's lexical mixing through her use of the expressed guess and repetition strategies thus providing the equivalent to the child. As for the type of lexical mixing, there was a tendency, across all the periods investigated but especially the later ones, to use a repetition in response to lexical items that were phonetically similar in Norwegian and English such as *milk* and *melk*. This repetition served to provide Siri with a model for pronunciation. Otherwise, particularly from when Siri was age 2;2, Siri's mother would issue a minimal grasp in response to a mix for which Siri knew the English equivalent, the only exception being politeness formulas which were accepted in either language (see Lanza 1997). Language socialization is not instantaneous and hence a developmental perspective on parent–child interactions is mandatory if we are to understand the impact of parental strategies on the child's language mixing. The analysis of parent–child interactions in Siri's family as presented in Lanza (1997), and how they contributed to Siri's language socialization, is essentially a qualitative, interactional, and developmental analysis. The focus of the analysis was on lexical mixing as Siri demonstrated clear signs of overall dominance in Norwegian, the main language in her environment.

5.   A note on the minimal grasp

As noted in the introduction, Auer (1995) has pointed out that the same contextualization cue may receive a different interpretation on different occasions. This comes out especially clearly in the use of the minimal grasp. It is important to point out that minimal grasps can function as requests for clarification which have the *potential* for opening negotiations for a monolingual context. However, these clarification requests are by their nature plurifunctional and must be analysed in relation to the parent's overall interactional style with the child. In (10) and (11) we see how Siri already at the age of 2;2 manages to locate the trouble spot in her utterances in conversation with her mother and repairs them in order to meet her interactional demands. In (10) she increases the volume of her voice and in (11) she extends her reference thereby making it clearer for her mother.

(10)   [Siri (2;2) and her mother are looking at a book (Lanza 1997: 278)]

SIRI	MOTHER
	Where's the kitty cat?
(p) hop/	
	Hm?
hop/	
	Uhuh. It's hopped up in the window. Jumped up in the window.

(11)   [Siri (2;2) is playing with her doll and wants to dress it. (Lanza 1997: 278)]

SIRI	MOTHER
	Clothes?
yeah on/ clothes on/	
clothes on/	
	Hm?
baby clothes on/	

In (12) Siri locates the trouble spot as that of language choice, and repairs her mixed utterance.

(12)   [Siri (2;2) had just clapped her hands. (Lanza 1997: 279)]

SIRI	MOTHER
klappe hand/	
'clap'	
	Hm?
clap hand/	

Siri's mother's recurrent use of *hm?* as a prompt for repair provides an interesting locus for investigating the extent to which Siri exhibited sensitivity to her mother's interactional demands. In the data for Siri at the age of 2;2, her mother used *hm?* 32 times in conversations with her daughter. 29 of these did not involve a mix on the part of Siri. And what is interesting is that there is not a single case in which Siri responds with a mix to the query *hm?* when issued to a non-mix. That is, she interprets the repair cue as a signal to attend to some other aspect of the utterance as exemplified in (10) and (11) above.

Siri's interactions with her father were essentially bilingual in nature so that when her father did use open-ended minimal grasps, she understood the trouble spot to be something else than language mixing as we see demonstrated in (13) taken from a conversation when Siri was 2;7. By this time Siri has already been socialized into a particular interactional style with her father.

(13)   [Siri (2;7) and her father are talking about a visit to her Norwegian grandmother (*Bestemor*) who has been sick. They will be taking some medicine to her.]

SIRI	FATHER
1 Uhuh/⟨?⟩/	
give Bestemor/	
'**give**+e[4] Grandmother'	
2	Hva sier du?
	'What are you saying?'
3 **give** Bestemor det/	
'**give**+e Grandmother that'	
4	Skal vi gi det til Bestemor?
	'Shall we give that to Grand-
	mother?'
5 ja/	
'yes'	
6	Ja.
	'yes'
7 er du syks?	
'are you sicks?'	
8	Om jeg er syk?
	'If I am sick?'
9 ja↑/	
10	Nei, jeg er ikke syk.
	'No, I am not sick.'

After an initial unintelligible utterance, Siri uses a mixed utterance. In reply to her father's minimal grasp in line 2, Siri specifies her reference more clearly in line 3 all the while maintaining the English lexical item in her utterance. In line 4 her father issues an expressed guess to which Siri replies affirmatively. From then on the discourse continues with convergent language choices.

That children can and do isolate the source of trouble spots in a conversation has been documented in the literature. What is a trouble spot has to be analyzed interactionally. Moreover, we saw this clearly with Siri's responses to her mother's minimal grasps in examples (10), (11), and (12). With her father Siri reacted differently. That a young bilingual child does not switch languages upon a minimal grasp does not necessarily mean that he/she has not acquired the competence to make inferences. Socialization is interactional and hence both parties may perceive the context differently. Hence Siri responds differentially to the minimal grasp strategy dependent upon her interlocutor. Thus we see the importance of analyzing situated meaning, as discussed above. What these representative conversational exchanges show is that language socialization is interactive and that the child is not merely a passive recipient of sociocultural knowledge, but rather actively contributes to the meaning and outcome of interactions with others in a social group. Methodological consequences of this would be that an analytic approach that quantifies the use of this strategy across families without taking into account individual children's interactions is inherently incompatible with the theoretical approach that I have advocated in this chapter. Hence an emphasis on the local creation of social meaning constrains somewhat the applicability of quantitative approaches to discourse.

A close look at conversation sequences of language negotiation reveal a number of structural features. Auer (1998: 13) points out that a sequential approach to code-switching serves to ground "microscopic aspects of conversational organisation" in "ethnographically documented wider (macroscopic) structures". The meaning that is attached to language mixing or the alternation of codes is only conveyed as part of the interactive process and hence cannot be discussed without reference to the conversational context. Siri's parents' preferences for Siri's use of the one language or the other are highlighted in conversational sequences of language negotiation, and are thus amenable to sequential analysis. This is precisely why I have done microanalyses of the instances of language mixing for Siri in interactions with each of her parents with the continuum of discourse strategies serving as a heuristic. A qualitative discourse analysis is indeed an analysis, and hence it is unfortunate that such an analysis be referred to as anecdotal.

6. A bilingual conversation with a monolingual?

The continuum of discourse strategies has been especially applied to parent–child interactions not only to follow the child's development within a language socialization perspective but also to understand the context of the child's utterance. This discourse perspective on language contact can indeed be applied to all interactions involving speakers of more than one language, just as language negotiation sequences like those in Figure 1 can occur in any bilingual interaction. However, a conversation between a true monolingual adult speaker (as opposed to one who feigns monolingualism) and a bilingual 2-year-old may actually don some characteristics of a bilingual interaction. In a recording made in the U.S. between Siri (2;0) and her American grandmother (who speaks no Norwegian), the grandmother actually responded to Siri's mixing, that is, indicated comprehension and even repeated some of Siri's Norwegian words. Consider the following example:

(14)   [Siri's mother has gone to pick up her husband at the airport.]

	SIRI	GRANDMOTHER
1		Where did Mama go?
2	Daddy/	
3		What's Daddy coming in on?
4	**fly**/	
	'airplane'	
5		What's Daddy coming in on?
6	huh?/	
7		What's Daddy coming in on?
8	huh?/	
9		An airplane.
10	**fly**/ //**fly**]/	//Air]plane.
	'airplane'	
11	**nei**/ **fly**/	
	'no'	
12		A **fly**.

The first time Siri's grandmother asks her what her father was arriving on, Siri responds with the Norwegian equivalent *fly* (/ fly: /) in line 4. After two unsuccessful attempts to get an answer in lines 5 and 7, she supplies Siri with the response *an airplane*. Avoiding a breakdown in communication, the grandmother eventually repeats Siri's word in line 12 and the conversation moves on. After a few minutes of discourse, the topic was recycled: the grandmother posed the same question and received the same answer from Siri, and the conversation moved on.

In another example Siri's grandmother incorporated Siri's Norwegian utterance without any further negotiation, truly a result of the phonetic similarity between the Norwegian word and the English equivalent, plus the fact that the conversation was about the here-and-now. Why does Siri's grandmother who is a monolingual speaker of English accept some instances of Siri's use of Norwegian? It would seem likely that she wants to avoid communication breakdowns, so that when understanding is not seriously hampered, the conversation can continue. We can ask what effect this may have had on Siri's perception of the context and on her language choices, that is, on Siri's perception of her grandmother's competence in Norwegian. McClure (1981) found that very young bilingual children made binary judgments of linguistic competence — either the interlocutor knows a language, or he or she does not. Hence even conversations with monolinguals must be carefully examined. Conversation is indeed a cooperative endeavor, especially conversation between adult and child where a great deal of interpretation and negotiation is often required on the part of the adult in order to avoid a communication breakdown.

A similar situation to this is reported on in Deuchar and Quay (2000: 105) in which little M at the age of 1;7.12 is in interaction with her grandmother and her mother. M was acquiring English and Spanish in England. Her mother, a native speaker of English, would speak either English or Spanish with her daughter depending upon the others in the interaction. In the interaction with the monolingual English-speaking grandmother, both adults used a move on strategy very frequently, a strategy which I propose contributes to a negotiation of a bilingual context. Deuchar and Quay conclude (2000: 105) that "what at first sight looks like a *bilingual* strategy may in fact be a strategy to avoid communication breakdown, a goal often sought after in conversations between an adult and a child, whether bilingual or monolingual". Whatever the motivation for, or level of awareness of, the use of the move on strategy by the grandmother, it is clear that the result was the negotiation of a bilingual discourse with the child. Interestingly, Deuchar and Quay (2000: 106) state that the monolingual grandmother's tendency to be less insistent upon a monolingual conversation than was the case for the child's Spanish-speaking yet bilingual father may explain why there was an overall greater tendency for the child to produce Spanish words in an English context than for English words to be produced in a Spanish context. Another important aspect of some of the interactions in the study labelled as English-context sessions, however, is that they were not dyadic but rather triadic with both the grandmother and the bilingual mother in interaction with the young girl M.

7. Dyadic vs. triadic interactions

This issue of the impact of the participants in an interaction is an important aspect of conversational discourse — the *participation framework* (Goffman 1981). Schiffrin (1990: 241) defines participation framework as "a set of positions which individuals within perceptual range of an utterance may take in relation to what is said". Those individuals in the participation framework whom the speakers know are there, but who have not been ratified as participants, may be referred to as *overhearers*, and then there are the *eavesdroppers*. Ratified participants in an interaction include the addressed recipient and the unaddressed recipient, or *auditor*. An auditor is thus part of the interaction, as opposed to the *overhearer*. And although a speaker may address another participant in an interaction directly, the *auditor* is still part of the interaction. In a study on language style and audience design, Bell (1984) revealed that third persons including *overhearers* as well as *auditors*, who are ratified participants in the conversation, affect style and hence language choice to a lesser but regular degree. Speakers, however, provide primary accommodation to their addressee.

In a dyadic conversation, identifying the recipient of an utterance may pose no problems. In triadic parent–child interactions, however, can we assume that conversation is merely a succession of dyadic exchanges? The child may, for example, address both parents simultaneously, and likewise the parent may be speaking to the other parent and child at the same time. An *auditor*, who is a ratified participant must not be treated as an *overhearer*, thus implying that the conversational exchange is merely dyadic. Hence using triadic interactions to form dyadic models of communication assumes a dyadic nature in multi-party interactions which indeed may not be the case. From a language socialization perspective, we may ask whether the interactional styles and roles displayed in dyadic parent–child interaction are similar to those in triadic interactions, particularly in the case of language mixing (Lanza 1996).

The analysis I presented above of the Siri data was on the basis of dyadic interactions. The triadic interactions in the Siri data are mainly dinner table conversations. Dinnertime is an important time of the day in the family life of many, a time for intense interaction as members discuss past, present and future events and as such, dinnertime is an important arena for language socialization (Ochs and Taylor 1992). In Siri's family, both languages are used at the dinner table, and that Siri uses language choice to single out her addressee is evident in many cases. In contrast with her communicative strategies in dyadic interaction, Siri's mother would actually encourage Siri's use of Norwegian especially by prompting her to tell her father about the day's events; hence she would elicit Norwegian for Siri's father to respond to. Consider example (15).

(15) [Siri (2;3) and her parents are eating dinner and talking about Siri's skiing earlier that day and a skiing trip when both parents had fallen.]

	SIRI	PARENTS
1		F: **Både Mamma og Pappa har nok falt.**
		'Both Mama and Papa have fallen.'
2	**// jeg falt]/**	M: **//Ja].**
	'I fell'	'Yes.'
3		F: **Ja, du falt du óg.**
		'Yes, you fell, you too.'
4		M: You went all the way back past our house and to the garage. On skis today.
5	fall/	
6		M: Mm. You fell sometimes.
7	**nesten/nesten/nesten/**	
	'almost/almost/almost/'	
8		F: **Nesten?**
		'Almost?'
9	ja/	
	'yes'	
10		M: Almost what?
11	almost fall/	

As we see in (15), all three members of the family co-construct the narrative of Siri's skiing escapade. Siri's mother does not respond to Siri's use of Norwegian lexical items in lines 2 and 7, rather she allows the father to follow up. In line 10 she responds with an expressed guess strategy, following up on the father's query in line 8. In other interactions, Siri's mother could also function as an interpreter for Siri when her father didn't understand even if this meant repeating Siri's utterance in Norwegian.

The distinction between dyadic and triadic (or multiparty) interactions is an important one with methodological consequences. Separating these two main types of interactions in the Siri data revealed a difference in the mother's strategies dependent upon whether or not Siri's Norwegian-speaking father was present. This in turn provided a more differentiated picture of Siri's language socialization in the home. The parents (especially her mother) responded in differential ways. In triadic conversations Siri's mother would display her bilingual identity and usually move on in the conversation allowing the father to pick up on Siri's Norwegian bids for conversation although she would also at times provide English equivalents for Norwegian items as exemplified in line 10 in the example above. This points out the need to build dyadic models of communication on dyadic interactions only and not on interactions when both parents are present. Triadic interactions are not merely a series of dyadic exchanges. Had a dyadic model of interaction between Siri and her mother been developed on the basis of triadic conversations, a very different picture would have emerged than the one depicted in the dyadic conversations. Hence a discourse perspective on language contact in parent–child interaction, or in any interaction, involves sensitivity to the participation framework of the conversation.

8. Some other studies of early bilingualism

Other studies of bilingual first language acquisition lend support to the importance of adopting a language socialization perspective and thereby examining the micro-level of interaction in parent–child conversations. As noted above, Döpke (1992) stresses the importance of what she calls *insisting strategies* (more or less corresponding to the minimal grasp strategy, including requests for translation). The only children in her study who acquired active command of the minority language were those met with these high constraint insisting strategies. This aspect of interaction seemed to be more decisive than the child-centered mode of interaction on which her book focuses.

Both Garau (1996) and Mishina (1997) have examined parent–child interaction based on the approach in Lanza (1992), that is presented in this chapter. In Garau's (1996) study of a Catalan-English child, both parents used strategies that were more bilingually oriented. Interestingly, however, as the child approached the age of 3, the English-speaking father changed his interactional style considerably, and started using more monolingually oriented strategies towards the child's use of Catalan. As Garau (1996: 326) points out, "Andreu responded to his father's change in interactional style with a dramatic progression in his active use of English". The father was persistent enough in his use of requests for clarification to make the child aware that the trouble spot in the conversation was mixing, but at the same time he was flexible enough not to endanger communication with him at any time, as she states. Mishina's (1997) study of the early bilingual development of two Japanese-English bilingual children states specifically in her conclusion that although the parents' adherence to his/her native language appeared to play a role, the analyses revealed that the parental response strategies to the children's mixing best explain the different language choice patterns in the children's speech with each of their parents. Mishina (1997: 162) states: "Parental response strategy may be the most crucial factor contributing to the strict separation of the two languages according to the interlocutor". In other words, it was not merely the fact that the parents each only used his or her language, rather the indexical value of the response strategy to the child's language mixing played an important role.

Another study (Christiansen 1995) which attempted to sort out various types of mixing and resorted to a discourse perspective involves another 2-year-old child, bilingual in Norwegian and English, who also had an American mother and a Norwegian father. What Christiansen found was that of the 307 mixed utterances in the corpus, 215 involved the combination of Norwegian grammatical morphemes with English lexical morphemes, thus indicating the child's dominance in Norwegian (cf. Petersen 1988), similar to Siri. Petersen (1988) had proposed that the directionality of mixing would be a strong indicator of language dominance. Christensen found, however, that 92 mixed utterances in the data involved the combination of English grammatical morphemes with Norwegian lexical morphemes. By looking at the use of these mixed utterances in interaction, she noticed that those involving Norwegian grammatical morphemes occurred in interactions with the father and the mother while those utterances involving English grammatical morphemes only occurred in interactions with the mother. Hence the child was dominant in Norwegian, but why did he use Norwegian lexical morphemes with his English-speaking mother? An analysis of the parents' discourse strategies, similar to the analysis presented above, showed that both parents used response strategies that were *bilingually* oriented, that is, that opened up for lexical mixing, and were contexts in the code-switching mode (Grosjean 1998). This case shows us the importance of examining the interrelationship between the child's linguistic development and his language socialization within which this development is embedded. A discourse-analytic approach provides the means for investigating this.

Recently, Nicoladis and Genesee (1998) have taken issue with the findings in Lanza (1992). Whereas my study focused on the bilingual development of a young girl in a Norwegian-American family in Norway, Nicoladis and

Genesee's study was on bilingual family communication in bilingual Montréal. The results of Nicoladis and Genesee's study did not support what they refer to as *the parental discourse hypothesis*, as originally proposed in my work (Lanza 1992). Nicoladis and Genesee suggest that the different sociolinguistic context between the two studies may explain the different results, that is, a case of family bilingualism as opposed to societal bilingualism. This is an interesting hypothesis concerning the impact of the ambient input. However, language negotiation can occur in all bilingual contexts in the context of *societal* bilingualism as well as *family* bilingualism. The negotiation of language choice/language context occurs in any potentially bilingual encounter, not just in parent–child conversations (see Auer 1998). Thus in societal bilingualism the analysis would then require investigating more types of interaction in which the young child engages, in order to gain a comprehensive picture of the child's language socialization into the use of two languages.

Nonetheless it is important to recall, as pointed out in Lanza (1999), that the analytical methods we employ in our research reflect our theoretical assumptions. Indeed Schiffrin (1997: 88) points out "that the methods used to analyze discourse stem from implicit theoretical assumptions about the nature of language, the goals of linguistic inquiry, and the complex of relationships among cognition, language, communication, social life, and culture".

Nicoladis and Genesee's (1998) study is interesting in its attempts to quantify results across a larger sample of children; however, it is neither a developmental nor an interactional study and as such they operate with different theoretical assumptions as implied in their analysis. Hence their analytical approach is not in line with the language socialization approach that I have advocated. Pooling elements of discourse across various developmental periods and conversations involving different interlocutors results in numbers large enough to quantify. However, such quantification may fail to capture the true significance of discourse and its impact on language socialization. Indeed in Lanza (1999), a recalculation of Siri's data according to the criteria carefully described in Nicoladis and Genesee (1998), I obtained the same results as they did, that is, no relationship between parental discourse strategy and mixing rate. However, an indepth interactional and developmental analysis of the data as done in Lanza (1997) has shown that that is not what is going on in Siri's family.

My study of Siri indicated that mixing rates varied developmentally, with more mixing with her mother initially. Moreover, similar to Garau's (1996) study, especially the mother's strategy towards Siri's lexical mixing changed from when Siri was 2;0 to 2;1, and this corresponded to the decrease in Siri's mixing. At this point Siri's mother felt that Siri should be aware of her two languages and she started to negotiate more of a monolingual context with her child. Siri's mother feared that Siri would not acquire English. Note that language socialization is an interactive and developmental process also involving changing parental beliefs and attitudes towards the child's developing language competence (see also De Houwer 1998c). More work both quantitative as well as qualitative should be done to test the approach advocated in this chapter, although as noted above, there are caveats to heed in regard to quantification in discourse. Moreover, I will hold that developmental and interactional perspectives are essential for determining the extent to which parental discourse strategies have an impact on the child's language choice, regardless of whether we have family bilingualism or societal bilingualism.

9. Conclusion

In this chapter I have presented a discourse perspective on language contact in parent–child interactions. With a view towards understanding the child's language socialization in the family, we should examine everyday conversations in order to obtain insight into the extent to which the parents encourage or discourage language mixing. The analyses presented were of language negotiation sequences, focusing on participant-related switching. I have argued that such analyses must be sensitive to issues of contextuality, sequentiality, and interactional achievement in discourse. These aspects must also be included in any analysis investigating the interrelationship between parental discourse and bilingual child language mixing, at the micro-level of interaction.

Auer (1995: 128) has stated that "due to undefined situations or non-determined language choices, processes of language negotiation occur (and are open to conversation analytic treatment)". This we have seen in the examples from the parent–child interaction in Siri's home. The young bilingual child is in the process of learning to define situations within the home. Language socialization is a process in which the child through interaction is socialized into conversational styles relevant for the community he or she is growing up in, both the community of the family and that of the larger society. Hence we must follow these conversational exchanges from a developmental perspective as language socialization is not instantaneous. The effect may not be immediate particularly in the very early stages of language acquisition.

There has been a tendency in studies of bilingual first language acquisition to focus on dyadic interactions, and in some cases to treat multi-party interactions as a series of dyadic exchanges. We need to investigate the social embedding of the young bilingual child's language acquisition in interaction, by taking into account the multiplexity of that interaction. The study of bilingual first language acquisition can draw a lot of insight from theoretical approaches in discourse analysis and studies of conversational code-switching. The language socialization approach provides us with the necessary theoretical framework for analyzing the micro-level of interaction in bilingual acquisition.

In Siri's family each parent used his or her respective language with the child. The analyses that I presented focused on how the parents responded to Siri's mixing, hence a focus on participant-related switching. In other bilingual families the parents will indeed initiate mixing in conversation with their child. In this case we will need to carefully examine discourse-related switching in addition to participant-related switching, in the terms of Auer's model. Such a discourse perspective will thus render a more comprehensive picture of the bilingual child's language socialization in families in which the child is actually socialized into code-switching.

Notes

* I am grateful to Peter Auer, Li Wei, and the editors for helpful comments and suggestions on an earlier version of this chapter.

1. Auer's model focuses on language alternation clearly exemplified in (2). From a language socialization perspective, it is the use of the other language, also within a mixed utterance, that is of interest in order to see how open the caregiver is for the child's mixing in discourse and how more of a monolingual or bilingual context is negotiated.

2. The transcription conventions used in the examples from Lanza (1997) are noted in the appendix at the end of the chapter.

3. A Norwegian verbal inflection is attached to the English verb. See Lanza (1997: 107–14) for a discussion of the problems of interpretation for this form.

4. Cf. note 3.

Appendix: Transcription conventions used

Note that child utterances in my data are presented in a separate column adjacent to adult utterances, so that the reader may clearly see each participant's contribution to the conversation (also see Ochs 1979).

bold	forms written in bold type indicate language mixing in dyadic conversations. In triadic conversations, bold forms indicate one language in contrast with the other.
→	points to the focus of attention
/	marks child's utterance boundary (determined by intonation)
//]	overlapping:
	// placed at beginning of overlap
	] placed at end of overlapped utterances
=	latching: placed between utterances with no time gap
≠	latching between child utterances
⟨?⟩	indicates unintelligible utterance
↑	marks low rise intonation
′	high rise intonation as in an echo question
(.)	slight pause
(p)	piano, softly spoken utterance
::	lengthened syllable, each colon counting as one beat
hug	underlining to mark stress

CHAPTER 9

Bilingual children's repair strategies during dyadic communication

Liane Comeau and Fred Genesee

1. Introduction

The simultaneous acquisition of two languages during early childhood is a common phenomenon that has recently received considerable scientific attention (see De Houwer 1995, for a review). While important advances have been made in our understanding of bilingual language acquisition as a result of this research, most research has focused on children's ability to differentiate their two languages and on their syntactic development (Döpke 1998; Paradis to appear; Paradis and Genesee 1996; Meisel 1994a; Müller 1999). Little attention has been paid to the development of their communicative competence, that is, how bilingual children learn the various pragmatic abilities necessary for effective communication.

Young children learn more than a linguistic code when they acquire language; they also acquire a number of skills that allow them to communicate with others. For example, they learn how to participate in conversations, how to use different genres of language in different contexts (e.g. formal vs. colloquial language), and how to clarify their utterances when others fail to understand them. Likewise, children who grow up learning two languages learn more than two linguistic codes; they acquire the same communication skills as monolingual children and, in addition, those skills that are specific to bilingual communication. For instance, bilingual children must learn to make decisions about which language(s) to use with their interlocutors and, in particular, with interlocutors who understand only one language. While several studies have shown that bilingual children can make appropriate language choices when speaking with bilinguals and monolinguals (e.g. De Houwer 1990; Genesee, Nicoladis and Paradis 1995; Genesee, Boivin and Nicoladis 1996; Lanza 1997; Meisel 1994a; Padilla and Liebman 1975;

Saunders 1988), little is known about the specific cues bilingual children use to make such language choices.

The research reported in this chapter explored the development of bilingual children's communicative competence by examining their ability to repair communication breakdowns. All children experience breakdowns during dyadic communication for multiple reasons — speaking too softly, pronouncing words inaccurately, poor lexical choice, or providing vague explanations. Breakdowns in communication owing to these problems typically elicit feedback in the form of clarification requests. Such requests are not always specific or explicit, so children often need to infer the cause of the breakdowns in order to select appropriate repair strategies. For bilingual children, language choice is an additional possible cause of breakdowns. Thus, bilingual children must determine whether their interlocutor's requests for clarification are intended as requests for a change in language or for another type of repair if they are to reply appropriately.

While examples extracted from case studies suggest that young bilingual children can repair communication breakdowns due to language choice by translating their utterances (De Houwer 1990; Lanza 1997; Jarovinskij and Fabricius 1987; Vihman and McLaughlin 1982), this ability has not been investigated systematically. Before articulating the precise goals of the present study, we review extant research on bilingual children's communicative competence and relevant findings on monolingual children's ability to respond to their interlocutors' feedback.

1.1 Bilingual children's communicative competence

A central issue in bilingual acquisition research has been whether young bilingual children go through a stage when their two language systems are fused or whether they can differentiate their languages early on. This has important implications for communicative competence as making any kind of language choice requires that children have two languages to choose from. The fact that many bilingual children code-mix (that is, they use elements and structures from both of their languages within the same utterance or conversation) has been interpreted by some as evidence for fusion of their linguistic systems (e.g., Volterra and Taeschner 1978; Redlinger and Park 1980; Vihman 1985). However, recent studies have challenged this interpretation and argue that bilingual children may code-mix, not because their linguistic systems are fused, but for largely proficiency-based reasons, such as filling in gaps in their vocabulary (Quay 1995; see also Genesee 1989). Other explanations related to parental discourse strategies have also been suggested (Lanza 1997).

Genesee *et al.* (1995) compared French–English bilingual 2-year-olds' language use with each of their parents. In the five participating families, English was the mother's language and French was the father's language. These parents used mostly their native language when speaking with their children. Although the children mixed their languages when speaking with their parents, they used a higher proportion of the mother's language with their mothers than with their fathers, and vice-versa for the father's language. Such pragmatic differentiation constitutes evidence that bilingual children as young as 2 years of age have separate language systems and suggests that they can appropriately associate each of their languages with one of their parents (see also Goodz 1994; Lanza 1992, 1997). This association may take place over time as a result of continuously hearing each parent speak one language. While learning to use both languages appropriately within one's family is a critical aspect of bilingual children's communicative competence, bilingual children must also learn to make appropriate language choices with unfamiliar interlocutors.

Unlike monolingual children, who generally interact with adults who are more linguistically competent, bilingual children can encounter adults who only speak and understand one language, and in this sense they are less competent than the children. To communicate with such adults, bilingual children must have the ability to make on-line adjustments in their language use that reflect their interlocutor's linguistic proficiency. Genesee *et al.* (1996) investigated whether young bilingual children possess this ability. They observed four French–English bilingual 2-year-olds on separate occasions while they played with each parent as well as with an unfamiliar monolingual adult. As in the study by Genesee and his colleagues (1995), the children used their languages differentially and appropriately with their parents. Moreover, three of the children adjusted their language use to accommodate the unfamiliar interlocutor: They used a higher proportion of the experimenter's language with the experimenter than with the parent who spoke the same language as the experimenter. This suggests that young bilingual children are sensitive to the linguistic proficiency of others, even unfamiliar others, and can adjust their language use on-line in accordance with their perceptions. However, research is needed to investigate in more detail the circumstances under which they can adjust their language use and their understanding of cues for language change.

The present study further investigates young bilingual children's communicative competence by examining their repairs of communication breakdowns.

We were especially interested in their ability to repair breakdowns in communication due to language choice and in their ability to differentiate such breakdowns from breakdowns due to other causes. Unlike language-based breakdowns, the latter are experienced by both bilingual and monolingual children. Monolingual children's ability to repair communication breakdowns and related communication skills, such as their understanding of their interlocutors' feedback, their sensitivity to the needs of their interlocutors, and their ability to select relevant means of meeting those needs, have been the object of much research. This literature provides an essential framework for investigating bilingual children's repairs of communication breakdowns.

1.2 Monolingual children's communication skills

In the same way as young bilingual children are sensitive to the linguistic proficiency of others and can adjust their language choice accordingly, monolingual preschoolers have been found to be sensitive to characteristics of their interlocutors and to be capable of taking these characteristics into account when communicating with them. For example, Gelman and Shatz (1977) have shown that 4-year-olds are sensitive to younger children's limited abilities — they use shorter utterances and more attention-getting devices and directives when speaking to 2-year-olds than when speaking to peers and adults. Menig-Peterson (1975) also found that 3- and 4-year-olds are capable of modifying their explanations as a function of the amount of knowledge they share with their interlocutor. When describing an event to an adult, the children they studied provided more information to naive listeners than to listeners who were present when the event in question took place. Similar findings have been obtained by other studies investigating children's ability to take into account the extent of their listener's knowledge or their perspective when communicating with them (Maratsos 1973; Perner and Leekam 1986; Peterson, Danner and Flavell 1972). The ability to adapt one's communication strategies in accordance with the needs of others is an important component of communicative competence and, moreover, it plays an important role in more complex discourse, such as responding to the feedback of one's interlocutors and repairing breakdowns in communication.

Communicative competence entails responsivity to feedback from one's interlocutors concerning the effectiveness or appropriateness of one's message. Clarification requests in particular play a critical role in regulating conversation, and children need to learn the conversational rules for using and interpreting these requests. Two classic studies have shown that children can integrate clarification requests and responses to requests in their conversations from a young age. Gallagher (1977), for example, observed children at Brown's Stages I, II, and III while they were playing with an experimenter who asked *What?* every three minutes. Children from all three stages seemed to understand that such requests required a response, and they provided adequate responses, such as repeating or revising their initial utterance. She found that the children seldom responded inappropriately (e.g., by changing the subject), and they rarely ignored the experimenter's requests. The more linguistically advanced children (Stage II) were capable of using a wider range of responses than the Stage I children (see also Konefal and Fokes 1984). Garvey's (1977) observations of 2- to 5-year-olds' conversations revealed that they could respond appropriately to each other's clarification requests and were capable of embedding breakdown-repair sequences in their conversations without disrupting turn-taking, much like adults do; that is, the children who made clarification requests gave the floor back to their conversational partners once their requests were answered. Thus, it appears that young children have a good grasp of the rules for using clarification requests.

As noted earlier, children experience multiple types of breakdowns when communicating with others. Consequently, they receive multiple and varied forms of feedback from their conversational partners: requests for clarification, requests for more information, feedback indicating that the meaning of their utterances was incorrectly interpreted, etc. To investigate whether young children recognize that different types of feedback require different types of responses, Wilcox and Webster (1984) examined 17 to 24 month-old children's responses to two types of feedback. In one condition, the experimenter responded to the children's requests for objects as if they were declarative statements, a form of indirect feedback indicating that the interlocutor did not correctly understand the intent of the child's utterance. The children's preferred strategy in this case was to reformulate their initial utterance, presumably because they recognized that the intent of their original utterance had been misunderstood and so they needed to reconvey this intent in a different way. In the second condition, the experimenter made a clarification request that did not require a specific response (i.e. *What?*). The children did not favor a particular response, suggesting that they understood that this was a generic request that did not focus on a particular cause for the breakdown. In a similar study, Marcos and Bernicot (1994) found that children as young as 18 months of age were capable of providing different responses to three types of feedback from an adult experimenter. Taken together, these findings suggest that children's responses to their interlocutors are influenced by the form of the feedback they receive.

Researchers have investigated whether children's responses are also influenced by other aspects of the situation, such as characteristics of their interlocutors. Tomasello, Farrar and Dines (1984) compared the responses of children in Brown's Stages I and II to specific clarification requests (i.e. *What do you want?*) in two contexts: while playing with their mothers and with an unfamiliar experimenter. They found that the Stage I and Stage II children's responses were guided by different factors. The Stage II children relied on the form of the clarification request in that they provided only the specific information that was requested by their interlocutors. Their familiarity with the interlocutor (mother vs. unfamiliar experimenter) did not influence their responses. For their part, the Stage I children did not seem to appreciate that the interlocutor's request called for a specific response, as they often provided more information in their responses than was required (e.g. by adding novel lexical items), especially when responding to the unfamiliar interlocutor. It appears that they assumed that the unfamiliar adult required more clarification than their mother. Thus, they appeared to rely on the familiarity of their interlocutor when making a response rather than on the form of the request.

In a subsequent study, Anselmi, Tomasello and Acunzo (1986) compared children's responses to two types of clarification requests: the generic request *What?*, and specific requests, such as *You went where?* or *You did what?*. The children were 1;8 to 3;8 years of age. As in the previous study by Tomasello and his colleagues (1984), the children were observed on separate occasions while playing with their mother and with an unfamiliar adult. Anselmi and colleagues found that most of the children responded differentially to the two types of clarification requests. In response to the specific queries, the children tended to provide only the information that was required, thereby indicating that they were sensitive to the specificity of the request. This contrasted with the high number of repetitions the children used in response to the generic question *What?*. Repetition is a reasonable response to this question since it often indicates that one's utterance was not heard. The difference in the children's responses to the two types of clarification requests was more pronounced when they interacted with their mothers than with the unfamiliar interlocutors.

The combined findings of the studies on monolingual children suggest that they rely on characteristics of their interlocutors as well as the form of the feedback they receive when formulating a response to feedback concerning their utterances. These studies indicate that preschool children develop a wide range of communication skills. At the same time, research has revealed additional abilities when children are given more than one opportunity to respond by conversational partners who provide feedback for two or more consecutive turns (that is, they answer children's responses to a request for clarification with another request, thereby indicating that they require additional clarification). Researchers who examined young monolingual children's responses to consecutive clarification requests during conversations have observed phenomena that do not occur in simpler exchanges. Langford (1981) studied conversations between 4-year-olds and their caregivers and found that children often persisted in answering their interlocutors' requests until they were satisfied that their intent had been understood, suggesting that children are compelled to put effort into getting their meanings across and accommodating their conversational partners. In a similar study, Spilton and Lee (1977) observed naturally-occurring breakdown-repair sequences in four-year-old dyads. They argue that observing children as they make successive attempts to respond to clarification requests provides useful information about their ability to cooperate with their interlocutor. When asked more than one question concerning a failed communication attempt, children are forced to evaluate why their previous response has not been sufficient to clarify their utterance and to make other attempts at repairing the breakdown. Indeed, the responses of the 4-year-olds examined by Spilton and Lee changed as a function of both the form of the request and of the position of the request within the sequence.

Brinton, Fujiki, Loeb and Winkler (1986) also explored children's ability to answer sequences of clarification requests by examining their responses to three consecutive non-specific requests during a referential communication task. They found that all children responded appropriately to the first request, but preschool-aged children responded less frequently to the second and third requests than did older children. It is possible that the younger children lacked the linguistic ability to provide other responses, or perhaps they could not determine what kind of additional information to provide. These possibilities could be tested by investigating whether young children can respond to a second or third clarification request if these requests explicitly state what kind of information is needed.

In sum, the extant research on monolingual children indicates that even before children acquire their native language fully, they attain relatively high levels of communicative competence. More specifically, they master important conversational skills, such as the ability to repair communication breakdowns, and they are capable of responding differentially to various types of feedback.

These findings suggest that children are aware that breakdowns in communication can occur for a number of reasons and they are capable of inferring probable causes for such breakdowns. Furthermore, in many cases they can provide responses that are appropriate given the needs of their interlocutors.

1.3   Goals of the present study

The present study contributes to this body of research in a unique way by investigating the repair strategies of children for whom language choice is an additional cause of communication breakdowns. During conversations between a monolingual adult and a bilingual child, the same clarification request from an adult can indicate either that the child needs to translate or reformulate his/her utterance in the other language or that the child should attempt to repair the breakdown without changing language (e.g. by repeating his/her initial utterance in whole or in part or by reformulating it). Young bilingual children's ability to infer the intent of their interlocutor's clarification requests was investigated by comparing their repairs of both breakdowns that were due to their language choice (language-based breakdowns) and breakdowns that occurred for other reasons (other breakdowns). We used consecutive clarification requests ranging from non-specific to explicit to investigate whether the children would make appropriate repairs in response to non-specific clarification requests or whether they would need explicit feedback concerning the cause of the breakdowns. If children translate or rephrase their initial utterances in their other language only when attempting to repair language-based breakdowns and are able to do so in response to non-specific clarification requests, this would constitute evidence that the children can readily identify language choice as the cause of communication breakdowns. This would be an impressive demonstration of children's sensitivity to the specific needs of their interlocutors and would contribute to our understanding of the development of bilingual children's communicative competence.

2.   Method

2.1   Participants

Eighteen French–English bilingual children from the Montreal area participated in this study. There were twelve 3-year-olds (6 girls and 6 boys) and six 5-year-olds (three girls and three boys). The number of 5-year-olds is relatively small because we quickly noticed that they reached ceiling on our measures. The results concerning this age group will thus be described only briefly. All the children, except one, were acquiring French and English from their parents in the home since birth. The exception was a 3-year-old girl (CEC) whose parents used only French in the home, but she had been attending an English daycare full-time since she was 9 months old. In most of the other families, French was the native language of one parent and English the native language of the other. Two of the parents were raised bilingually and considered both French and English to be their native languages. The parents claimed that they used their native language most of the time when addressing their children.

All the children used both languages spontaneously, but few were equally fluent in both according to parental reports. They were not regularly exposed to other languages, although some children had some infrequent exposure to

Table 1. Descriptive data on participants

Child	Age	Language used by experimenter	Child's MLU* in experimenter's language	PPVT (English)	EVIP (French)
ALX	3;2	French	2.0 (79)	121	141
CAR	3;4	French	3.2 (382)	97	100
CEC	3;0	English	1.6 (231)	75	82
CLA	3;2	English	2.7 (144)	109	105
JIA	3;2	English	3.2 (225)	106	103
JUL	3;2	English	2.5 (317)	67	129
JUS	3;5	English	2.5 (451)	91	88
KEL	3;5	French	4.1 (175)	95	97
MAR	3;5	French	2.4 (77)	96	76
NIC	3;2	French	2.6 (236)	104	87
NIS	3;5	French	4.0 (143)	118	105
OLI	3;2	English	5.1 (226)	116	78
Mean	3;3		3.0	99.6	99.3
AMA	5;6	English	5.0 (418)	100	123
BEN	5;1	French	4.6 (141)	73	137
COL	5;5	English	4.3 (488)	83	103
EMI	5;4	French	2.5 (154)	99	80
FEX	5;8	English	2.5 (135)	83	120
NER	5;0	French	2.9 (367)	111	66
Mean	5;4		3.6	91.5	104.8

Note: Number of utterances on which MLU is based is provided in parentheses

a third language when visiting their grandparents. The parents reported that the children had no known hearing or speech problem, nor were they suffering from any kind of developmental delay or disorder. Refer to Table 1 for a summary of the children's ages, their MLU's (based on their utterances during a play session with an adult interlocutor), and standardized scores on English and French receptive vocabulary measures (the *Peabody Picture Vocabulary Test*, PPVT-R, by Dunn and Dunn (1981), and its French adaptation, the *Echelle de vocabulaire en images Peabody*, EVIP, by Dunn, Thériault-Whalen and Dunn (1993)).

2.2 Procedure

Each child was visited at home on two occasions. The order of visits was counterbalanced. The receptive vocabulary tests were administered during one visit by a bilingual research assistant or the first author, who is also bilingual. This person also administered other tasks, but only the vocabulary measures will be discussed for the purposes of this report. These measures were used to get a rough measure of the children's ability in both languages. They were chosen because they can be administered quickly, and normative data are available for both languages. The children's scores fell within monolingual norms in at least one of their two languages, with half of the children performing within or above norms in both languages. Although great caution must be used when using monolingual norms for bilingual children (Umbel, Pearson, Fernandez and Oller 1992), it is striking that so many of their scores fell within norms developed for children acquiring only one language. This suggests that their receptive vocabulary in each language was not greatly influenced by the simultaneous acquisition of another language. Similar findings have been reported by Pearson, Fernandez and Oller (1993) and Umbel and colleagues.

During the other visit, the children were filmed for up to one hour by an observer (the person who administered the vocabulary tasks) while playing freely with an unfamiliar experimenter (either the first author or a trained research assistant). The researchers brought some toys to the families' homes (e.g. puzzles, sticker books and stuffed animals), but the children's toys were often used as well. Most parents left the room once the children felt comfortable with the experimenter. Those who preferred to stay nearby were instructed to limit their interactions with the child as much as possible and they were told not to help the children answer the experimenter's clarification requests. The observer who filmed the session rarely spoke, and on those few occasions she mainly used the language in which she was addressed. The experimenter used only the child's non-dominant language (the language typically used less often by the child during daily activities; this language coincided with the language in which the child was considered to be least advanced, as reported by the parents). The non-dominant language was chosen on the assumption that this would increase the child's use of the other language and, thus, incur more instances of language-based breakdowns. While parental reports are generally not deemed to be highly reliable, they were sufficient for our purposes here as it was not critical to observe the children using their non-dominant language. Incidentally, however, children's performance on the receptive vocabulary measures were consistent with parental reports in many cases. For the most part, the differences between each child's scores was negligible (less than the standard error of measurement) or went in the expected direction. Only three of the children performed better in their so-called non-dominant language on these tests.

While the experimenters who played with the children were not monolingual speakers of the children's non-dominant language, they were native speakers of this language. They made every effort to act as though they did not understand the children when they used their dominant language (hereafter referred to as the wrong language), nor did they use that language with anyone while in the children's presence. The fact that the experimenters were bilingual raises the possibility that the children noticed that their interlocutor did, in fact, understand both languages. However, during pilot testing, we observed that it was more difficult for monolingual experimenters to determine the language of a child's utterance than it was for bilingual experimenters. Since the language used by the children dictates the kind of clarification requests to be made by the experimenter, it was important that the experimenters be capable of easily identifying the language spoken by the child. In addition, bilingual experimenters could better judge whether the children provided satisfactory repairs of language-based breakdowns and, thus, could better determine when to stop making clarification requests.

Each time the child used the wrong language, the experimenter made up to five requests for clarification in the following increasing order of precision:

1. *What?* (Sometimes, this question was asked in a slightly different form, depending on the context: e.g., *A what?* or *The what?* This is a non-specific request that provides no indication that language is the cause of the breakdown).

2. *I don't understand* (This second non-specific request indicates that the child's first response was not successful in repairing the breakdown, but still provides no clue as to the cause of the breakdown).
3. *Can you tell me that so I can understand?* (This question indicates that some kind of reformulation of the initial utterance is required.)
4. *I don't speak French.* (This assertion provides the reason for the communication breakdown.)
5. *Can you tell me that in English?* (The experimenter explicitly states how the breakdown should be repaired.)

The least specific questions were asked first to investigate the children's understanding of implicit requests for language change. The more explicit requests at the end of the sequence allowed for the possibility that children have the linguistic proficiency to translate their initial utterance or to reformulate it in the other language, but fail to realize that this is the appropriate repair strategy unless they are told to do so explicitly. Requests were made until the child either (a) repaired the breakdown, (b) changed the subject or (c) did anything else that made it very difficult to continue making requests (e.g. left the room for a couple of minutes or became noticeably frustrated by the experimenter's requests).

The children's repairs of language-based breakdowns were compared to their repairs of other breakdowns to determine whether their use of strategies differed for the two breakdown types. This comparison is important because translating one's utterance to repair a language-based breakdown does not necessarily indicate that the child has identified the cause of the breakdown if the same child also translates his/her utterances when attempting to repair other kinds of breakdowns. In other words, studying children's responses to both types of breakdowns during a single play session is a better test of the children's ability to infer the intent of the experimenter's clarification requests than examining only repairs of language-based breakdowns. Some of the breakdowns that were not due to language choice occurred naturally and others were initiated by the experimenter when there was a plausible reason for doing so — e.g. the child's utterance was ambiguous, the pronunciation of a word differed from the target pronunciation, or the child spoke softly and was difficult to hear.

As with the language-based breakdowns, the experimenter made up to five requests following a breakdown. The first three requests in the sequence were the same as those used for language-based breakdowns. Using the same first three questions regardless of the cause of the breakdown allowed us to determine whether young bilingual children can differentiate language-based from other communication breakdowns without relying on the form of the request. The last two requests were adapted to each breakdown. The fourth request made the cause of the breakdown explicit and the last request provided the solution to repair the breakdown, as shown here:

1. *What?*
2. *I don't understand.*
3. *Can you tell me that so I can understand?*
4. *I can't hear you.*
5. *Can you speak more loudly?*

2.3 Transcription and coding

Twenty minutes of the videotaped interaction between the experimenter and each child were fully transcribed according to the CHAT system (MacWhinney, 2000) for the purpose of calculating the children's MLU in the language used by the experimenter. The children's utterances were coded for addressee and language (French, English, or mixed) to determine the extent to which the children used the same language as the experimenter. In addition, the children's responses to clarification requests throughout the filmed session were transcribed and coded for the following:

1. *Type of breakdown (language-based or other)*. A language-based breakdown is defined as any instance where the child's use of a mixed utterance or an utterance entirely in the wrong language was met by one or more requests for clarification from the experimenter. *Other* breakdowns occurred each time a child's potentially unclear utterance in the experimenter's language was met by one or more requests for clarification by the experimenter.
2. *Clarification request* to which the child is responding (i.e. *What?*, *I don't understand*, etc.)
3. *Repair strategy* (see Table 2 for descriptions and examples of strategies.)

These three types of codes allowed us to determine which repair strategies were used by the children and at what point in the sequence of five requests each strategy was used for each type of breakdown. In particular, they allowed us to determine whether children changed their language appropriately in response to clarification requests. Of all the verbal strategies, translation is the

Table 2. Repair strategies

Strategy	Definition and example
Translation	Translating/rephrasing the initial utterance in the other language, in whole or in part. JIA: Want to dessiner. ('Want to draw.') Experimenter: I don't understand. JIA: You want to draw.
Repetition	Repeating the initial utterance verbatim or in substance KEL: Arrose les fleurs. ('Water the flowers.') Experimenter: Quoi? ('What?') KEL: Arrose les fleurs. ('Water the flowers.')
Reformulation	Rephrasing the initial utterance in some way, either by adding, removing or substituting elements without any change in language CEC: Ah ah un mouton. ('Ah ah a sheep.') Experimenter: What? CEC: Ah chevre chevre. ('Ah goat goat.')
Subject Change	Introducing a new topic of conversation or activity. Sometimes, as in the example below, this involves a change in language. These instances were rare and are discussed separately in the text. JIA: Canards. ('Ducks.') Experimenter: I don't understand. JIA [pointing at something unrelated]: Hey look!
Yes/No	Answering in the negative or affirmative, often by saying yes or no. As with Subject Change, such responses sometimes involved a change in language. CLA: Anglais a mon papa. ('English to my dad.') Experimenter: Can you tell me that in English? CLA: No.

only adequate repair of language-based breakdowns. All responses including a partial or complete translation or reformulation of the children's utterance in the experimenter's language were coded as a translation. Other responses, such as changing the subject or responding with yes or no, sometimes also involve a change in language, but they are not conducive to repairing communication breakdowns so they were analyzed separately. Responses such as repetition and reformulation do not involve a language change and so they are inappropriate for repairing language-based breakdowns, but they are adequate for repairing other breakdowns. All the data were coded by the first author. The repair strategies of three randomly chosen children (two 3-year-olds and one 5-year-old) were coded independently by a trained research

Table 2. (cont.)

Strategy	Definition and example
Asking for help	Asking a third party to help respond to the request. NER: toi c'est buyer toute le choses d'accord? ('You buy all the things okay?') Experimenter: est-ce que tu peux dire ca pour que je comprenne? ('Can you say that so I can understand?') NER [to observer filming the play session]: quoi c'est ('What is it?')
Change of pronunciation	Changing the pronunciation of all or part of the initial utterance to make it sound like the other language. This strategy was never used on its own, but it was used in combination with other modifications of the initial utterance. JUL [normal French pronunciation]: Mesurer. ('Measure.') Experimenter: Can you say that so I'll understand? JUL [The r-sound is pronounced in English]: Ruban a mesurer. ('Measuring tape.')
Combination	Using any combination of two or more strategies in response to a single clarification request. In this example, the child first provides a Yes/No-type answer , and then reformulates his utterance into the experimenter's language (Translation). OLI: Oui ca va comme ca. ('Yes it goes like this.') Experimenter: Can you say that in English? OLI: Hmm non je sais connais pas. ('Hmm no I know don't know.') OLI: I will just show you how to do neat and square.
Non-verbal	Gesturing (e.g. pointing to an object, miming an action). ALX: Hum this is a saw. Experimenter: Quoi? ('What?') ALX: [points to his toy saw]
No response	Providing no verbal or non-verbal response to the clarification request.

assistant. Interrater reliability was 85 per cent and disagreements were resolved by discussion.

3. Results

3.1 Frequency of communication breakdowns

Sixty-one breakdowns were excluded from the analyses. In 11 cases, the nature of the breakdown (language-based vs. other) could not be determined because the children's utterances were unintelligible. The other 50 breakdowns were excluded because of experimenter error (i.e. making the same request more than once, making requests that were different from the pre-established set of clarification requests, and not giving children time to answer one request before making the next request).

The remaining breakdowns were distributed unevenly among the children. Table 3 shows important individual differences in the number of language-based and other breakdowns. The number of language-based breakdowns was determined by the extent to which the children used the wrong language. Nearly all of these breakdowns (90 per cent) occurred with the 3-year-olds. Individual differences in the number of other breakdowns depended on a number of factors, including whether a particular child pronounced words clearly, whether she/he showed signs of fatigue or annoyance with the experimenter's questions, and her/his choice of language. Indeed, with respect to the latter factor, some children used so little of the experimenter's language that the experimenter had few opportunities to request clarification of a breakdown that was not due to the children's use of the wrong language.

Table 3. Number of language-based and other breakdowns experienced by each child

	Name	Language-Based	Other
3-year-olds	ALX	36	2
	CAR	11	11
	CEC	3	4
	CLA	6	6
	JIA	11	5
	JUL	18	17
	JUS	0	9
	KEL	5	16
	MAR	10	1
	NIC	4	6
	NIS	0	4
	OLI	10	4
	Total	114	85
5-year-olds	AMA	3	3
	BEN	0	4
	COL	1	22
	EMI	0	13
	FEX	1	6
	NER	7	6
	Total	12	54

It should be noted that, since up to 5 requests for clarification were made for each breakdown in communication, the number of requests made to the children exceeds the number of breakdowns. When reporting the children's repair strategies in subsequent sections, we use the number of requests to which the children responded as the unit of analysis rather than the number of breakdowns. Table 4 indicates the number of breakdowns for which one, two, three, four, or five requests were made, as well as the total number of clarification requests made for each type of breakdown (language-based vs. other) and for each age group. There were seldom more than one or two requests per breakdown, and this applies to both language-based and other breakdowns.

Table 4. Number of breakdowns for which one to five requests were made and number of clarification requests by breakdown type and by age group

	3-year-olds					5-year-olds				
	Language-based breakdowns									
# of requests	1	2	3	4	5	1	2	3	4	5
# of breakdowns	24	35	20	1	34	3	5	0	0	4
Total # of requests	328					33				
	Other breakdowns									
# of requests	1	2	3	4	5	1	2	3	4	5
# of breakdowns	65	12	5	1	2	45	7	1	1	0
Total # of requests	118					66				

3.2 Children's overall language use

Many of the children had low MLU's in the language used by the experimenter, as shown in Table 1. In spite of this, most of the children were capable of using this language in greater proportion than the wrong language during the play sessions. Figures 1 and 2 show that all children except two (ALX and MAR) produced more utterances in the experimenter's language than mixed utterances or utterances entirely in the wrong language. Two other children (JUS and EMI) demonstrated high levels of control over their languages by using the same language as the experimenter at all times. Incidentally, these two children's MLU's in the experimenter's language were quite low in comparison to the other children's. Thus, it appears that the appropriate use of one's languages is not highly correlated with linguistic ability. These findings corroborate those of Genesee et al. (1996) by showing that young

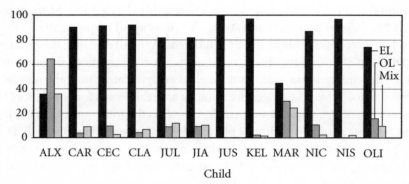

Figure 1. Percentage of utterances in each language (Experimenter's Language, Other Language, and Mixed) for each 3-year-old

bilingual children are capable of adapting their language choice to match the language used by an unfamiliar interlocutor.

The 5-year-olds, on average, used the experimenter's language in greater proportion than the younger children (97 per cent vs. 82 per cent, respectively). Thus, in general, the 5-year-olds appear to have had better control than the younger children over their language use. The fact that the older children used very little of the wrong language accounts for the low number of language-based breakdowns they experienced. Exact percentages and raw frequencies of utterances in each language can be found in Appendix 1.

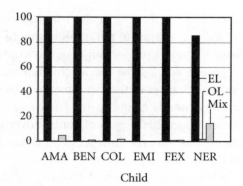

Figure 2. Percentage of utterances in each language (Experimenter's language, Other Language, and Mixed) for each 5-year-old

3.3 Three-year-olds' repair strategies

The 3-year-old children used a number of different repair strategies in response to the experimenter's requests for clarification, whether they were
repairing language-based or other breakdowns. While there were individual
differences in the proportional use of certain strategies, only aggregated data
will be presented here and only the main findings will be discussed.

Ten of the 3-year-olds experienced language-based breakdowns. All of
them appropriately translated their utterances in response to some requests for
clarification, but they differed from each other with respect to the number of
times they used this strategy (range: 3 to 11). The examples below illustrate
how some of the children translated their utterances:

(1) NIC (3;4)

NIC:	N'est pas une boat. ('Is not a boat.')
Experimenter:	Quoi? ('What?')
NIC:	Euh, c'est bateau bateau. ('Uh, it's boat boat.')

In this example, the child reformulated his utterance in the appropriate
language in response to the experimenter's first request for clarification.

(2) ALX (3;2)

ALX:	There's water right there.
Experimenter:	Quoi? ('What?')
ALX:	Water!
Experimenter:	Je comprends pas. ('I don't understand.')
ALX:	De l'eau! ('Some water!')

(3) MAR (3;5)

MAR:	First the apple apple.
Experimenter:	Quoi? ('What?')
MAR:	Apple.
Experimenter:	Hmm je comprends pas la. ('Hmm I don't understand.')
MAR:	Uh. [child pauses]
Experimenter:	Est ce que tu peux me dire pour que je comprenne? ('Can you say that so I can understand?')
MAR:	Uh pomme pomme! ('Apple apple!')

In the second and third examples, the children answered in the wrong language at first (by repeating a portion of their initial utterance), but translated after the second and third requests, respectively.

The majority of the 3-year-old children's translations (88 per cent) were made after the first, second, or third clarification request, none of which provide explicit information about the cause of the breakdown (Figure 3). Thus, the children were capable of correctly interpreting the experimenter's requests for clarifications as implicit requests for language change. Translations account for 17 per cent of the 3-year-olds' total responses to clarification requests. An additional 7 per cent of their responses were also in the appropriate language but were not translations of the children's initial utterances. These responses consisted of subject changes, yes/no answers, and short utterances accompanying gestures such as *Look* and *Like this*, as shown in the following example:

(4)   JUL (3;2)

        JUL: And a scie. ('And a saw.')
        Experimenter: A what?
        JUL: Scie. ('Saw.')
        Experimenter: I don't understand.
        JUL: A scie. ('A saw.')
        Experimenter: Can you say that so I can understand?
        JUL: For . . . [child shows how to cut with a saw]

Here, the child uses the wrong language when responding to the first two requests for clarification. The child then repairs the breakdown by demonstrating the action of sawing for the experimenter and accompanies this gesture with a word in the appropriate language. While this response involves a language change, the child did not translate or reformulate his initial utterance in the appropriate language.

At times, the children also made inappropriate language changes; that is, they shifted from their initial mixed utterances to the wrong language only, or they added novel words from the wrong language in their responses. They responded in this way 5 per cent of the time. (Seven of the children did this at least once: ALX, CAR, CLA, JUL, KEL, MAR, and OLI. JUL responded in this way the most, for a total of eight times.) Combining all responses that entailed an appropriate language change, almost 25 per cent of the children's responses to a request for clarification when the wrong language had been used initially were in the experimenter's language.

Strategies used by the 3-year-olds when repairing language-based vs. other

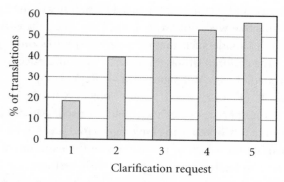

Figure 3. Cumulative frequency of translations made by 3-year-olds in response to each type of clarification request (language-based breakdowns)

breakdowns were compared to determine whether the children used their repair strategies differentially for the two types of breakdowns (see Figure 4). A 2×4 repeated measures ANOVA revealed that while there was no main effect for Type of breakdown, $F (1, 3)=0.21$, $p>.05$, there was a significant interaction between Type of breakdown and Repair strategy, $F (1, 3)=9.74$, $p<.01$. Post-hoc comparisons using an alpha level of .01 as the cutoff for significance showed that this interaction was due to a significant difference in children's use of Translation. They translated their utterances significantly more when attempting to repair language-based breakdowns than when attempting to repair other breakdowns, $F (1)=17.41$, $p<.005$. Indeed, children translated their utterance 17 per cent of the time when repairing a language-

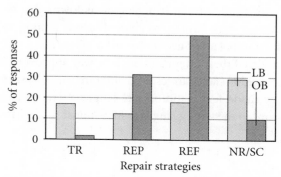

Figure 4. Percentage of repair strategies of 3-year-olds following language-based versus other breakdowns: Translation (TR), Repetition (RE), Reformulation (REF), and No Response/Subject Change (NR/SC)

based breakdowns, and virtually never used this strategy when attempting to repair breakdowns that were not due to language choice: the two children who did (KEL and JUL) made such inappropriate responses only one time each (1.7 per cent of the children's total responses). The differences observed in the use of other strategies were not significant — Repetition, F (1)=3.05, $p>.10$; Reformulation, F (1)=5.2, $p>.01$; and Subject Change/No Response, F (1)=2.02, $p>.10$. Other strategies were seldom used. Although gestures are also an appropriate way of repairing language-based breakdowns and could be used to compensate for a lack of proficiency in the experimenter's language, less than 5 per cent of requests were met with gestures for both types of breakdowns. Strategies such as answering with only yes or no, combining two strategies, changing one's pronunciation, and asking for help were seldom used. Changing one's pronunciation, in particular, was never used on its own but only in combination with other responses. The percentages on which the statistical analyses above are based and the percentage and frequency of use of different repair strategies for 3- and 5-year-olds can be found in Appendix 2.

3.4 Five-year-olds' repair strategies

While 5-year-olds experienced few language-based communication breakdowns, all of those who did eventually translated their initial utterances or responded in a way that showed they understood the cause of the breakdown (i.e. by stating that they did not know the word in the other language, or by incorrectly claiming that they were in fact using the appropriate language). None of the 3-year-olds made such metalinguistic comments. The distribution of 5-year-olds' responses when attempting to repair breakdowns that were not due to language choice was very similar to that observed among the 3-year-olds. Repetitions of their initial utterance accounted for 38 per cent of their responses, and they reformulated their utterances in some way approximately 50 per cent of the time. They seldom failed to respond and rarely used gestures, and like the 3-year-olds, they made few inappropriate language changes. Only one child (NER) used a word in the wrong language in response to a clarification request.

4.   Discussion

The 5-year-olds we observed experienced few language-based breakdowns because they used the same language as their interlocutor most of the time.

When such breakdowns occurred, they demonstrated that they had an explicit understanding of their cause, as evidenced by their metalinguistic comments to the experimenter in response to clarification requests and their use of translation as a repair strategy.

In comparison, the 3-year-olds experienced a larger number of language-based breakdowns, with some children making extensive use of the wrong language. Nonetheless, the ability to repair language-based breakdowns appears to be a part of bilingual children's communicative competence by 3 years of age. Although the children we observed often failed to provide adequate repairs of language-based breakdowns, a quarter of their responses to requests for clarification consisted of translations or reformulations of their utterances in the appropriate language. Moreover, almost all of these appropriate responses were made in response to non-specific clarification requests, indicating that the children had identified language choice as the cause of the breakdown relatively easily. This is further confirmed by the fact that the distribution of the strategies used to repair language-based breakdowns differed from the pattern used to repair other types of breakdowns. In particular, they often translated or reformulated their initial utterance in the appropriate language when attempting to repair language-based breakdowns, but only twice changed their language when attempting to repair other breakdowns. Thus, there is evidence that the children were capable of differentiating the two types of breakdowns and of understanding the intent of the experimenter's clarification requests without explicit feedback concerning the cause of the breakdowns. Their use of inappropriate strategies when attempting to repair language-based breakdowns, such as repeating their initial utterance or reformulating it without changing language, is arguably due to performance factors such as a lack of vocabulary in the experimenter's language rather than to a lack of communicative competence.

Investigating bilingual children's repair strategies during dyadic communication allows us to observe manifestations of communicative competence that are not seen in monolingual populations, as bilingual children experience breakdowns that are due to language choice in addition to the variety of breakdowns that also occur in monolingual discourse. The children in this study demonstrated that they were capable of using appropriate strategies for repairing both language-based and other breakdowns. The strategies they used in the latter case are the same as those reported to be used by monolingual children (Anselmi *et al.* 1986; Gallagher 1977; Marcos and Bernicot 1994; Tomasello *et al.* 1984; see also De Houwer 1990, who compared the repair strategies of the bilingual child she studied to those of monolingual children). Thus, it appears that young bilingual children possess the same ability to repair communication breakdowns as monolingual children as well as abilities that are specific to bilinguals. Moreover, young bilingual children can infer the precise cause of breakdowns in communication without receiving explicit feedback. These findings suggest that the extent of preschoolers' communicative competence has not been fully appreciated by previous research on monolingual children.

We are presently analyzing data on age-matched monolingual children to compare their responses to those of bilinguals. We will examine more closely whether bilingual children's repairs of breakdowns not due to language choice differ in some ways from those of monolinguals by using the same sequence of clarification requests as in our bilingual samples. We will also examine younger bilingual children's repairs of communication breakdowns to investigate when children acquire the ability to repair language-based breakdowns.

Appendix 1. Percentage and frequency (in parentheses) of children's utterances in each language

Child	Experimenter's Language	Other language	Mixed
ALX	34.8 % (79)	61.7 % (140)	3.5 % (8)
CAR	91.0 % (382)	1.7 % (7)	7.3 % (31)
CEC	92.8 % (231)	6.4 % (16)	0.8 % (2)
CLA	93.0 % (144)	1.9 % (3)	5.1 % (8)
JIA	82.1 % (225)	6.6 % (18)	11.3 % (31)
JUL	83.0 % (317)	7.3 % (28)	9.7 % (37)
JUS	100.0 % (451)	0	0
KEL	96.2 % (175)	2.2 % (4)	1.6 % (3)
MAR	46.7 % (77)	27.9 % (46)	25.4 % (42)
NIC	91.8 % (236)	5.8 % (15)	2.3 % (6)
NIS	97.9 % (143)	0	2.1 % (3)
OLI	73.4 % (226)	16.2 % (50)	10.4 % (32)
MEAN	81.9 %	11.5 %	6.6 %
AMA	99.1 % (418)	0	0.9 % (4)
BEN	99.3 % (141)	0	0.7 % (1)
COL	98.8 % (488)	0	1.2 % (6)
EMI	100.0 % (154)	0	0
FEX	98.5 % (135)	0.7% (1)	0.7 % (1)
NER	83.6 % (367)	1.1% (5)	15.3 % (67)
MEAN	96.5 %	0.3 %	3.1 %

Appendix 2. Percentages and frequencies (in parentheses) of strategies by age group for language-based and other breakdowns

	Strategy	Language-based	Other	Total (freq.)
3-year-olds	Translation	17.1 % (56)	1.7 % (2)	58
	Other lg. change	7.3 % (24)	0	24
	Repetition	12.5 % (41)	30.5 % (36)	77
	Reformulation	18.0 % (59)	50.0 % (59)	118
	Gestures	4.6 % (15)	4.2 % (5)	20
	Subject change	3.7 % (12)	1.7 % (2)	14
	No response	24.7 % (81)	7.6 % (9)	90
	Inappropriate lg. change	4.9 % (16)	N/A*	16
	Other strategies**	7.3 % (24)	4.2 % (5)	29
	Total	*100 % (328)*	*100 % (118)*	*446*
5-year-olds	Translation	12.1 % (4)	1.5 % (1)	5
	Other lan. change	0	0	0
	Repetition	12.1 % (4)	37.9 % (25)	29
	Reformulation	15.2 % (5)	54.5 % (36)	41
	Gestures	3.0 % (1)	1.5 % (1)	2
	Subject change	3.0 % (1)	1.5 % (1)	2
	No response	15.2 % (5)	1.5 % (1)	6
	Inappropriate lg. change	0	N/A*	0
	Other strategies**	39.4 % (13)	1.5 % (1)	14
	Total	*100 % (33)*	*100 % (66)*	*99*

* For "other" breakdowns, Translation and Inappropriate language change are the same thing.
** Other strategies: Low-frequency strategies such as Yes/No, Asking for help, Changing the pronunciation, and all possible combinations of two or more strategies.

Last words

Brian MacWhinney

The study of childhood bilingualism has made rapid advances in recent years. This progress is being driven by work in three major traditions, each of which is reflected in this volume. One tradition views bilingualism through the eyes of the sociolinguist trying to understand how the child learns to select, mix, and switch between languages on the basis of the social situation and the abilities of the interlocutors. A second tradition views bilingualism through the eyes of the psycholinguist who wants to understand how the young bilingual manages to keep languages separate in terms of their formal structures. A third tradition, which is the newest of the three, views bilingualism through the eyes of the infancy researcher who sees bilingualism as a searchlight that illuminates the perceptual, motor, and cognitive capacities of the infant.

The current volume invites the reader to develop a new view of emergent bilingualism by bringing these three traditions together. The chapters themselves do not produce a unified view. Rather, the unification is left as an assignment to the reader; and it is an assignment very much worth completing. The issue that lies at the core of this unification is the problem of language differentiation. The chapters in this volume are unanimous in their rejection of the idea (Volterra and Taeschner 1978) that the bilingual child begins with a single undifferentiated language. However, the reasons for rejecting this hypothesis are as various as the perspectives of each of the authors.

When we look at this issue from the viewpoint of the infancy researchers, the idea that the infant raised in a bilingual environment would operate with an undifferentiated auditory system seems singularly unlikely. For example, the studies of Bosch and Sebastián-Galles argue in favor of strong perceptual differentiation between languages in the first few months of life. If a fairly high level of language differentiation can be achieved at such a young age, it would seem strange to imagine that languages would be undifferentiated at age 3. We know from studies with monolinguals (Bahrick and Pickens 1988; Mehler, Jusczyk, Lambertz, Halsted, Bertoncini and Amiel-Tison 1988) that two month olds prefer to listen to their native language, rather than a very different foreign language. More recent studies indicate that this preference is present just after birth (Moon, Cooper and Fifer 1993), and that it is largely grounded on the use of prosodic cues (Dehaene-Lambertz and Houston 1998). The fact that prosodic cues are central to the early preference for L1 is important for two reasons. First, it leaves open the possibility that these preferences are acquired inside the womb when listening to the rhythm of the mother's voice, since prosodic characteristics of speech transmit through the amniotic fluid better than segmental characteristics. Second, it means that research on bilingual infants must pay careful attention to prosodic differences between languages.

Unfortunately, the researcher's job of nailing down the perceptual basis of language differentiation in bilingual infants is more difficult technically than the parallel problem for monolinguals. When working with bilinguals, it is important to control the distance between the two native languages in terms of prosody, phonetic features, and the segmental inventory. We know that, by about 5 months, monolinguals can begin to differentiate their native language from a prosodically similar foreign language (Nazzi, Jusczyk and Johnson 2000), and that they can also discriminate between two prosodically similar foreign languages. Using the combined training and preference paradigm that has been used in much recent work (de Boysson-Bardies 1999), Bosch and Sebastián-Galles show that bilingual infants can distinguish two native languages as similar prosodically as Spanish and Catalan.

When Bosch and Sebastián-Galles (1997a) relied on an eye-movement latency measure, rather than their current training-plus-preference method, they found slightly different results. In that study, monolingual four-month-olds oriented more quickly to their native language than to a foreign language. For bilinguals, the reverse was true, since they oriented more quickly to sounds in the unfamiliar, novel language. Concerned that this effect might represent a transient period for the bilinguals, the authors then replicated the study with six-month-olds and found, perhaps to their surprise, the same effect. They seem at a loss to explain the results from these two different paradigms. However, it seems to me that the results are not as puzzling as they suggest. In the training-plus-preference method, the infants are being habituated to the language of the training set. If they then show a novelty preference during testing, this probably reflects more the special characteristics of this procedure than everyday, natural mechanisms. However, using this procedure we find that bilinguals can discriminate between languages as well as monolinguals. The eye-movement latency procedure measures reactions more directly. In this case, bilingual children are illustrating the fact that they have learned not to ignore interesting new linguistic stimuli. Because they are being faced daily with important discriminations, they tend to orient to new materials more than monolinguals, who are learning to simply ignore certain signals as irrelevant to their language learning (Werker 1995). For our present purposes, what is important here is not the fact that bilinguals can behave differently in certain tasks, but that both monolinguals and bilinguals show clear and early auditory discrimination between languages.

When we turn to the literature on early babbling, the picture is somewhat different. In that area, it is often assumed that the child produces babbling without attention to the exact form of the native language. The fact that deaf children babble normally up to six months (Lenneberg 1967; Oller 1991) suggests that early babbling may not be tightly coupled to audition (Oller and Eilers 1988). This initial decoupling may explain why *babbling drift* during the first year is relatively difficult to quantify (Atkinson, MacWhinney and Stoel 1970). Recent work has attempted to specify some parameters of drift (de Boysson-Bardies and Vihman 1991). However, the trends identified so far are statistically weak and many of the differences are confined to overall prosodic characteristics (Whalen, Levitt and Wang 1991). Given the weakness of the monolingual evidence for babbling drift, it is not surprising that Poulin-Dubois and Goodz found that French-English bilingual infants showed no clear language-based differentiation when babbling in the company of the French-speaking parent vs. the English-speaking parent. Moreover, they found that the children tended to favor French patterns over English patterns in their babbling. Since 10 of the 12 children had French-speaking mothers, this is not a surprising result. But the authors note that there is another, more interesting, account of these results. This is that the children found the syllable timing of French more to their liking and used it more as a model for their babbling.

Research on early speech perception by monolingual children provides much clearer evidence for language discrimination and differentiation than does research on early babbling. This is not a problem for views that emphasize early differentiation, since advances in comprehension are typically viewed as driving later advances in production. But should we not expect some form of differentiation in production as the child begins to produce the first words? To further explore this issue, we need to turn to the second major tradition represented in this volume, the sociolinguistic tradition that examines the child's use of languages in context. Perhaps the most forceful spokesperson for this tradition is Lanza who outlines the view that socialization of the bilingual occurs in an interactive, contextualized, and sequential discourse process. Specifically, she argues that parents respond to children's language mixing with one of five possible strategies: minimal grasp, expressed guess, repetition, move-on, and code-switching. By selecting one of these options, the child and the parent co-construct a unique bilingual environment. This co-construction begins with the child's first words and continues throughout the years of language acquisition. As Lanza notes, even children growing up in a one-parent–one-language environment learn subtle patterns of code-switching, as evidenced by her case study of a Norwegian-English child bilingual.

Lanza's analysis underscores the extent to which child bilinguals are receiving input that strengthens both differentiation and mixing at the same time. They are taught a rich set of expectations for using a particular code, acceptable ways of mixing codes, methods for negotiating code selection, and ways of expressing communicative failure. Parents are able to socialize children into these expected behaviors without interfering with basic communication. Sometimes these patterns are fairly subtle. For example, both Nicoladis and Genesee (1998) and Lanza were unable to detect a direct relation between parental use of the five proposed discourse strategies and mixing rate. However, when children are observed more closely and across a wider developmental period, these relations emerge more clearly. The chapter by Comeau and Genesee further underscores the extent to which child bilinguals have achieved a high level of control of language switching, particularly in the context of communicative breakdowns. In this way, the child can use knowledge about the pragmatics of code-switching to compensate for early deficits in lexical or syntactic knowledge.

The emphasis in the chapters by Lanza and Comeau and Genesee on the smooth acquisition of a sophisticated ability to switch codes tends to mask the existence of an early period in language acquisition at which code-switching is less adequately controlled (Köppe 1997; Nicoladis and Genesee 1996). During the first months of productive language use, children are happy that they can produce any words at all. At this time, they may implicitly recognize the provenance of their first words, but lack the ability to avoid code-switching and inappropriate code usage. This early blending could be misinterpreted as evidence for incomplete differentiation or as evidence of ignorance of the importance of code selection. But it would be better to interpret these early errors as signs of incomplete language learning. The trilingual child studied by Quay faced an even more complex challenge that he resolved by speaking primarily in Japanese and passively comprehending input in German and

English. Here, again, we see that the cognitive complexity of the first stages of language learning makes it difficult for the child to show complete control of all of the input languages from the very beginning. But this does not mean that the child fails to differentiate languages in the second year.

The evidence from both infant perception and early bilingual socialization supports a view of the child as working with a well-differentiated set of codes. At the same time, the child's mastery of the adult target languages remains highly incomplete. These gaps and ambiguities in knowledge drive the processes of language transfer and mixing that have been detected in later years (Döpke 2000; Hulk and Müller in press). Given the extent to which the child has achieved differentiation in audition and language use, it is almost surprising to see that there is still a debate regarding language differentiation in syntax. At first glance, it might seem as if the early fusion hypothesis is being used as a straw man to motivate specific further analyses. However, the issue is deeper than this. The problem in the area of grammatical development, as reflected in the chapter by Meisel, is figuring out how to treat cross-language influences in the context of a differentiated system. Meisel argues convincingly that children use language-specific patterns in early multi-word utterances. This claim matches up well with cross-linguistic comprehension and production data collected in the framework of the Competition Model (MacWhinney and Bates 1989). Meisel contrasts his early differentiation analysis with the early fusion analysis of Deuchar and Quay (1998) and Deuchar (1999). Although Meisel accepts the data which Deuchar and Quay present, he is unwilling to accept their suggestion that the child is using a "rudimentary syntax, based on a predicate-argument structure".

Meisel criticizes the Deuchar-Quay approach as formally vague. However, the notion of predicate-argument structure they are using is one of the most basic and well-defined concepts in all of logic and automata theory. It is a core concept underlying categorical grammar, Montague grammar, and word grammar. Perhaps Meisel is linking the Deuchar and Quay analysis with the older and much less useful (MacWhinney 1975) concept of topic-comment structure. However, the Deuchar-Quay proposal should be viewed in its own light as emphasizing the role of item-based patterns (MacWhinney 1982). In this light, the predicate-argument structure that obtains between *más* or *more* and its nucleus is nothing more than an item-based predicate argument structure of the type outlined by MacWhinney (1975, 1982) and by Serratrice in this volume.

In her analysis of verb morphology in an English–Italian bilingual, Serratrice argues that the child begins learning aspectual marking and subject-verb agreement by acquiring individual constructions without analysis from the adult input. For example, the child might say *That's a cat* without really controlling subject-verb agreement productively. The *that's a X* form is used in a limited, constructional way and not composed from its pieces. As a result, there are few errors in English verb morphology, but also little productivity. On the other hand, this rigidity leads to many errors of omission. In Italian, the child is also learning verbs in a case-by-case way, although the forms are in advance of parallel forms in English. Although Serratrice believes that conservative, word-based acquisition is at the core of initial learning, she recognizes that, with advancing competence and the learning of path-breaking verbs, there is increasing productivity and generality in the verb morphology system. Although her research shows clearly that Italian leads English in this regard, it is not clear whether this lead-lag relation between Italian and English results in changes to the pattern of English development in this child.

Idiazabal and Almgren provide further support for the input-driven nature of early verb acquisition. In their study, the focus is on the treatment of aspectual and tense marking in Spanish and Basque. They find that, in their Basque-Spanish bilingual, the earliest Spanish past tenses are in the imperfect. This pattern is unlike that found in Spanish monolinguals, where the preterite typically precedes the imperfect. However, it appears that this preference for the imperfective in Spanish is driven by the fact that M.'s father used large numbers of imperfectives in story telling. When the perfective enters, it is used to describe real events. In Basque, on the contrary, there are few examples of past tense verb forms referring to pretend activities. This appears to reflect the fact that the Basque input to the bilingual child emphasized the use of the perfective. Thus, it appears that statistical features of the bilingual input can deviate from and override features of the standard monolingual input.

As the bilingual child acquires increasingly complex grammars in the two languages, the period of early item-based patterns gives way to a period of syntactic transfer, bootstrapping, lead-lag patterns, and interaction (Gawlitzek-Maiwald and Tracy 1996; Hulk and Müller in press; Döpke 2000). Meisel questions this line of research by casting doubt either on the nature of the subjects, the analyses, or the grammatical theory being utilized. In order to evaluate Meisel's interpretations of these issues, readers will want to read the original reports. Ideally, they would also like to match up the published literature with the original transcript data in order to better understand the relative frequency of specific types of cross-language interactions. This level of analysis is important, because many of the issues here depend on the ways in

which specific structures are coded and counted. For example, transfer phenomena could well be interpreted as errors, unless their frequency is impres-
sively large and their distribution theoretically predicted. To fully evaluate these
issues, additional comparisons based on the raw data will be needed. This type
of analysis will become possible when more of the relevant data are made
publicly available in the CHILDES database (MacWhinney 2000).

So far, we have contrasted work from three very different traditions, all
directed toward the central issue of language differentiation. Work on early
audition shows that the infant is able to differentiate codes perceptually in the
first months. When the child comes to learn the first words, they are already
differentiated in prosodic and segmental terms. However, syntactic development is at first highly conservative and lexically based. Until syntactic patterns
become more general, there may be little evidence for rampant overgeneralization. This does not mean that the two codes are mixed, only that they
remain lexically based and not yet capable of strong syntactic transfer. As
syntactic patterns grow in strength, we begin to see evidence for language
mixing. However, this mixing is further shaped and controlled by interactional
processes modeled by the parents and other adults.

As these details begin to sort themselves out, I believe that work on child
bilingualism will move in new directions. One promising application is the use
of child bilingualism as a way of informing our theories of monolingual
acquisition. For example, bilingual children have provided us with clear
evidence that children can cheerfully violate the mutual exclusivity constraint
(Markman 1989) by accepting two names for a single object (Au and Glusman
1990; Davidson, Jergovic, Imami and Theodos 1997; McClure 1997). Bilingual
children have helped illuminate the relative strength or markedness of phonological processes (Deuchar and Clark 1996; Faingold 1996; Zlatic, MacNeilage,
Matyear and Davis 1997) and morphological devices (De Houwer 1990; Klinge
1990; De Houwer 1997; Sinka and Schelleter 1998). Bilingual children can also
help us understand how word segmentation strategies interact with different
prosodic structures. Poulin-Dubois and Goodz (this volume) have suggested
that French-English bilingual children may prefer the syllable-timed structures
of French as models for early babbling. The study by Nicoladis constructs a
similar type of analysis for early segmentation and word learning. Nicoladis
focuses on the fact that English tends to place mostly nouns in sentence-final
position, whereas Portuguese presents the child with nouns, verbs, and other
forms in this same position. If the child is strongly biased to acquire nouns
from final position, as Tardif, Shatz, and Naigles (1997) have argued, then

Nicoladis' young English–Portuguese bilingual Carlo should have acquired relatively more nouns in English than in Portuguese. In fact, this is not what happened at all. Actually, Carlo learned more nouns than verbs in both English and Portuguese. This indicates that the child was basically set to learn nouns. However, it may well have been the case that his acquisition of English was speeded by the fact that the words he wanted to learn appeared in a position that made them easy to spot and learn. Although the results of this single case study are far from definitive, they show how bilinguals help illuminate core processes in language learning. In the case investigated by Nicoladis, further comparisons would need to compare languages such as Korean and English that treat verbs in markedly different ways. Of course, finding balanced bilingual children who speak exactly the correct combination of languages is no easy matter. However, the logic of such comparisons is quite powerful.

Returning to the issues with which we began, we see how the perspectives of infant perception, socialization, and grammatical analysis have enriched our ideas about language differentiation. We now see the bilingual child as working with two complex systems that are clearly distinguishable, but which interact in important ways. We also see that studies of children learning two languages of markedly different structure can shed light on basic issues in language processing. We can look to ongoing developments in the study of child bilingualism as a way of further explicating the nature of language learning, social interactions, and the human mind.

References

Aarsen, J., Akinci, M-A., Yagmur, K. 2001. "Development of Turkish clause linkage in narrative texts. A comparison of bilingual children in Australia, France and the Netherlands." In *Research on Child Language Acquisition*, M. Almgren, A. Barreña, M-J. Ezeizabarrena, I. Idiazabal and B. MacWhinney (eds.), 41–56. Somerville, MA: Cascadilla Press.

Abercrombie, D. 1967. *Elements of General Phonetics*. Edinburgh: Edinburgh University Press.

Aguirre, C. 1995. *La adquisición de las categorías gramaticales del español*. Ph.D. Dissertation, Autonomous University of Madrid.

Akhtar, N. 1999. "Acquiring basic word order: Evidence for data-driven learning of syntactic structure." *Journal of Child Language* 26: 339–56.

—— and Tomasello, M. 1997. "Young children's productivity with word order and verb morphology." *Developmental Psychology* 33: 952–65.

Akinci, M-A. 2001. "Development of perspective in narrative texts of Turkish-French bilingual children in France." In *Research on Child Language Acquisition*, M. Almgren, A. Barreña, M.-J. Ezeizabarrena, I. Idiazabal and B. MacWhinney (eds.), 55–77. Somerville, MA: Cascadilla Press.

Aksu-Koç, A. 1988. *The Acquisition of Aspect and Modality. The Case of Past References in Turkish*. Cambridge: Cambridge University Press.

Aldridge, M. 1989. *The Acquisition of INFL*. Bloomington: Indiana University Linguistics Club Publications.

Allen, S. E. M. 1996. *Aspects of Argument Structure Acquisition in Inuktitut*. Amsterdam: John Benjamins.

Andersen, R. W. 1989. "La Adquisición de la Morfología Verbal." *Lingüística* 1: 90–142.

Antelmi, D. 1997. *La Prima Grammatica dell'Italiano: Indagine Longitudinale sull'Acquisizione della Morfosintassi Italiana*. Bologna: Il Mulino.

—— Tomasello, M. and Acunzo, M. 1986. "Young children's responses to neutral and specific contingent queries." *Journal of Child Language* 13: 135–44.

Antinucci, F. and Miller, R. 1976. "How children talk about what happened." *Journal of Child Language* 3: 167–90.

Arnberg, L. 1987. *Raising Children Bilingually: The Pre-school Years*. Clevedon, Avon: Multilingual Matters.

Atkinson, K., MacWhinney, B. and Stoel, C. 1970. "An experiment on the recognition of babbling." *Papers and Reports on Child Language Development* 5: 1–8.

Au, T. K. and Glusman, M. 1990. "The principle of mutual exclusivity in word learning: To honor or not to honor?" *Child Development* 61: 1474–90.

—— Dapretto, M. and Song, Y.-K. 1994. "Input vs constraints: Early word acquisition in Korean and English." *Journal of Memory and Language* 33: 567–82.

Auer, P. 1984. *Bilingual Conversation*. Amsterdam: John Benjamins.

—— 1995. "The pragmatics of code-switching: A sequential approach." In *One Speaker, Two Languages. Cross-disciplinary Perspectives on Code-switching*, L. Milroy and P. Muysken (eds.), 115–35. Cambridge: Cambridge University Press.

—— 1998. *Bilingual Conversation* revisited. In *Code-switching in Conversation. Language, Interaction, and Identity*, P. Auer (ed.), 1–24. London: Routledge.

Bahrick, L. E. and Pickens, J. N. 1988. "Classification of bimodal English and Spanish language passages by infants." *Infant behavior and Development* 11: 277–96.

Bassano, D. 1996. "Early lexical development in French: Formal and functional aspects of word class acquisition." Paper presented at the *Seventh International Congress for the Study of Child Language*, Istanbul, Turkey, July.

Bates, E. 1976. *Language and Context: The Acquisition of Pragmatics*. New York: Academic Press.

—— and Goodman, J. C. 1997. "On the inseparability of grammar and the lexicon: evidence from acquisition, aphasia, and real-time processing." *Language and Cognitive Processes* 12: 507–86.

—— —— 1999. "On the emergence of grammar from the lexicon." In *The Emergence of Language*, B. MacWhinney (ed.), 29–79. Mahwah, NJ: Erlbaum.

—— Marchman, V., Thal, D., Fenson, L., Dale, P., Reznick, J. S., Reilly, J. and Hartung, J. 1994. "Developmental and stylistic variation in the composition of early vocabulary." *Journal of Child Language* 21: 85–123.

—— Thal, D., Fenson, L., Whitesell, K. and Oakes, L. M. 1989. "Integrating language and gesture in infancy." *Developmental Psychology* 25: 1004–19.

Barron-Hauwaert, S. 2000. "Issues surrounding trilingual families: Children with simultaneous exposure to three languages." *Zeitschrift für Interkulturellen Fremdsprachenunterricht* [Online] 5 (1): 13 pp. Available at: http:// www.ualberta.ca/~german/ejournal/barron.htm (1 May 2000).

Bell, A. 1984. "Language style as audience design." *Language in Society* 13: 145–204.

Bennet-Kastor, T. 1986. "Cohesion and predication in child narrative." *Journal of child language* 13: 353–70.

Benveniste, E. 1966. *Problèmes de Linguistique Générale I*. Paris: Gallimard.

Berger, P. and Luckmann, T. 1966. *The Social Construction of Reality*. London: Penguin Books.

Berglund, E. 1999. *Early Communicative and Language Development in Swedish Children: Methods, results, clinical implications, and prospects for the future*. Edsbruk: Akademitryck AB.

Berman, R. and Slobin, D. I. 1994. *Relating Events in Narrative. A Crosslinguistic Developmental Study*. Hillsdale, N. J.: Lawrence Erlbaum Associates.

Bhatia, T. K. and Ritchie, W. C. 1999. "The bilingual child: Some issues and perspectives." In *Handbook of Child Language Acquisition*, W. C. Ritchie and T. K. Bhatia (eds.), 569–643. San Diego: Academic Press.

Bickerton, D. 1981. *Roots of Language*. Ann Arbor, MI: Karoma.

—— 1990. "Syntactic development: The brain just does it." Manuscript, University of Hawai'i at Manoa.

Bloom, L. 1970. *Language Development: Form and Function in Emerging Grammars*. Cambridge, MA: The MIT Press.

—— Lifter, K. and Hafitz, J. 1980. "Semantics of verbs and the development of verb inflection in child language." *Language* 56: 386–412.

—— Tinker, E. and Margulis, C. 1993. "The words children learn: Evidence against a noun bias in early vocabularies." *Cognitive Development* 8: 431–50.

Bloom, P. 2000. *How Children Learn the Meanings of Words*. Cambridge, MA: MIT Press.

Bonnotte, I., Kaifer, A., Fayol, M. and Idiazabal, I. 1991. "La Representación Cognitiva de los Verbos. Aproximación descriptiva y evolutiva." *Infancia y Aprendizaje* 54: 102–15.

—— —— —— —— 1993. "Rôle des types de procès et du co-texte dans l'emploi des formes verbales de la narration. *Langue Française* 97: 81–101.

Bosch, L. and Sebastián-Gallés, N. 1997a. "Native-language recognition abilities in four-month-old infants from monolingual and bilingual environments." *Cognition* 65: 33–69.

—— —— 1997b. "The role of prosody in infants' native-language discrimination abilities: the case of two phonologically close languages." *Proceedings 5th European Conference on Speech Communication and Technology. Rhodes (Greece)*: 231–4.

—— —— 2001. "Evidence of early language discrimination abilities in infants from bilingual environments." *Infancy* 2 (1): 29–49.

—— —— In preparation. "Exploring four-month-old infants' abilities to discriminate languages from the same rhythmic class."

—— Cortès, C. and Sebastián-Gallés, N. 2001. "El reconocimiento temprano de la lengua materna: un estudio basado en la voz masculina." *Infancia y Aprendizaje* 24: 197–213.

Brinton, B., Fujiki, M., Loeb, D. F. and Winkler, E. 1986. "Development of conversational repair strategies in response to requests for clarification." *Journal of Speech and Hearing Research* 29: 75–81.

Bronckart, J. P. 1976. *Genèse et organisation des formes verbales chez l'enfant*. Bruxelles: Mardaga.

—— 1982. "Verbe et catégories verbales: Vers un approche textuelle." *Bulletin CILA* 35: 7–20.

—— 1996. *Activité Langagière. Textes et Discours*. Lausanne: Delachaux et Niestlé.

—— and Sinclair, H. 1973. "Time, tense and aspect." *Cognition* 2: 107–30.

Brown, R. 1958. *Words and Things*. Glencoe, Il: Free Press.

—— 1973. *A First Language: the Early Stages*. London: George Allen and Unwin.

Caselli, M. C., Bates, E., Casadio, P., Fenson, J., Fenson, L., Sanderl, L. and Weir, J. 1995. "A cross-linguistic study of early lexical development." *Cognitive Development* 10: 159–99.

Cazden, C. 1968. "The acquisition of noun and verb inflections." *Child Development* 39: 433–48.

Cenoz, J. and Genesee, F. (eds.) 1998. *Beyond Bilingualism: Multilingualism and Multilingual Education*. Clevedon, UK: Multilingual Matters.

—— Hufeisen, B. and Jessner, U. (eds.) 2000. *Trilingualism — Tertiary Languages — German in a multilingual world*. Special issue of *Zeitschrift für Interkulturellen Fremdsprachenunterricht* 5 (1). Available at: http//www.ualberta.ca/~german/ejournal/ejournal.html

Cenoz, J. and Jessner, U. 2000. *English in Europe: the Acquisition of a Third Language*. Clevedon: Multilingual Matters.

Choi, S. and Gopnik, A. 1995. "Early acquisition of verbs in Korean: A cross-linguistic study." *Journal of Child Language* 22: 497–529.

Chomsky, N. 1965. *Aspects of the Theory of Syntax.* Cambridge, MA: The M. I. T. Press.

Christiansen, K. M. H. 1995. '*Ka looking for du?*' *A study of language differentiation and the effect of context on language mixing.* Thesis presented for the degree of Cand. Philol., University of Bergen, Norway.

Christophe, A. and Morton, J. 1998. "Is Dutch native English? Linguistic analysis by 2-month-olds." *Developmental Science* 1: 215–19.

Clahsen, H. and Muysken, P. 1996. "How adult second language learning differs from child first language development." *Behavioral and Brain Sciences* 19: 721–3.

Clark, E. V. 1978. "Discovering what words can do." *Papers from the Parasession on the Lexicon, CLS* 14: 34–57. Chicago: University of Chicago Press.

—— 1987. "The principle of contrast: A constraint on language acquisition." In *Mechanisms of language acquisition,* B. MacWhinney (ed.), 1–33. Hillsdale, NJ: Lawrence Erlbaum Associates.

—— 1993. *The Lexicon in Acquisition.* Cambridge: Cambridge University Press.

Cohen, M. 1969. "Sur l'étude du langage enfantin." *Enfance* 22: 203–72.

Comrie, B. 1976. *Aspect.* Cambridge: Cambridge University Press.

—— 1985. *Tense.* Cambridge: Cambridge University Press.

Cook-Gumperz, J. 1986. "Caught in a web of words: some considerations on language socialization and language acquisition." In *Children's Worlds and Children's Language,* J. Cook-Gumperz, W. Corsaro and J. Streeck (eds.), 37–64. Berlin: Mouton de Gruyter.

Cutler, A. and Otake, T. 1994. "Mora or phoneme? Further evidence for language specific listening." *Journal of Memory and Language* 33: 824–44.

—— Mehler, J., Norris, D. G. and Seguí, J. 1983. "A language-specific comprehension strategy." *Nature* 304: 159–60.

—— —— —— —— 1992. "The monolingual nature of speech segmentation by bilinguals." *Cognitive Psychology* 24: 381–410.

Davidson, D., Jergovic, D., Imami, Z. and Theodos, V. 1997. "Monolingual and bilingual children's use of the mutuall exclusivity constraint." *Journal of Child Language* 24: 3–24.

de Boysson-Bardies, B. (ed.) 1999. *How Language Comes to Children: From Birth to Two Years.* Cambridge, MA: MIT Press.

—— Vihman, M. M. 1991. "Adaptation to language: Evidence from babbling and first words in four languages." *Language* 67: 297–319.

—— —— Roug-Hellichius, L., Durand, C., Landberg, I. and Arao, F. 1992. "Material evidence of infant selection from the target language: A cross linguistic phonemic study." In *Phonological Development: Models, Research, Implications,* C. Ferguson, L. Menn and C. Stoel Gammon (eds.), 369–91. Timonium, MD: York Press.

de Houwer, A. 1990. *The Acquisition of Two Languages from Birth: A Case Study.* Cambridge, MA: Cambridge University Press.

—— 1995. "Bilingual language acquisition." In *The Handbook of Child Language,* P. Fletcher and B. MacWhinney (eds.), 219–50. Oxford: Blackwell.

—— 1997. "The role of input in the acquisition of past verb forms in English and Dutch: Evidence from a bilingual child." In *Proceedings of the 28th Stanford Child Language Research Forum,* E. Clark (ed.), 153–62. Stanford: CSLI.

—— 1998a. "By way of introduction: Methods in studies of bilingual first language acquisition." *The International Journal of Bilingualism* 2: 249–63.

—— 1998b. "Comparing error frequencies in monolingual and bilingual acquisition. Peer Commentaries." *Bilingualism: Language and Cognition* 1: 173–4.

—— 1998c. "Environmental factors in early bilingual development: The role of parental beliefs and attitudes." In *Bilingualism and Migration*, G. Extra and L. Verhoeven (eds.), 75–95. Berlin/New York: Mouton de Gruyter.

—— and Gillis, S. 1998. "Dutch child Language: An overview." In *The Acquisition of Dutch*, A. De Houwer and S. Gillis (eds.), 27–48. Amsterdam/Philadelphia: John Benjamins.

—— and Meisel, J. M. 1996. "Analyzing the relationship between two developing languages in bilingual first language acquisition: Methodology, data, findings." Paper presented at the *Workshop on Language Contact: Linking Different Levels of Analysis*. Wassenaar: Netherlands Institute for Advanced Study.

de Jong, E. 1986. *The Bilingual Experience*. Cambridge: Cambridge University Press.

de Lemos, C. 1981. "Interactional processes in the child's construction of language." In *The child's construction of language*, W. Deutsch (ed.), 57–75. London: London Academic Press.

De León, L. 1999. "Why Tzotzil (Mayan) children prefer verbs over nouns?: Input and interaction vs. cognitive constraints." Paper presented at the *Eighth International Congress for the Study of Child Language*, San Sebastian, Basque Country/Spain. July.

Dehaene-Lambertz, G. 1995. *Capacités linguistiques précoces et leurs bases cérébrales*. Unpublished PhD Thesis, Université Paris VI, Paris.

—— and Houston, D. 1998. "Faster orientation latencies toward native language in two-month old infants." *Language and Speech* 41 (1): 21–43.

Descoeudres, A. 1930. *Le développement de l'enfant de deux à sept ans*. Neuchatel: Delachaux and Niestlé S. A.

Deuchar, M. 1999. "Are function words non-language-specific in early bilingual two-word utterances?" *Bilingualism: Language and Cognition* 2 (1): 23–34.

—— and Clark, A. 1996. "Early bilingual acquisition of the voicing contrast in English and Spanish." *Journal of Phonetics* 24: 351–65.

—— and Quay, S. 1998. "How early is it possible to establish one vs. two systems in bilingual syntactic development?" *Bilingualism: Language and Cognition* 1 (3): 231–43.

—— —— 2000. *Bilingual Acquisition. Theoretical Implications of a Case Study*. Oxford: Oxford University Press.

Dolz, J. 1987. "Imparfait Passé-Simple et superstructure des contes d'enfants." *Feuillets* 86/87: 147–79.

—— 1990. *Catégorie verbale et action langagière. Le fonctionnement des temps du verbe dans les textes écrits des enfants catalans*. Ph.D. dissertation, University of Geneva, F. P. S. E.

—— Plazaola, I., Rosat, M.-C., Schneuwly, B., and Trevisi, S. 1988. "Ancrage textuel et temps du verbe dans cinq langues chez des élèves de 14 ans." In *II Congreso Mundial Vasco. Euskara Biltzarra Vol. I*, 41–52. Gasteiz: Servicio de publicaciones del Gobierno Vasco.

Döpke, S. 1992. *One Parent — One Language: An Interactional Approach*. Amsterdam: John Benjamins.

Döpke, S. 1997a. "German-English simultaneous bilingualism: window into input process-ing during primary language acquisition." Paper presented at the *First International Symposium on Bilingualism*, University of Newcastle.

—— 1997b. "Is the simultaneous acquisition of two languages in early childhood equal to acquiring each of the two languages individually?" In *The Proceedings of the Twenty-eighth Annual Child Language Research Forum*, E. Clark (ed.), 95–112. Stanford: Centre for the Study of Language Information.

—— 1998. "Competing language structures: The acquisition of verb placement by bilingual German-English children." *Journal of Child Language* 25: 555–84.

—— 2000. "Generation of and retraction from cross-linguistically motivated structures in bilingual first language acquisition." *Bilingualism: Language and Cognition* 3 (3): 209–26.

Dore, J. 1985. "Holophrases revisited: Their 'logical' development from dialog." In *Children's Single Word Speech*, M. D. Barrett (ed.), 23–58. New York: Wiley.

Dromi, E. 1987. *Early Lexical Development*. Cambridge: Cambridge University Press.

Dunn, L. M. and Dunn, L. M. 1981. *Peabody Picture Vocabulary Test-Revised*. Circle Pines, Minnesota: American Guidance Service.

—— Thériault-Whalen, C. M. and Dunn, L. M. 1993. *Échelle de vocabulaire en images Peabody*. Toronto: Psycan.

Duranti, A. 1988. "The ethnography of speaking: Toward a linguistics of the praxis." In *Linguistics: The Cambridge Survey*, Vol. 4: *Language: The Socio-Cultural Context*, F. Newmeyer (ed.), 210–28. Cambridge: Cambridge University Press.

—— 1997. *Linguistic Anthropology*. Cambridge: Cambridge University Press.

—— and Goodwin, C. (eds.). 1992. *Rethinking Context: Language as an Interactive Phenom-enon*. Cambridge: Cambridge University Press.

Egger, M. E. 1879. *Observations et réflexions sur le développement de l'intelligence et du langage chez les enfants*. Paris: Alphonse Picard.

EGLU 1997. *Euskal Gramatika. Lehen Urratsak. II*. Bilbao: Euskaltzaindia.

Eilers, R. E., Oller, D. K. and Benito-Garcia, C. R. 1984. "The acquisition of voicing contrasts in Spanish-and English learning infants and children." *Journal of Child Language* 11: 313–36.

Ezeizabarrena, M. J. 1991. "Ezeztapenerako formen bilakaera bi haur elebidunen eta elebakar baten hizkuntz jabekuntzan." In *Adquisición del lenguaje en niños bilingües y monolingües*, I. Idiazabal (ed.), 183–95. San Sebastián: Universidad del País Vasco.

Faingold, E. 1996. "Variation in the applicaiton of natural processes: Language-dependent constraints in the phonological acquisition of bilingual children." *Journal of Psycholin-guistic Research* 25: 515–26.

Fayol, M. 1985. "L'emploi des temps verbaux dans les récits éscrits. Etudes chez l'enfant, l'adulte et l'adolescent." *Bulletin de Psychologie* 38: 683–703.

Fenson, L., Pethick, S. and Cox, J. L. 1994. "The MacArthur Communicative Development Inventories: Short form versions." Unpublished manuscript. Department of Psychol-ogy, San Diego State University, San Diego CA.

Fernald, A., Taeschner, T., Dunn, J., Papousek, M., de Boysson-Bardies, B. and Fukui, I. 1989. "A cross-language study of prosodic modifications in mothers' and fathers' speech to preverbal infants." *Journal of Child Language* 16: 477–501.

Fodor, J. D. 1998. "Unambiguous triggers." *Linguistic Inquiry* 29: 1–36.

Gallagher, T. 1977. "Revision strategies in the speech of normal children developing language." *Journal of Speech and Hearing Research* 20: 303–18.

Garau, M. J. 1996. *Language Development in a Catalan-English Bilingual Between the Ages of 1 and 3*. Doctoral Dissertation, Universidad Pompeu Fabra.

Garvey, C. 1977. "The contingent query: A dependant act in conversation." In *Interaction, Conversation, and the Development of Language: The Origins of Behavior, Vol. 5*, M. Lewis and L. Rosenblum (eds.), 63–93. New York: Wiley.

Gathercole, V., Sebastián, E. and Soto, P. 1999. "The early acquisition of Spanish verbal morphology: across the board or piecemeal knowledge?" *International Journal of Bilingualism* 3: 133–82.

—— —— —— 2000. "Lexically specified patterns in early verbal morphology in Spanish." In *New Directions in Language Development and Disorder*, M. R. Perkins and S. J. Howard (eds.), 149–68. London: Plenum.

Gawlitzek-Maiwald, I. and Tracy, R. 1996. "Bilingual bootstrapping." *Linguistics* 34: 901–26.

Gelman, R. and Schatz, M. 1977. "Appropriate speech adjustments: The operation of conversational constraints on talk to 2-year-olds." In *Interaction, Conversation, and the Development of Language: The Origins of Behavior Vol. 5*, M. Lewis and M. Rosenblum (eds.), 27–61. New York: Wiley.

Genesee, F. 1988. "Bilingual language development in preschool children." In *Language Development in Exceptional Circumstances*, D. Bishop and K. Mogford (eds.), 62–79. Edinburgh: Churchill Livingston.

—— 1989. "Early bilingual development: one language or two?" *Journal of Child Language* 16: 161–79.

—— 2000. "Bilingual first language acquistion: Exploring the limits of the language faculty." In *21st Annual Review of Applied Linguistics*, M. McGroarty (ed.), 153–68. Cambridge: Cambridge University Press.

—— In press. "Rethinking bilingual acquisition." In *Bilingualism: Challenges and Directions for Future Research*, J. M. Dewaele (ed.). Clevedon: Multilingual Matters.

—— Boivin, I. and Nicoladis, E. 1996. "Talking with strangers: A study of bilingual children's communicative competence." *Applied Psycholinguistics* 17: 427–42.

—— Nicoladis, E. and Paradis, J. 1995. "Language differentiation in early bilingual development." *Journal of Child Language* 22: 611–31.

Gentner, D. 1982. "Why nouns are learned before verbs: Linguistic relativity versus natural partitioning." In *Language Development: Language, Culture, and Cognition*, S. Kucazj (ed.), 301–34. Hillsdale, NJ: Lawrence Erlbaum.

Gili Gaya, S. 1972. *Estudios de lenguaje infantil*. Barcelona: Bibliograf.

Givón, T. 1979. *On Understanding Grammar*. New York: Academic Press.

Goffman, E. 1969. *Strategic Interaction*. Philadelphia: University of Pennsylvania Press.

—— 1981. *Forms of Talk*. Philadelphia: University of Pennsylvania Press.

Goldberg, A. E. 1998. "Patterns of experience in patterns of language." In *The New Psychology of Language*, M. Tomasello (ed.), 203–19. Mahwah, NJ: Erlbaum.

Goldfield, B. A. 1993. "Noun bias in maternal speech to one-year-olds." *Journal of Child Language* 20: 85–99.

Golinkoff, R. M. and Hirsh-Pasek, K. 1999. *How Babies Talk: The Magic and Mystery of Language in the First Three Years of Life.* New York: Dutton.

—— Mervis, C. B. and Hirsh-Pasek, K. 1994. "Early object labels: The case for a developmental lexical principles framework." *Journal of Child Language* 21: 125–55.

Goodz, N. S. 1989. "Parental language mixing in bilingual families." *Infant Mental Health Journal* 10: 25–43.

—— 1994. "Interactions between parents and children in bilingual families." In *Educating Second Language Children: The Whole Child, The Whole Curriculum, The Whole Community,* F. Genesee (ed.), 61–82. Cambridge: Cambridge University Press.

Grimm, H., Doil, H., Müller, C. and Wilde, S. 1996. "Elternfragebogen für die differentielle Erfassung früher sprachlicher Fähigkeiten" (Parent questionnaire for the differential assessment of early language abilities). *Sprache and Kognition* 15: 32–45.

Groat, E. 1995. "English expletives: a minimalist approach." *Linguistic Inquiry* 26: 354–65.

Gropen, J., Pinker, S., Hollander, M., Goldberg, R. and Wilson, R. 1989. "Learnability and acquisition of the dative alternation in English." *Language* 65: 203–57.

Grosjean, F. 1998. "Studying bilinguals: Methodological and conceptual issues." *Bilingualism: Language and Cognition* 1 (2): 131–49.

—— 2000. "The bilingual's language modes." In *One Mind, Two Languages: Bilingual Language Processing,* J. L. Nicol (ed.), 1–25. Oxford: Blackwell.

Guasti, M. T. 1993/94. "Verb syntax in Italian child grammar: finite and non-finite verbs." *Language Acquisition* 3: 1–40.

Guilfoyle, E. and Noonan, M. 1988. "Functional categories and language acquisition." Unpublished manuscript, McGill University, Montreal.

Gumperz, J. J. 1982. *Discourse Strategies.* Cambridge: Cambridge University Press.

Harding, E. and Riley, P. 1986. *The Bilingual Family — A Handbook for Parents.* Cambridge: Cambridge University Press.

Hart, B. and Risley, T. R. 1999. *The Social World of Children Learning to Talk.* Baltimore: Paul H. Brookes Publishing Co.

Hernández Pina, F. 1984. *Teorías psicolingüísticas y su aplicación a la adquisición del español como lengua materna.* Madrid: Siglo XXI.

Hoekstra, T. and Hyams, N. 1998. "Aspects of root infinitives." *Lingua* 106: 81–112.

Hoffmann, C. 1985. "Language acquisition in two trilingual children." *Journal of Multilingual and Multicultural Development* 6 (6): 479–95.

—— and Widdicombe, S. 1999. "Code-switching and language dominance in the trilingual child." *AILE Proceedings of 8th EUROSLA Conference Paris,* vol. 1, Special Issue: 51–62.

Hulk, A. and Müller, N. 2000. "Bilingual first language acquisition at the interface between syntax and pragmatics." In *Bilingualism, Language and Cognition* 3: 227–44.

—— and Van der Linden, E. 1997. "Language mixing in a French-Dutch bilingual child." Paper presented at the *First International Symposium on Bilingualism,* University of Newcastle.

—— 1998. "Evidence for transfer in bilingual children?" *Bilingualism: Language and Cognition* 1: 177–80.

Huss, L. M. 1991. *Simultan tvåspråkighet i svensk-finsk kontext.* Uppsala: Studia Uralica Upsaliensia 21.

Hyams, N. 1986. *Language Acquisition and the Theory of Parameters.* Dordrecht: Reidel.

—— 1992. "Morphosyntactic development in Italian and its relevance to parameter-setting models: comments on the paper by Pizzuto and Caselli." *Journal of Child Language* 19: 695–709.

Ingham, R. 1998. "Tense without agreement in early clause structure." *Language Acquisition* 7: 51–81.

Iverson, J. M., Capirici, O. and Caselli, M. C. 1994. "From communication to language in two modalities." *Cognitive Development* 9: 23–43.

Jacobsen, T. 1986."¿Aspecto antes que tiempo? Una mirada a la adquisición temprana del español." In *Adquisición del lenguaje*, J. M. Meisel (ed.), 97–114. Frankfurt am Main: Verwuert.

Jarovinskij, A. and Fabricius, I. 1987. "On communicative competence of a bilingual child: A case study." *Acta Linguistica Academiae Scientarum Hungaricae* 37: 177–87.

Jekat, S. 1985. *Die Entwicklung des Wortschatzes bei bilingualen Kindern (Französisch-Deutsch) in den ersten vier Lebensjahren.* Unpublished Master's Thesis, University of Hamburg.

Johnson, C. and Lancaster, P. 1998. "The development of more than one phonology: A case study of a Norwegian-English bilingual child." *International Journal of Bilingualism* 2: 265–300.

Johnson, M. H., Posner, M. I. and Rothbart, M. K. 1991. "Components of visual orienting in early infancy: contingency learning, anticipatory looking and disengaging." *Journal of Cognitive Neuroscience* 3 (4): 335–44.

Jusczyk, P. W. 1997. *The Discovery of Spoken Language.* Cambridge, MA: MIT Press.

—— and Aslin, R. N. 1995. "Infants' detection of sound patterns of words in fluent speech." *Cognitive Psychology* 29: 1–23.

—— Hohne, E. A., Jusczyk, A. M. and Redanz, N. J. 1993. "Infants' sensitivity to the sound patterns of native language words." *Journal of Memory and Language* 32: 402–20.

Kaiser, G. A. 1998. *Verb-Zweit-Effekte in der Romania: Eine diachronische Studie mit besonderer Berücksichtigung des Französischen.* Habilitation Dissertation, University of Hamburg.

Kasuya, H. 1998. "Determinants of language choice in bilingual children: The role of input." *International Journal of Bilingualism* 2 (3): 327–46.

Kayne, R. 1989. "Notes on English agreement." Manuscript, CUNY.

Kazazis, Kostas. 1970. "A case of interference in the Greek grammar of a trilingual child." *Neo-Hellenika: Annual Publication of the Center for Neo-Hellenic Studies* 1: 191–95.

Kemler-Nelson, D. G., Jusczyk, P. W., Mandel, D. R., Myers, J., Turk, A. and Gerken, L. A. 1995. "The Head-Turn Preference procedure for testing auditory perception." *Infant Behavior and Development* 18: 111–16.

Klinge, S. 1990. "Prepositions in bilingual language acquisition." In *Two first languages — Early grammatical development in bilingual children*, J. M. Meisel (ed.), 123–56. Dordrecht: Foris.

Konefal, J. A. and Fokes, J. 1984. "Linguistic analysis of children's conversational repairs." *Journal of Psycholinguistic Research* 13: 1–11.

Köppe, R. 1996. "Language differentiation in bilingual children: The development of grammatical and pragmatic competence." *Linguistics* 34: 927–54.

—— 1997. *Sprachentrennung im frühen bilingualen Erstspracherwerb: Französisch/Deutsch.* Tübingen: Narr.

Krasinski, E. 1995. "The development of past marking in a bilingual child and the punctual–nonpunctual distinction." *First Language* 15: 277–300.

Ladefoged, P. 1975. *A Course in Phonetics*. New York: Harcourt, Brace Jovanovich.

Langford, D. 1981. "The clarification request sequence in conversation between mothers and their children." In *Adult-Child Conversation*, P. French and M. Maclure (eds.), 159–74. London: Croom Helm.

Lanza, E. 1988. "Language strategies in the home: Linguistic input and infant bilingualism." In *Bilingualism and the Individual: Copenhagen Studies in Bilingualism, Vol. 4*, A. Holmen, E. Hansen, J. Gimbel and J. N. Jørgensen (eds.), 69–84. Clevedon: Multilingual Matters.

—— 1992. "Can bilingual two-year-olds code-switch?" *Journal of Child Language* 19 (3): 633–58.

—— 1993. "Language mixing and language dominance in bilingual first language acquisition." In *The Proceedings of the Twenty-fourth Annual Child Language Research Forum*, E. V. Clark (ed.), 197–208. Stanford University: Center for the Study of Language and Information Conference Series.

—— 1996. "L'input parental et la différentiation linguistique chez une bilingue de deux ans: Interactions dyadiques et triadiques. "*AILE (Acquisition et Interaction en Langue Étrangère)* 6: 11–37.

—— 1997. *Language Mixing in Infant Bilingualism: A Sociolinguistic Perspective*. Oxford: Oxford University Press.

—— 1998a. "Cross-linguistic influence, input and the young bilingual child. Commentary to N. Müller, *Transfer in bilingual first language acquisition*." *Bilingualism: Language and Cognition* 1 (3): 181–2.

—— 1998b. "Indexicality and language socialization in bilingual first language acquisition." Paper presented at the 6th International Pragmatics Conference, Reims, France.

—— 1999. "Parental discourse and language mixing in bilingual children revisited." Paper presented at the *VIII International Congress for the Study of Child Language*, San Sebastian, Spain, July. To be submitted for publication in *The International Journal of Bilingualism*.

—— 2001. "Concluding remarks: Language contact — A dilemma for the bilingual child or for the linguist?" In *Cross-Linguistic Structures in Simultaneous Bilingualism*, S. Döpke (ed.), 227–45. Amsterdam: John Benjamins.

Lebeaux, D. S. 1988. *Language Acquisition and the Form of Grammar*. PhD dissertation, University of Massachusetts.

Lenneberg, E. H. 1967. *Biological foundations of language*. New York: Wiley.

Leopold, W. 1939. *Speech development of a bilingual child: A linguist's record: Vol. I. Vocabulary growth in the first two years*. Evanston, Il: Northwestern University Press.

—— 1949. *Speech development of bilingual child: A linguist's record: Vol. III. Grammar and general problems*. Evanston, Il.: Northwestern University Press.

—— 1954. A child's learning of two languages. In *Georgetown University Round Table on Languages and Linguistics*, 19–30. Washington: Georgetown University Press.

—— 1978. "A child's learning of two languages." In *Second language acquisition: A book of readings*, E. Hatch (ed.), 23–32. Rowley, MA: Newbury House.

Levinson, S. 1993. *Pragmatics*. Cambridge: Cambridge University Press.

Levy, Y. 1985. "Theoretical gains from the study of bilingualism: A case report." *Language Learning* 35: 541–54.

Li Wei. 1998. "The 'why' and 'how' questions in the analysis of conversational code-switching." In *Code-switching in Conversation. Language, Interaction, and Identity*, P. Auer (ed.), 156–76. London: Routledge.

—— and Milroy, L. 1995. "Conversational codeswitching in a Chinese community in Britain." *Journal of Pragmatics* 23: 281–99.

Lieven, E., Pine, J. and Baldwin. G. 1997. "Lexically-based learning and early grammatical development." *Journal of Child Language* 24: 187–219.

López Ornat, S. 1994. *La adquisición de la lengua española*. Madrid: Siglo XXI.

Lyons, J. 1968. *Introduction to Theoretical Linguistics*. London/New York: Cambridge University Press.

McArthur, T. 1998. *The English languages*. London: Cambridge University Press.

McClure, E. 1981. "Formal and functional aspects of the code-switched discourse of bilingual children." In *Latino Language and Communicative Behavior*, R. Durán (ed.), 69–94. Norwood, N. J.: Ablex.

McClure, K. 1997. "Evidence against mutual exclusivity." In *Proceedings of the GALA '97 Conference on Language Acquisition*, A. Sorace, C. Heycock and R. Shillock (eds.), 102–8. Edinburgh: Edinburgh University.

McCune-Nicolich, L. 1981. "The cognitive bases of relational words in the single word period." *Journal of Child Language* 8: 15–34.

McLaughlin, B. 1978. *Second-language acquisition in childhood*. Hillsdale, NJ: Lawrence Erlbaum Associates Inc.

MacNamara, J. 1982. *Names for Things*. Cambridge, MA: The MIT Press.

MacWhinney, B. 1975. "Pragmatic patterns in child syntax." *Stanford Papers And Reports on Child Language Development* 10: 153–65.

—— 1982. "Basic syntactic processes." In *Language Acquisition: Vol. 1. Syntax and semantics*, S. Kuczaj (ed.), 73–136. Hillsdale, NJ: Lawrence Erlbaum.

—— 1991. *The CHILDES Project: Tools for Analyzing Talk*. Hillsdale, NJ: Lawrence Erlbaum Associates.

—— 1995. *The CHILDES Project: Tools for Analysing Talk*. Second edition. Hillsdale, NJ: Lawrence Erlbaum Associates.

—— 2000. *The CHILDES Project: Tools for Analyzing talk*. Third Edition. Mahwah, NJ: Lawrence Erlbaum Associates.

—— and Bates, E. (eds.). 1989. *The Crosslinguistic Study of Sentence Processing*. New York: Cambridge University Press.

Mahlau, A. 1994. "El proyecto BUSDE. Corpus y metodología." In *La adquisición del vasco y del castellano en niños bilingües*, J. M. Meisel (ed.), 69–111. Frankfurt and Madrid: Vervuert.

Maratsos, M. P. 1973. "Nonegocentric communication abilities in preschool children." *Child Development* 44: 697–700.

—— 1988. "The acquisition of formal word classes." In *Categories and Processes in Language Acquisition*, Y. Levy, I. Schlesinger and M. Braine (eds.), 31–44. Hillsdale, NJ: Lawrence Erlbaum.

Marchman, V. and Bates, E. 1994. "Continuity in lexical and morphological development: a test of the critical mass hypothesis." *Journal of Child Language* 21: 339–66.

Marcos, H. and Bernicot, J. 1994. "Addressee cooperation and request reformulation in young children." *Journal of Child Language* 21: 677–92.

Marcus, G. F., Vijayan, S., Bandi Rao, S. and Vishton, P. M. 1999. "Rule learning by seven-month-old infants." *Science* 283: 77–80.

Markman, E. 1989. *Categorization and naming in children: Problems of induction.* Cambrdige, MA: MIT Press.

—— 1990. "Constraints children place on word meanings." *Cognitive Science* 14: 57–77.

Mayer, M. 1969. *Frog where are you?* New York: Dial Press

Mead, G. 1934. *Mind, Self and Society.* Chicago: University of Chicago Press.

Mehler, J. and Christophe, A. 1994. "Language in the infant's mind." *Philosophical Transactions of the Royal Society of London B* 346: 13–20.

—— and Christophe, A. 1995. "Maturation and learning of language in the first year of life." In *The Cognitive Neurosciences*, M. S. Gazzaniga (ed.), 943–54. Cambridge, Mass.: Bradford Books, MIT Press.

—— Dupoux, E., Nazzi, T. and Dehaene-Lambertz, G. 1996. "Coping with linguistic diversity: the infant's viewpoint." In *Signal to Syntax*, J. L. Morgan and K. Demuth (eds.), 101–16. Mahwah, NJ: Lawrence Erlbaum Associates.

—— Frauenfelder, U. and Segui, J. 1981. "Phoneme monitoring, syllable monitoring and lexical access." *British Journal of Psychology* 72: 471–7.

—— Jusczyk, P. W., Lambertz, G., Halsted, N., Bertoncini, J. and Amiel-Tison, C. 1988. "A precursor of language acquisition in young infants". *Cognition* 29: 143–78.

Meisel, J. M. 1986. "Word order and case marking in early child language. Evidence from simultaneous acquisition of two first languages: French and German." *Linguistics* 24: 123–83.

—— 1989. "Early differentiation of languages in bilingual children." In *Bilingualism Across the Lifespan: Aspects of Acquisition, Maturity, and Loss,* K. Hyltenstam and L. Obler (eds.), 13–40. Cambridge: Cambridge University Press.

—— 1990a. "INFL-ection: Subjects and subject-verb agreement." In *Two First Languages: Early Grammatical Development in Bilingual Children,* J. M. Meisel (ed.), 237–98. Dordrecht: Foris.

—— (ed.). 1990b. *Two First Languages: Early Grammatical Development in Bilingual Children.* Dordrecht: Foris.

—— (ed.). 1994a. *Bilingual First Language Acquisition: French and German Grammatical Development.* Amsterdam: John Benjamins.

—— 1994b. "Code-switching in young bilingual children: The acquisition of grammatical constraints." *Studies in Second Language Acquisition* 16: 413–39.

—— 1994c. "Getting FAT. Finiteness, Agreement and Tense in early grammars." In *Bilingual First Language Acquisition. French and German Grammatical Development,* J. M. Meisel (ed.), 89–129. Amsterdam: John Benjamins.

—— 1994d. "La adquisición de la negación en euskera y castellano." In *La adquisición del vasco y del español en niños bilingües,* J. M. Meisel (ed.), 151–80. Frankfurt/M: Vervuert.

—— (ed.). 1994e. *La adquisición del vasco y del español en niños bilingües.* Frankfurt am Main: Vervuert.

—— 1995. "Parameters in acquisition." In *A Handbook of Child Language*, P. Fletcher and B. MacWhinney (eds.), 10–35. Oxford: Blackwell.

—— 1997a. "The acquisition of the syntax of negation in French and German: Contrasting first and second language acquisition." *Second Language Research* 13: 227–63.

—— 1997b. "The L2 Basic Variety as an i-language." *Second Language Research* 13: 374–85.

Menig-Peterson, C. L. 1975. "The modification of communicative behavior in preschool-aged children as a function of the listener's perspective." *Child Development* 46: 1015–18.

Menn, L., O'Connor, M., Obler, L. K. and Holland, A. 1995. *Non-fluent Aphasia in a Multilingual Word*. Amsterdam: John Benjamins.

Mikès, M. 1990. "Some issues of lexical development in early bi- and trilinguals." In *Children's Language*, vol 7, G. Conti-Ramsden and C. Snow (eds.), 103–20. Hillsdale, N. J.: Lawrence Erlbaum.

Milroy, L. and Muysken, P. (eds.). 1995. *One Speaker, two Languages: Cross-Disciplinary Perspectives on Code-Switching*. Cambridge: Cambridge University Press.

Mishina, S. 1997. *Language Separation in Early Bilingual Development: A Longitudinal Study of Japanese/English Bilingual Children*. Doctoral dissertation, University of California, Los Angeles.

Moon, C., Cooper, R. and Fifer, W. 1993. "Two-day-olds prefer their native language." *Infant Behavior and Development* 16: 495–500.

Morgan, J. L. 1994. "Converging measures of speech segmentation in preverbal infants." *Infant Behavior and Development* 17: 389–403.

Müller, N. 1998. "Transfer in bilingual first language acquisition." *Bilingualism: Language and Cognition* 1: 151–92.

—— 1999. "Crosslinguistic influence in bilingual children: Comparing German/French and German/Italian." Paper presented at the *Eighteenth International Congress for the Study of Child Language*, San Sebastian, Spain.

—— and Hulk, A. to appear. "Crosslinguistic influence in bilingual language acquisition: Italian and French as recipient languages." *Bilingualism: Language and Cognition*.

Myers-Scotton, C. 1993. *Social Motivations for Codeswitching*. Oxford: Oxford University Press.

Naka, N., Miyata, S. and Nisisawa, H. 1999. "Measuring vocabulary in Japanese." Paper presented at the 12th World Congress of Applied Linguistics AILA '99 Tokyo.

Navracsics, J. 1999. *The Acquisition of Hungarian by Trilingual Children*. Ph.D. dissertation, University of Vesprém, Vesprém-Pécs.

Nazzi, T., Bertoncini, J. and Mehler, J. 1998. "Language discrimination by newborns: towards an understanding of the role of rhythm." *Journal of Experimental Psychology: Human Perception and Performance* 24: 756–66.

—— Juscyk, P. W. and Johnson, E. K. 2000. "Discriminating languages from the same rhythmic class: Evidence from English-learning 5-month-olds." *Journal of Memory and Language* 43(1): 1–19.

Nelson, K. 1973. "Structure and strategy for learning to talk." *Monograph of the Society for Research in Child Development* 38: serial no. 1–2.

—— Hampson, J. and Shaw, L. K. 1993. "Nouns in early lexicons: Evidence, explanations and implications." *Journal of Child Language* 20: 61–84.

Nelson, K. and Lucariello, J. 1985. "The development of meaning in first words." In *Children's Single Word Speech*, M. D. Barrett (ed.), 59–86. New York: Wiley.

Newport, E. L., Gleitman, H. and Gleitman, L. R. 1977. "Mother, I'd rather do it myself: Some effects and non-effects of maternal speech style." In *Talking to Children: Language Input and Acquisition*, C. A. Ferguson and C. E. Snow (eds.), 109–49. Cambridge: Cambridge University Press.

Nicoladis, E. 1994. *Code-mixing in Young Bilingual Children*. Ph.D. dissertation, McGill University, Montreal.

—— and Genesee, F. 1996. "A longitudinal study of pragmatic differentiation in young bilingual children." *Language Learning* 46 (3): 439–64.

—— —— 1997a. "Language development in preschool bilingual children." *Journal of Speech-Language Pathology and Audiology* 21: 258–70.

—— —— 1997b. "The role of parental input and language dominance in bilingual children's code-mixing." *Proceedings of the Annual Boston University Conference on Language Development* 21 (2): 422–32.

—— —— 1998. "Parental discourse and codemixing in bilingual children." *International Journal of Bilingualism*, 2 (1): 85–99.

—— —— Mayberry, R. and Genesee, F. 1999. "Gesture and early bilingual development." *Developmental Psychology* 35: 514–26.

Ninio, A. 1988. "On formal grammatical categories in early child language." In *Categories and Processes in Language Acquisition*, Y. Levy, I. Schlesinger and M. Braine (eds.), 99–119. Hillsdale, NJ: Lawrence Erlbaum.

—— 1999. "Pathbreaking verbs in syntactic development and the question of prototypical transitivity." *Journal of Child Language* 26: 619–53.

—— and Snow, C. E. 1996. *Pragmatic Development*. Boulder, CO: Westview Press.

Ochs, E. 1979. "Transcription as theory". In *Developmental Pragmatics*, E. Ochs and B. Schieffelin (eds.), 43–72. New York: Academic Press.

—— 1988. *Culture and Language Development: Language Acquisition and Language Socialization in a Samoan Village*. Cambridge: Cambridge University Press.

—— 1996. "Linguistic resources for socializing humanity." In *Rethinking Linguistic Relativity*, J. J. Gumperz and S. Levinson (eds.), 407–37. Cambridge: Cambridge University Press.

—— and Schieffelin, B. 1995. "The impact of language socialization on grammatical development." In *The Handbook of Child Language*, P. Fletcher and B. MacWhinney (eds.), 73–94. Oxford: Blackwell.

—— and Taylor, C. 1992. "Family narrative as political activity." *Discourse and Society* 3 (3): 301–40.

Ogura, T. 1998. *Makkaasaa nyuuyouji gengo hattatsu shitsumonshi no kaihatsu to kenkyuu* (The development and study of the MacArthur Communicative Development Inventories). Kobe: Kobe University Press.

—— Yamashita, Y. and Murase, T. 1998. "Shokigengo hattatsu inbentori no datousei oyobi goi chekkurisuto no kentoo" (The validity and the analysis of vocabulary checklist in the first version of the Japanese Early Communicative Development Inventory). *Kobe Daigaku Hattatsu Kagaku Kenkyukiyou* (*Kobe University Developmental Science Bulletin*) 5 (2): 261–76.

Oksaar, E. 1978. "Preschool trilingualism: A case study." In *Language Acquisition and Developmental Kinesics*, F. C. Peng and W. von Raffler-Engel (eds.), 129–38. Hiroshima: Bunka Hyoron Publishing Co.

Olguin, R. and Tomasello, M. 1993. "Twenty-five-month-old children do not have a grammatical category of verb." *Cognitive Development* 8: 245–72.

Oller, D. K. 1991. "Similarities and differences in vocalizations of deaf and hearing infants: Future directions for research." In *Research on Child Language Disorders: A Decade of Progress*, J. Miller (ed.), 125–38. Austin, TX: Pro-Ed.

—— and Eilers, R. E. 1982. "Similarities of babbling in Spanish-and English-learning babies." *Journal of Child Language* 21: 33–58.

—— —— 1988. "The role of audition in infant babbling." *Child Development* 59: 441–9.

—— Urbano, R. and Cobo-Lewis, A. B. 1997. "Development of precursors to speech in infants exposed to two languages." *Journal of Child Language* 24: 407–25.

Otake, T. and Cutler, A. 1996. *Phonological Structure and Language Processing: Crosslinguistic Studies*. Berlin: Mouton de Gruyter.

Padilla, A. M. and Liebman, E. 1975. "Language acquisition in the bilingual child." *Bilingual Review* 2: 34–55.

Pallier, C., Sebastián-Gallés, N., Dupoux, E., Christophe, A. and Mehler, J. 1998. "Perceptual adjustment to time-compressed speech: A cross-linguistic study." *Memory and Cognition* 26 (4): 844–51.

Paradis, J. 1996. "Phonological differentiation in a bilingual child: Hildegard revisited." In *Proceedings of the 20th Annual Boston University Conference on Language Development*, A. Stringfellow, D. Cahana-Amitay, E. Hughes and A. Zukowski (eds.), 428–39. Somerville, MA: Cascadilla Press.

—— To appear. "Beyond 'one system or two?': Degrees of separation between the languages of French-English bilingual children." In *Cross-linguistic Structures in Simultaneous Bilingualism*, S. Döpke (ed.). Amsterdam/Philadelphia: John Benjamins.

—— and Genesee, F. 1996. "Syntactic acquisition in bilingual children: autonomous or interdependent?" *Studies in Second Language Acquisition* 18: 1–25.

—— —— 1997. "On continuity and the emergence of functional categories in bilingual first language acquisition." *Language Acquisition* 6: 91–124.

Pearson, B. Z. 1998. "Assessing lexical development in bilingual babies and toddlers." *International Journal of Bilingualism* 2 (3): 347–72.

—— Fernández, S. C. and Oller, D. K. 1993. "Lexical development in bilingual infants and toddlers: Comparison to monolingual norms." *Language Learning* 43: 93–120.

—— —— —— 1995. "Cross-language synonyms in the lexicons of bilingual infants: one language or two?" *Journal of Child Language* 22: 345–68.

—— —— Lewedag, V. and Oller, D. K. 1997. "The relation of input factors to lexical learning by bilingual infants (ages 10 to 30 months)." *Applied Psycholinguistics* 18: 41–58.

Perner, J. and Leekam, S. R. 1986. "Belief and quantity: three-year-olds' adaptation to listener's knowledge." *Journal of Child Language* 13: 305–15.

Petersen, J. 1988. "Word-internal code-switching constraints in a bilingual child's grammar." *Linguistics* 26: 479–93.

Peterson, C. L., Danner, F. W. and Flavell, J. H. 1972. "Developmental changes in children's response to three indications of communicative failure." *Child Development* 43: 1463–8.

Pine, J., Lieven, E. and Rowland, C. 1996. "Observational and checklist measures of vocabulary composition: what do they mean?" *Journal of Child Language* 23: 573–89.

——— ——— ——— 1998. "Comparing different models of the development of the English verb category." *Linguistics* 36: 4–40.

Pizzuto, E. and Caselli, M. C. 1992. "The acquisition of Italian morphology: implications for models of language development." *Journal of Child Language* 19: 491–557.

——— ——— 1993. "L'acquisizione della morfologia flessiva nel linguaggio spontaneo: evidenza per i modelli innatisti o cognitivisti?" In *Ricerche sull'Acquisizione dell'Italiano*, E. Cresti and M. Moneglia (eds.), 165–87. Roma: Bulzoni.

——— ——— 1994. "The acquisition of Italian verb morphology in a cross-linguistic perspective." In *Other Children, Other Languages*, Y. Levy (ed.), 137–87. Hillsdale, NJ: Erlbaum.

Plazaola, I. 1993. *Analyse du fonctionnement de trois types de discours en basque. Eléments historiques et linguistiques pour une didactique des formes verbales et des marques de personne.* Ph.D. dissertation, University of Geneva, F. P. S. E.

Poeppel, D. and Wexler, K. 1993. "The full competence hypothesis of clause structure." *Language* 69: 1–33.

Pye, C. 1986. "One lexicon or two?: An alternative interpretation of early bilingual speech." *Journal of Child Language* 13: 591–3.

Quay, S. 1995. "The bilingual lexicon: Implications for studies of language choice." *Journal of Child Language* 22: 369–87.

Radford, A. 1990. *Syntactic Theory and the Acquisition of English Syntax.* Oxford: Blackwell.

——— 1996. "Towards a structure-building model of acquisition." In *Generative Perspectives on Language Acquisition*, H. Clahsen (ed.), 43–90. Amsterdam: John Benjamins.

Ramus, F., and Mehler, J. 1999. "Language identification with suprasegmental cues: A study based on speech resynthesis." *Journal of the Acoustical Society of America* 105 (1): 512–21.

——— Nespor, M. and Mehler, J. 1999. "Correlates of linguistic rhythm in the speech signal." *Cognition* 73: 265–92.

Redlinger, W. E. and Park, T.-Z. 1980. "Language mixing in young bilinguals." *Journal of Child Language* 7: 337–52.

Robinson, B. F. and Mervis, C. B. 1999. "Comparing productive vocabulary measures from the CDI and a systematic diary study." *Journal of Child Language* 26: 177–85.

Roeper, T. 1999. "Universal bilingualism." *Bilingualism: Language and Cognition* 2 (3): 169–86.

Romaine, S. 1995. *Bilingualism.* 2nd ed. Oxford, U. K.: Blackwell.

——— 1999. "Bilingual language development." In *The Development of Language*, M. Barrett (ed.), 251–75. Philadelphia, PA: Psychology Press.

Ronjat, J. 1913. *Le développement du langage observé chez un enfant bilingue.* Paris: Champion.

Rubino, R. and Pine, J. 1998. "Subject-verb agreement in Brazilian Portuguese: what low error rates hide." *Journal of Child Language* 25: 35–59.

Saffran, J. R., Aslin, R. N. and Newport, E. L. 1996. "Statistical learning by 8-month-old infants." *Science* 274: 1926–8.

Sakurai, C. 1999. "A cross-linguistic study of early acquisition of nouns and verbs in English and Japanese." In *Cognition and Function in Language*, B. A. Fox, D. Jarafsky and L. Michaelis (eds.), 136–42. Stanford: CSLI Publications.

Saunders, G. 1988. *Bilingual children: From birth to teens*. Clevedon, Avon: Multilingual Matters.

Schieffelin, B. 1990. *The Give and Take of Everyday Life. Language Socialization of Kaluli Children*. Cambridge: Cambridge University Press.

—— and Ochs, E. 1986. Language socialization. *Annual Review of Anthropology* 15: 163–91.

Schiffrin, D. 1984. "Review of John J. Gumperz, *Discourse Strategies*, and John J. Gumperz (ed.), *Language and Social Identity*." *Language* 60(4): 953–9.

—— 1990. "The management of a co-operative self during argument: the role of opinions and stories." In *Conflict Talk*, A. Grimshaw (ed.), 241–59. Cambridge: Cambridge University Press.

—— 1994. *Approaches to Discourse*. Oxford: Blackwell.

—— 1997. "Theory and method in discourse analysis: What context for what unit?" *Language and Communication* 17(2): 75–92.

Schlyter, S. 1990. "The acquisition of tense and aspect." In *Two First Languages — Early Grammatical Development in Bilingual Children*, J. M. Meisel (ed.), 87–122. Dordrecht: Foris.

—— 1993. "The weaker language in bilingual Swedish-French children." In *Progression and Regression in Language: Sociocultural, Neuropsychological and Linguistic Perspectives*, K. Hyltenstam and A. Viberg (eds.), 289–308. Cambridge: Cambridge University Press.

—— 1994. "Early morphology in Swedish as the weaker language in French-Swedish bilingual children." *Scandinavian Working Papers on Bilingualism* 9: 67–86.

Schütze, C. and Wexler, K. 1996. "Subject case licensing and root infinitives." In *BUCLD 20 Proceedings*, A. Stringfellow, D. Cahana-Amitay, E. Hughes and A. Zukowsky (eds.), 670–81. Somerville, Mass.: Cascadilla Press.

Sebastián, E. 1989. *Tiempo y Aspecto Verbal en el Lenguaje Infantil*. Ph.D. dissertation, Autonomous University of Madrid.

Sebastián-Gallés, N., Dupoux, E., Segui, J. and Mehler, J. 1992. "Contrasting syllabic effects in Catalan and Spanish." *Journal of Memory and Language* 31: 18–32.

Serratrice, L. 1999. *The Emergence of Functional Categories in Bilingual First Language Acquisition*. Ph.D. dissertation, University of Edinburgh.

Shin, S. J. and Milroy, L. 2000. "Conversational codeswitching among Korean-English bilingual children." *International Journal of Bilingualism* 4 (3): 351–83.

Shirai, Y. and Andersen, R. W. 1995. "The Acquisition of Tense-Aspect Morphology: A Prototype Account." *Language* 71: 743–62.

Sinka, I. and Schelletter, C. 1998. "Morphosyntactic development in bilingual children." *International Journal of Bilingualism* 2: 301–26.

Slobin, D. I. 1985. "Crosslinguistic evidence for the Language-Making Capacity." In *The Crosslinguistic Study of Language Acquisition 2: Theoretical Issues*, D. I. Slobin (ed.), 1157–256. Hillsdale, NJ: Lawrence Erlbaum.

—— (ed.). 1997. *The Crosslinguistic Study of Language Acquisition Volume 5: Expanding Contexts*. Mahwah, NJ: Lawrence Erlbaum.

Smith, C. S. 1983. "A theory of aspectual choice." *Language* 59: 470–501.

Smoczynska, M. 1985. "The Acquisition of Polish." In *The Cross-linguistic Study of Language Acquisition Vol. I*, D. I. Slobin (ed.), 595–686. Hillsdale, N. J.: Lawrence Erlbaum Associates.

—— 1996. "Polish Tense and Aspect Systems." Ms. *VIIth International Congress for the Study of Child Language*, Istanbul, July 14–19, 1996.

Snow, C. E. 1995. "Issues in the study of input: Finetuning, universality, individual and developmental differences, and necessary causes." In *The Handbook of Child Language*, P. Fletcher and B. MacWhinney (eds.), 180–93. Oxford: Blackwell.

Sokolov, J. L. and Snow, C. E. (eds.). 1993. *Handbook of Research in Language Using CHILDES*. Hillsdale, NJ: Lawrence Erlbaum Associates, Publishers.

Spilton, D. and Lee, L. C. 1977. "Some determinants of effective communication in four-year-olds." *Child Development* 48: 968–77.

Stavans, A. 1992. "Sociolinguistic factors affecting codeswitches produced by trilingual children." *Language, Culture and Curriculum* 5 (1): 41–53.

Taeschner, T. 1983. *The Sun is Feminine. A Study on Language Acquisition in Bilingual Children*. Berlin: Springer-Verlag.

Tardif, T. 1996. "Nouns are not always learned before verbs: Evidence from Mandarin speakers' early vocabularies." *Developmental Psychology* 32: 492–504.

—— Shatz, M. and Naigles, L. 1997. "Caregiver speech and children's use of nouns versus verbs: A comparison of English, Italian, and Mandarin" *Journal of Child Language* 24: 535–65.

Thal, D. and Bates, E. 1988. "Language and gesture in late talkers." *Journal of Speech and Hearing Research* 31: 115–23.

Tomasello, M. 1992. *First Verbs: a Case Study of Early Grammatical Development*. Cambridge: Cambridge University Press.

—— 2000. "Do young children have adult syntactic competence?" *Cognition* 74: 209–53.

—— and Brooks, P. 1999. "Early syntactic development: a Construction Grammar approach." In *The Development of Language*, M. Barrett (ed.), 161–90. Hove: Psychology Press.

—— and Merriman, W. E. (eds.). 1995. *Beyond Names for Things*. Hillsdale, NJ: Lawrence Erlbaum Associates.

—— Farrar, M. J. and Dines, J. 1984. "Children's speech revisions for a familiar and an unfamiliar adult." *Journal of Speech and Hearing Research* 27: 359–63.

—— Strosber, R. and Akhtar, N. 1996. "Eighteen-month-old children learn words in non-ostensive contexts." *Journal of Child Language* 23: 157–76.

Tracy, R. 1995. *Child Languages in Contact: Bilingual Language Acquisition*. Habilitation Thesis, University of Tübingen.

Tucker, G. R. 1998. "A global perspective on multilingualism and multilingual education". In *Beyond Bilingualism: Multilingualism and Multilingual Education*, J. Cenoz and F. Genesee (eds.), 3–15. Clevedon: Multilingual Matters.

Ullman, S. 1963. "Semantic universals." In *Universals of Language*, J. H. Greenberg (ed.), 217–62. Cambridge, MA: M. I. T. Press.

Umbel, V. M., Pearson, B. Z., Fernandez, M. C. and Oller, D. K. 1992. "Measuring bilingual children's receptive vocabularies." *Child Development* 63: 1012–20.

Vihman, M. M. 1985. "Language differentiation by the bilingual infant." *Journal of Child Language* 12: 297–324.

—— 1986. "More on language differentiation." *Journal of Child Language* 13: 595–7.

—— and McCune, L. 1994. "When is a word a word?" *Journal of Child Language* 21: 517–42.

—— and McLaughlin, B. 1982. "Bilingualism and second language acquisition in preschool children." In *Verbal Processes in Children*, C. Brainard and M. Pressley (eds.), 35–58. New York: Springer Verlag.

Volterra, V. and Taeschner, T. 1978. "The acquisition and development of language by bilingual children." *Journal of Child Language* 5: 311–26.

Weist, R. M., Wysocka, H., Witkowska-Stadnik, K. and Buczowska Y Koniecza, E. 1984. "The Defective Tense Hypothesis: on the emergence of Tense and Aspect in Child Polish." *Journal of Child Language* 11: 347–74.

Werker, J. F. 1995. "Exploring developmental changes in cross-language speech perception." In *An Invitation to Cognitive Science. Language Volume 1*, L. Gleitman and M. Liberman (eds.), 87–106. Cambridge, MA: MIT Press.

—— and Tees, R. C. 1984. "Cross-language speech perception: evidence for perceptual reorganization during the first year of life." *Infant Behavior and Development* 7: 49–63.

—— —— 1999. "Influences on infant speech processing: Toward a new synthesis." *Annual Review of Psychology* 50: 509–35.

Westbury, C. and Nicoladis, E. 1998. "Meaning in children's first words: Implications for a theory of lexical ontology." In *Proceedings of the 22nd Annual Boston University Conference on Language Development*, A. Greenhill, M. Hughes, H. Littlefield and H. Walsh (eds.), 768–78. Somerville, MA: Cascadilla Press.

Wexler, K. 1994. "Optional infinitives, head movement and the economy of derivations." In *Verb Movement*, D. Lightfoot and N. Hornstein (eds.), 305–50. Cambridge: Cambridge University Press.

—— 1998. "Very early parameter setting and the unique checking constraint: a new explanation of the optional infinitive stage." *Lingua* 106: 23–79.

Whalen, D. H., Levitt, A. G. and Wang, Q. 1991. "Intonational differences between the reduplicative babbling of French-and English-learning infants." *Journal of Child Language* 18: 501–16.

Wilcox, M. J. and Webster, E. J. 1980. "Early discourse behavior: An analysis of children's responses to listener feedback." *Child Development* 51: 1120–5.

Yelland, G. W., Pollard, J. and Mercuri, A. 1993. "The metalinguistic benefits of limited contact with a second language." *Applied Psycholinguistics* 14: 423–44.

Zlatic, L., MacNeilage, P., Matyear, C. and Davis, B. 1997. "Babbling of twins in a bilingual environment." *Applied Psycholinguistics* 18: 453–69.

Zubiri, J. J. 1997. *Izen Sintagmaren Determinazioaren eta Kasuen Jabekuntza eta Garapena Hiru Urte Arte. (Goizuetako bi haur euskaldun elebakarren jarraipena)* Ph.D. dissertation, University of the Basque Country, Gasteiz.

Index